HUDSON PUBLIC LIBRARY
3 WASHINGTON STREET
HUDSON, MA 01749
ADULT: 978-568-9644
CHILDREN: 978-568-9645
www.hudsonpubliclibrary.com

THE BIRTH OF THE FBI

THE BIRTH OF THE FBI

Teddy Roosevelt, the Secret Service, and the Fight Over America's Premier Law Enforcement Agency

Willard M. Oliver

Rowman & Littlefield
Lanham • Boulder • New York • London

Published by Rowman & Littlefield
An imprint of The Rowman & Littlefield Publishing Group, Inc.
4501 Forbes Boulevard, Suite 200, Lanham, Maryland 20706
www.rowman.com

6 Tinworth Street, London SE11 5AL, United Kingdom

British Library Cataloguing in Publication Information Available

Library of Congress Cataloging-in-Publication Data

Names: Oliver, Willard M., author.
Title: The birth of the FBI: Teddy Roosevelt, the Secret Service, and the fight
over America's premier law enforcement agency /
    Willard M. Oliver.
Description: Lanham : Rowman & Littlefield, [2019] I Includes
    bibliographical references and index.
Identifiers: LCCN 2018054400 (print) I LCCN 2019001800 (ebook) I ISBN
    9781442265042 (Electronic) I ISBN 9781442265035 (cloth : alk. paper)
Subjects: LCSH: United States. Federal Bureau of Investigation—History—
    20th century. I United States. Secret Service—History—20th century. I
    Law enforcement—Political aspects—United States—History—20th
    century. I Roosevelt, Theodore, 1858-1919. I Tawney, James A. (James
    Albertus), 1855-1919. I United States. Congress--History--20th century. I
    Public land sales—United States—History—20th century. I Political
    corruption—United States—History—20th century. I United States—
    Politics and government—1901-1909.
Classification: LCC HV8144.F43 (ebook) I LCC HV8144.F43 O43 2019 (print) I
    DDC 363.250973/09041—dc23
LC record available at https://lccn.loc.gov/2018054400

To Beatriz Oliver
Welcome to the family!

Contents

Prologue

The Federal Bureau of Investigation was originally simply called the Bureau of Investigation when it was founded on July 26, 1908. To most people, however, the FBI is more closely associated with its most famous director, J. Edgar Hoover, whom many believe created the agency and served as its first director. By the time Hoover assumed the directorship, however, the Bureau had already existed under four previous presidential administrations with four directors and one interim director. This early history of the FBI is often forgotten, largely because Hoover's tenure, which itself ran through eight presidential administrations in a span of forty-eight years, overshadowed everything about that agency.

It is not too surprising that many people do not know the origins of the FBI, let alone that it was originally called the Bureau of Investigation. Several recent books, both excellent reads, are subtitled in such a way as to perpetuate the myth that the agency started under J. Edgar Hoover: Bryan Burrough's *Public Enemies: America's Greatest Crime Wave and the Birth of the FBI, 1933–34* and David Grann's *Killers of the Flower Moon: The Osage Murders and the Birth of the FBI*.[1] Both books deal with events that took place early in J. Edgar Hoover's career, suggesting that they were what gave rise to the FBI. While the books themselves are clear about the agency's timeline, they still advance the notion that it was Hoover who really created the FBI.

The true birth of the FBI traces back to the presidential administration of Theodore Roosevelt, who created the Bureau of Investigation with the help of his attorney general, Charles Joseph Bonaparte. Although it could be said that the Bureau was created to respond to serious federal land fraud, the reality is that the FBI emerged from a political fight. President Theodore Roosevelt, finding himself in a political row with Congress over the Secret Service, found a political solution to the problem by creating the Bureau of Investigation. So the true origins of the FBI have little to do with crime waves and criminal investigations but, rather, are shrouded in the mystery of politics.

In order to understand the fight between the president and Congress in the last years of Roosevelt's administration, one must understand its antecedents. When drafting the Constitution, the Founding Fathers had failed to empower any agency to enforce federal laws. At first, the government relied on the US Marshals Service to perform this function and later the Pinkerton National Detective Agency. During the Civil War, the government faced yet another criminal problem—curtailing economically debilitating counterfeiting. The government responded by creating a second federal law-enforcement agency, the United States Secret Service. After three presidential assassinations, that agency also took on the responsibility of protecting America's presidents. When Roosevelt came into office because of an assassin's bullet, he brought with him his penchant for fighting corruption and his love of the outdoors. His conservation beliefs, mixed with his belief in law enforcement, led him to use the powers of his administration to tenaciously fight the land thieves that had become problematic in the West as a result of abuses of the Homestead Acts. When Roosevelt borrowed Secret Service operatives, as they were then called, to investigate fraudulent land deals, Congress became involved in the issue, in part because some of their own had been caught committing those very crimes. After Congressman James A. Tawney attached an amendment to an appropriations bill preventing Roosevelt from borrowing Secret Service operatives to investigate land frauds, Roosevelt created the Bureau of Investigation in response. The fight was now on between Roosevelt and Tawney, and at stake was the very survival of Roosevelt's newly created law-enforcement agency.

This is the true story of the birth of the FBI.

Early photo of US Deputy Marshals at the US Land Office in the Oklahoma Territory. Until the Civil War, they were the only federal law enforcement agency widely available to the federal government.

Photo number 49-AR-35 courtesy of the National Archives and Records Administration.

1

Federal Law Enforcement

The federal law-enforcement agencies that we are so familiar with today—the Drug Enforcement Administration, the US Border Patrol, and the Bureau of Alcohol, Tobacco, Firearms and Explosives—are all administrative inventions of the twentieth century. "Before the twentieth century," writes legal historian Lawrence M. Friedman, "criminal justice was overwhelmingly the business of the states, not the federal government."[1] This growth in federal power was primarily driven by the 1919 passage of the Volstead Act and in 1920 by the enactment of the "Great Experiment," Prohibition. Though intoxicating beverages were no longer legal in the United States, the public remained thirsty, and a black market for the sale of alcohol thrived, which in turn gave rise to the mafia; in response, the powers of federal law-enforcement agencies were expanded. After Prohibition was overturned in 1933, the federal law-enforcement mechanism turned its attention to "dangerous narcotics," and by the late twentieth century America was fighting the so-called "war on drugs."[2] This, naturally, led to an ever-expanding number of federal law-enforcement agencies and their personnel. By the twenty-first century, because of the terrorist attacks of September 11, 2001, and a rise in global terrorism, the federal government established the Department of Homeland Security, which is today filled with all manner of new, reformed, and expanded law-enforcement agencies.

Before this twentieth-century expansion, however, law enforcement had been under the purview of local governments. As police historian Samuel Walker explains, "criminal law enforcement was mainly the responsibility of the county sheriff and the town constables."[3] In more rural areas, it was the sheriff who served as the chief law-enforcement officer, while in larger towns and cities constables typically oversaw the night watch and possibly a day ward—security practices that had been established in the Thirteen Colonies under English rule.[4]

The sheriffs "were initially appointed by the colonial governor, who was in turn appointed by the King of England."[5] Sheriffs were the primary law enforcers in the counties, but because they were commonly paid through a system of fees by the county courts, it was more profitable for them to perform civil duties, such as the issuance of subpoenas and collecting taxes. The career of a sheriff could be very lucrative indeed; as police historian Roger Lane explains, "the basic income, in addition to jailer's fees, was three dollars a day for attendance in court" and "to this was added a schedule of fees and expenses for over a dozen different kinds of services." But "the biggest gains lay in serving personal civil actions; the sheriff collected 4 per cent of damages and costs in judgments of up to one hundred dollars, 2 per cent between one and two hundred, and 1 per cent of all over two hundred dollars." This is why "the routine business of police simply did not occupy or concern" the typical sheriff.[6] Those routines were left to the constable and the watchmen.

Boston assembled the first night-watch system in America on April 12, 1631.[7] The watch initially served without a constable, but in 1634, the colonial courts created the position to further emulate the English system. The Boston night watch was to "see that all disturbances and disorders in the night shall be prevented and suppressed," by walking their rounds with a rattle, sounding the alarm by spinning it at the first sign of trouble.[8] This is why they were often referred to as the "rattle watch."[9]

The most serious danger against which the night watch stood guard was not so much criminal activity but fires, which posed the deadliest hazard to the all-wooden cities of the day, a lesson Boston learned all two well in 1652, when they suffered a series of horrendously deadly fires.[10] The watch was also tasked with lighting streetlamps at night and extinguishing them in the morning. For all of this they were paid a paltry sum. And on top of that, if they did have to appear in court, the night watch were only paid two dollars a day, not the three that sheriffs earned.[11]

The constable and watch systems were never highly respected in England or America, considered by most to be grossly ineffective. As far back as the late sixteenth century, the asinine Constable Dogberry and his night watchmen were written to be buffoons in Shakespeare's play *Much Ado About Nothing*. In one scene, when the aristocratic Conrade calls Constable Dogberry an ass, Dogberry accepts the title as one of nobility, imploring his masters to "remember that I am an ass; though it be not written down, yet forget not that I am an ass."[12]

The constable and watch system established in Boston fared little better than its English counterpart. Despite improvements in the payment system and the move to make watch service mandatory for all able-bodied males, many simply ignored the call or paid for a replacement, which meant the force was neither effective nor well respected. And even when those who could afford to avoid service on the watch made their payment, the money was never used to hire a suitable replacement: "The constable warned a number of housekeepers to attend him for the night," Benjamin Franklin complained of the Philadelphia watch, but "those who chose never to attend paid him six shillings a year to be excus'd which was suppos'd to be for hiring substitutes, but was, in reality, much more than was necessary for that purpose, and made the constableship a place of profit." "The constable, for a little drink," Franklin added, "often got such ragamuffins about him as a watch, that respectable housekeepers did not choose to mix with," and "walking the rounds, too, was often neglected, and most of the nights spent in tippling."[13]

It was the same situation all over the American colonies. One individual living in New York City in the 1750s complained the night watchmen there were "a parcel of idle, drinking, vigilant snorers, who never quell'd any nocturnal tumult in their lives; but would perhaps, be as ready to joining in burglary as any thief in Christendom."[14] In 1808 commentator in the *Louisiana Gazette* complained of the same problems in New Orleans, writing that "since substitutes have been allowed, the patrol is composed principally of the most worthless part of the community . . . it is like setting wolves to guard the sheep."[15] To improve the fitness and reliability of the watch, Franklin had advocated for a paid police force to be funded by levying a tax on property. Unfortunately for Franklin, it was not until 1838 that the city of Boston enacted such measures.

Even well into the nineteenth century, law enforcement wasn't much more sophisticated than the "rattle watch" of the early seventeenth century. In the early 1800s, the constables and "roundsmen" of New York City were known as the "leatherheads" for the tight-fitting leather helmets they wore. They were not well respected by the adults of New York City, and for the youth they often proved an abundant source of amusement. "Youthful and exuberant New Yorkers considered an evening out was not spent in the Orthodox manner unless they played some rough practical jokes on the poor, old, inoffensive Leatherheads," wrote retired Police Chief George Washington Walling, reminiscing about the early days of the force. "It is recorded of such a staid young man as Washington Irving [of *Legend of Sleepy Hollow* and *Rip Van Winkle* fame], even that he was in the habit of upsetting watch-boxes if he caught a 'Leatherhead' asleep inside; and on one occasion, so it is said, he lassoed the box with a stout rope, and with the aid of companions dragged it down Broadway, while the watchmen inside yelled loudly for help."[16] It was, in truth, so common to find the night watchmen asleep during Washington Irving's day that New Yorkers often quipped, "While the city sleeps, the watchmen do too."[17]

Such was the state—the sorry state—of early policing in the eighteenth century. So, when the United States of America formed its first government, it could not look to the local police to enforce its laws. The system of sheriffs, constables, and watchmen was grossly inadequate to the new national government's interests—not to mention it did not fall under the authority or control of the federal government. Indeed, it was that very fact that proved to be a selling point for ratification of the United States Constitution.

On Thursday, August 30, 1787, the members of the Constitutional Convention in Philadelphia took up the issue of law enforcement when they entertained Article XVIII, which became Article 4, Section 4, of the US Constitution. The proposed article read, "The United States shall guaranty to each State a Republican form of Government; and shall protect each State against foreign invasion, and on the application of its Legislature, against domestic violence."[18] There was little debate over the proposal—only the motion to drop the word *foreign* and a short debate over changing *domestic violence* to *insurrection*, although in the end that latter edit was dropped.[19] The vote was nine to two in favor of retaining the amendment, and the convention moved on.

This section of the Constitution was very intentionally constructed to prevent another Shays's Rebellion, which was still fresh in everyone's mind.[20] That short-lived rebellion had broken out in August of 1786 before finally being quelled in June of 1787. At the close of the American Revolution, many of the thirteen original states had found themselves deep in debt, unable to secure new lines of credit. In desperate need of income, their governments raised taxes on their own people—and this immediately after having just concluded a bloody war largely fought because of the oppressive taxes the English Crown had levied. But even more oppressive to the people was the heavy hand used in collecting those state taxes. Aggrieved, protesters gathered, with one farmer lamenting, "I have been greatly abused, have been obliged to do more than my part in the war, been loaded with class rates, town rates, province rates, Continental rates . . . been pulled and hauled by sheriffs, constables, and collectors, and had my cattle sold for less than they were worth." The farmer, whose alias was "Plough Jogger," called for rebellion: "The great men are going to get all we have," he told the assembly, "and I think it is time for us to rise and put a stop to it, and have no more courts, nor sheriffs, nor collectors, nor lawyers."[21] The crowd agreed, and eventually a reluctant Daniel

Shays was nominated from among them to serve as leader of the uprising.

These rebels, often referred to as the Shaysites, immediately sought to shut down the local courts through protests. The judges, not appreciating the disruption to their business, issued court orders for the rebels' arrest. This only succeeded in ratcheting up the tension. Everything came to a head on January 25, 1787, when the rebels decided to raid the Springfield Armory so as to properly arm themselves. The plan was a disaster, because half of the rebels failed to show on time and the militia had caught wind of the planned attack and were well prepared to face them. In that action, four of Shays's men were killed, another twenty were wounded, and the rest fled into the night. The hunt to bring the rebels to justice continued through most of the rest of 1787.[22]

As the roundup was still underway, the Constitutional Convention was convening in Philadelphia, and Shays's Rebellion was frequently discussed implicitly and explicitly in their debates. As to whether or not states would have the right to provide for their own protection, however, there was little debate: The members agreed that each state would be guaranteed a "Republican Form of Government."[23] Only when state governments were overwhelmed with some form of "domestic Violence" would the national government be permitted to step in and assist, and even then only upon the state's application to Congress.[24] It was clarified that were Congress not in session, the application was to be presented to the president. By virtue of this, states retained the right to enforce their own laws rather than having the national government step in to take control whenever it saw fit. This played an important role in the ratification of the Constitution.

The evening before John Bly and Charles Rose were to be hanged for their role in Shays's Rebellion, as Delaware and Pennsylvania were to take up the vote for ratification of the new US Constitution, *Publius* published the next installment of the Federalist Papers.[25] It was actually Alexander Hamilton who was claiming to be "of the people" and with James Madison and John Jay was penning the Federalist essays in the hopes of

convincing the citizens of each state, as well as their state representatives, to ratify the Constitution. In his third of six essays on
the limited powers of the presidency, known as Federalist #17,
Hamilton turned his attention to the administration of criminal
and civil justice.

Attempting to quell fears that ratifying the Constitution
would bestow the American president with the power of a des-
pot, Hamilton assured his readers that the chief executive would
have little power over the state governments. Hamilton promised "one transcendent advantage belonging to the province of
the State governments, which alone suffices to place the matter
in a clear and satisfactory light"—by which he meant "the ordinary administration of criminal and civil justice." He continued,
"This, of all others is the most powerful, most universal, and
most attractive source of popular obedience and attachment. It is
that which, being the immediate and visible guardian of life and
property, having its benefits and its terrors in constant activity
before the public eye, regulating all those personal interests and
familiar concerns to which the sensibility of individuals is more
immediately awake, contributes, more than any other circumstances, to impressing upon the minds of the people, affection,
esteem, and reverence toward the government."[26]

His assurance was that states, not the national government,
would have the power of both criminal justice and civil justice,
which would give them power commensurate to the national
government's, leaving little fear of a president-despot. For
even were the president to attempt tyranny, he would have no
criminal- or civil-justice powers by which to control the people:
effectively, he would have no police force.

Hamilton drove his point home: "This great cement of society" he wrote, "which will diffuse itself almost wholly through
the channels of the particular governments, independent of all
other causes of influence, would insure them so decided an empire over their respective citizens as to render them at all times a
complete counterpoise, and, not unfrequently, dangerous rivals
to the power of the Union."[27] In other words, were the national
government to try to wield its powers over the states, the states
and its people would have nothing to fear: they would have

leverage over the national government because they had the mechanisms of criminal and civil justice in their hands.

On June 21, 1788, delegates from New Hampshire cast the ninth vote in favor, ratifying the US Constitution. Now the country needed to begin implementing the Constitution. One of the first orders of business was to select a chief executive. That first presidential election was held between December 15, 1788, and January 10, 1789. When the electoral votes were tabulated, it was unanimous: George Washington was to become the first president of the United States. Elections for the first members of Congress were also held between December of 1788 and March of 1789, so come early April, the First Congress of the United States was seated, and on April 30, 1789, at Federal Hall in New York City, George Washington was inaugurated.

By the time Washington was seated as president, Congress was already hard at work. As Historian Gordon S. Wood explains, "the Senate immediately established a committee to draft a judiciary bill, chaired by Oliver Ellsworth, an experienced jurist from Connecticut who had . . . been a member of the Constitutional Convention."[28] Two months later, on June 12, 1789, Virginia's Senator Richard Henry Lee reported the first bill ever out of committee: Senate Bill Number 1 was known as the Judiciary Act of 1789.

Despite Hamilton's assurances to the contrary, Anti-Federalists were fearful that the judiciary act was nothing more than a power grab by the national government.[29] Ellsworth and committee, however, "were well aware of the fears of a national judiciary that the Anti-Federalists had aroused during the ratification debates, especially fears of a national judiciary that omitted certain common law rights like trial by jury"—which wouldn't be guaranteed until the Bill of Rights was ratified several years later, in 1791. They knew full well that "the possibility of conflict between the new federal government and the states was thus very great."[30]

After considerable debate, the Senate finally passed the act with a vote of fourteen to six, on July 17, 1789. It then went to the House of Representatives for consideration, which spanned the rest of July and all of August. For a first bill, it was highly contentious. But the stakes were high, for it was essentially creating the entire third branch of government, defining the powers of the executive branch. A vote was finally called on September 19, and it passed, thirty-seven to sixteen. But further amendments had been called for, which were voted on and passed on September 21. The final version was agreed upon that same day, and the bill was sent to the executive. On September 24, President George Washington signed into law the first Congressional act of the new government, which was, as Historian Wood summed it, "an ingenious bundle of compromises that allayed many of the Anti-Federalist suspicions."[31]

The compromise resulted in a three-tiered judiciary, with the Supreme Court at the head, a series of circuit appellate courts in between, and district courts at the bottom. The new law did not assume the authority or responsibility of the previously established state courts but allowed the federal courts to coexist alongside the state courts, sometimes sharing the same resources, often the very same courtrooms. This was common occurrence especially in the lower district courts, where it was generally the case that a local resident was selected to serve as the judge, thus deflecting any notion of outside control by the national government. These local courts were then responsible for the "fee schedules" and "modes of selecting jurors" and were to "have jurisdiction over admiralty cases, petty crimes, and revenue collection."[32]

As the district-court judges were to be appointed to serve as arbiters of the law, not administrators, Congress realized another person was needed to handle such things as the fee schedules, the formation of juries, and especially collection of revenue. Even more importantly, someone needed to be empowered to enforce the laws—a role certainly not suited to a member of the judiciary branch. And so, because the Judiciary Act had been based on "the organization and structure of the colonial and wartime admiralty courts,"[33] which itself had been based on the British vice-admiralty courts, Congress retained the title of the man who held those responsibilities: thus out of the Judiciary Act of 1789 was born the United States Marshals Service, "the oldest federal law-enforcement agency in the country."[34]

Section 27 of the Judiciary Act put forth "that a marshal shall be appointed in and for each district for the term of four years" in order to "execute throughout the district, all lawful precepts directed to him, and issued under the authority of the United States." It further stated the marshal "shall have power to command all necessary assistance in the execution of his duty, and to appoint as there shall be occasion, one or more deputies." This gave the district marshal the ability to not only appoint deputy marshals but also deputize civilians in a time of need. The section of the act also included the oath of office the marshal and his deputies would swear by:

> I, A. B., do solemnly swear or affirm, that I will faithfully execute all lawful precepts directed to the marshal of the district of _____ under the authority of the United States, and true returns make, and in all things well and truly, and without malice or partiality, perform the duties of the office of marshal (or marshal's deputy, as the case may be) of the district of _____, during my continuance in said office, and take only my lawful fees. So help me God.[35]

Further sections of the act describe the duties and responsibilities of the marshals, and they were many. "The primary function of the marshals," explains Frederick S. Calhoun, first historian of the US Marshals, "was to support the federal district courts. They served the subpoenas, summonses, writs, warrants, and other process issued by the courts; made all the arrests; and handled all prisoners. They also disbursed the money, paying the fees and expenses of the court clerks, US attorneys, jurors, and witnesses. They rented the courtrooms and jail space and hired the bailiffs, criers, and janitors. The marshals also took care of the details by making sure the water pitchers were filled, the prisoners were present, the jurors were available and the witnesses were on time."[36] A US marshal was clearly to be a jack-of-all-trades, shouldering all of the responsibilities necessary to ensure the district courts ran.

President Washington wasted little time in appointing US marshals to the original thirteen district courts.[37] His first appointment embodied Washington's ideal candidate: Nathaniel

Ramsay was named the first marshal of the Maryland district court partly as an act of political patronage and partly in reward for the bravery he had exhibited at the Battle of Monmouth.

When General Washington had arrived at Monmouth on June 28, 1778, he discovered that the British had surrounded the courthouse and that General Charles Lee had ordered his troops to flee soon after the British had opened fire.[38] Washington was livid. To prevent further loss and to turn the tide of the battle, he ordered Lieutenant Colonel Ramsay to take his regiments and hold the line: "I shall depend on your immediate exertion to check with your two regiments the progress of the enemy till I can form the main army." Ramsay's only reply? "We shall check them!"[39]

Ramsay immediately entered into combat with his two regiments against a much larger British force, and the fighting quickly devolved from rifles to pistols, and then from pistols to swords and hand-to-hand combat. Ramsay was wounded several times—including once when a pistol exploded near his face, permanently scarring him for life—but he fought on. The two regiments lost many soldiers that day, suffered many wounded, and saw scores of its men captured, including Ramsay. He had managed, however, to buy Washington the time he needed, and Washington was able to take the field with his Continental Army and eventually rout the British.

Ramsay himself spent the next several years as a British prisoner of war and was finally paroled in December of 1780. He retired from military duty a month later, returning home to Maryland to pursue a career in law. His practice was successful, and he invested heavily in local real estate. He then represented Maryland in the Second Continental Congress, where he supported passage of the Constitution, being a staunch Federalist. And so it was that, in light of his past bravery, his support of the Constitution, and the great respect he inspired locally in Maryland, President Washington appointed him the first US marshal. Ramsay's local ties would not make his appointment an affront to the people of Maryland, and his support of the Constitution Ramsay, Washington knew, meant he would understand that he worked for the national government, not the state government.

The fact he was a war hero and had valiantly served his state certainly did not hurt.

All of Washington's appointments to US marshalcies fell into this same pattern: whether it was Henry Dearborn of Maine or Isaac Huger in South Carolina, they were typically veterans of the American Revolution, enjoyed the respect of their communities (e.g., lawyers, businessmen, or sheriffs), and had openly supported the creation of the federal republic. Washington trusted that "the marshals would enforce the laws and orders of the federal government and its courts and administer its interests and affairs." This was important, because although the marshal's clients were, in effect, the district courts, "it was the presidency for whom they worked."[40]

Initially, Washington had his doubts about this newly created position, partly because, like most of his contemporaries, he did not believe the district courts would be overly busy. "How beneficial this office may be, I know not," he wrote Benjamin Lincoln regarding the marshal in Massachusetts. "At present, the mere emolument of it can not be, I should suppose, an object; but as a step, it may be desired by such as have nothing better in prospect."[41] In others words, the amount of money one could earn in the position of Marshal would not have been all that great, but if the person didn't have any better opportunities, it would suffice. Not only did Washington underestimate the opportunities for pay, he also underestimated how busy the US marshals would become.

Washington placed the supervision of the US marshals under his secretary of state, Thomas Jefferson. This was primarily because State had become the catchall department to deal with any bureaucratic function not concerning war or the treasury, the only other cabinet-level departments at the time. Although there was an attorney general in Washington's original cabinet, he merely served as the government's lawyer on retainer and had no administrative organization for which he was responsible—a part of the US attorney general's role that did not emerge until after the Civil War.

But it wasn't long before the importance of the US marshal became known. "When George Washington set up his first administration, and the first Congress began passing laws," explains Calhoun, "both branches of government quickly discovered an inconvenient gap in the constitutional design. It had no provision for a regional administrative structure stretching throughout the country."[42] Although state governments had an administrative mechanism by which they could communicate with their local constituents, the national government had nothing of equivalence. So they quickly came to rely on the US Marshals.

And Thomas Jefferson discovered this impediment early on in his role as secretary of state. A charge of his office was the promulgation of laws and proclamations, but there existed no method of delivering them to the citizens throughout the country.[43] Jefferson, therefore, found himself relying on the US marshals. So, for instance, when Washington issued his Thanksgiving Proclamation, Jefferson had the US marshals issue the proclamation to their respective states. In addition, because foreign diplomats had prosecutorial immunity and could not be summoned to court, the secretary of state requested that the US marshal in the District of Columbia maintain a list detailing who enjoyed the privilege at any given time. Still further, when Congress was ordered into special session, the secretary of state ordered the US marshals to notify their district's members of the House and Senate that they had been recalled. The US marshals soon found themselves tasked with nearly every possible responsibility of the national government because they were the only agency that could represent the government's interest at the local level. Not only was this true of the business of the district courts and the administration, but the Marshals also found themselves tasked by Congress with additional duties.

For instance, as Congress passed laws imposing tariffs on imported goods, they initially relied on the marshals to serve as customs and revenue collectors.[44] When Congress passed the Alien and Sedition Acts in 1798, they needed a means by which to enforce those laws.[45] If foreign nationals—aliens—needed to be rounded up and deported, they looked to the US marshals. If American citizens spoke critically of the United States government—sedition—and needed to be arrested, they turned to the US marshals. Further, when Congress passed the Militia Act of 1795, which mandated compulsory military duty in times of war, the US marshals were tasked with compelling service and bringing those who refused before the courts, as well as with collecting any punitive fines.[46] Although at the time the act passed it was commonly believed that America was about to go to war with England, the fragile peace was sustained until the War of 1812, when the marshals were again called upon to enforce conscription laws.

Perhaps the most burdensome task the US marshals were ever ordered by Congress to undertake was conducting the US Census.[47] Article I, Section 2, of the US Constitution apportions membership to the House of Representatives based upon population, necessitating a census. "The actual Enumeration," the Constitution reads, "shall be made within three Years after the first Meeting of the Congress of the United States, and within every subsequent Term of ten Years."[48] True to this requirement, on March 1, 1790, the First Congress approved An Act Providing for the Enumeration of the Inhabitants of the United States, charging that "the marshals of the several districts of the United States shall be, and they are hereby authorized and required to cause the number of the inhabitants within their respective districts to be taken."[49]

The US marshals were the only administrative entity that could carry out the task. They were already located within the districts, and they had the power to appoint deputy marshals to assist them in their duties. So the marshals divided their districts into sections and appointed assistant marshals to travel from home to home to count the people. As one can only imagine, this was an onerous duty for the marshals of the day, as finding some of the homes was probably nearly as difficult as it was getting to them. The task was of the utmost political importance, however, and the marshals persevered, continuing to coordinate the US census through 1870. In 1880, they passed the responsibility on to the newly formed US Bureau of the Census.

The US marshals in their first sixty years of existence were truly the representatives of the national government to the states and were the only federal law-enforcement agency in existence—other than postal inspectors. The marshals performed duties related to court administration, they were the local administrators for the government's administrative business, and they were often tasked by Congress with additional responsibilities, like taking the census. All of these duties tended to overshadow their law-enforcement duties, which made it easier to disregard somewhat the dangers of the job. They were, after all, only administrators. However, that all changed on January 11, 1794.

President Washington had appointed Robert Forsyth to be US marshal for the District Court of Georgia. During the American Revolution, Forsyth had served as captain of Light Dragoons in the cavalry of Henry "Light Horse Harry" Lee. After the war, Forsyth returned to Augusta, Georgia, where he engaged in farming, private businesses, and real estate. He served as a tax assessor and later a justice of the peace and was well known in the community. Forsyth met all of the qualities that Washington was looking for in his initial appointments. Like most other US marshals, Forsyth largely performed administrative duties—even on the day he became the first federal law-enforcement officer killed in the line of duty.

On January 11, 1794, Forsyth was serving Mr. Beverly Allen with civil papers.[50] Allen's reputation must have preceded him, for Forsyth had two deputy marshals accompany him. Upon their arrival, they discovered Allen and his brother speaking with some friends, and so, out of courtesy, Forsyth asked to speak privately with Allen outside. As Forsyth and his men went outside to wait, Allen and his brother ran upstairs and then locked themselves in a room. Forsyth and his deputies followed, approached the door, and knocked, demanding that Allen come out of the room. From inside the room, Allen fired a gun, and the bullet smashed through the door, striking Forsyth in the head. He was killed instantly. The deputy marshals arrested both Beverly Allen and his brother, William, but six weeks later the two escaped and were never recaptured. It was only recently that Retired US Marshal Rom Latham discovered that Allen had fled to Rogues' Harbor—a known criminal hideout in Logan County, Kentucky—where he had repented of his crime, begun to practice medicine, and quietly served his small community until his death twenty-three years later, in 1817.[51]

While Forsyth's murder did highlight the job's potential dangers, overall performing a marshal's duties was still largely seen as administrative and generally considered safe. And perhaps it generally was: for almost a half century after Robert Forsyth's murder, no US marshal lost his life to the job. But on February 2, 1839, Deputy Marshal John Gatewood was shot and killed when he and three other deputies were attempting to seize property under a court order—the circumstances pointedly similar to Forsyth's murder.[52] The next US marshal to lose his life was in enforcement of the Fugitive Slave Act of 1850.

As America drifted closer to civil war, the South seethed that escaped slaves found refuge among Abolitionists in the Northern states. And so, as part of the Compromise of 1850, an attempt to avoid war and retain the union of states, Congress passed the Fugitive Slave Act, which declared that Northern states could no longer harbor escaped slaves but, rather, must return them to their rightful owners. Congress turned to the US marshals to enforce their law.[53]

Enforcing the act taxed the marshals heavily, and in order to perform this duty they became dependent upon deputized citizens. On September 11, 1851, a landowner in Christiana, Pennsylvania, Edward Gorsuch, was deputized as part of a posse hunting four fugitive slaves believed to be hiding in town. It was discovered that a local group comprised of black and white abolitionists was harboring the fugitives, and a fight broke out as the posse attempted their recapture. Gorsuch was killed in the confrontation and two others were wounded. The violence soon came to be known as the Christiana Riot.[54]

Three years later, another deputy marshal was killed because of the Fugitive Slave Act. Anthony Burns had been a slave in Richmond, Virginia, but in 1853, at the age of nineteen, he had managed to escape. He successfully made his way north to Boston, where he found employment as a manual laborer for several local businessmen. The following year, on May 24, while walking down Court Street, he was arrested as a fugitive slave and taken to be held in the local courthouse. Word spread of Burns's arrest, and a crowd of abolitionists—black and white—ran to the courthouse, where their protest soon turned into mob violence. They stormed the courthouse in an attempt to free Burns, and in the melee Deputy US Marshal James Batchelder was fatally stabbed. The other marshals on duty and local police managed to maintain control of Burns, and after a trial he was returned to slavery in Virginia. His tragic case, however, galvanized abolitionist sentiment and exposed the difficulties of enforcing such laws.[55]

It was during this same period that the already-stretched Marshals Service was tasked with performing yet another service. The production and trade of counterfeit money by coneymen, as they were called, had been wreaking havoc on the US economy and was a growing national concern. The marshals were asked to find and arrest the counterfeiters, but for the first time they would have some help enforcing the law of the land, when the government began contracting with the Pinkerton National Detective Agency.[56]

Allan Pinkerton, who created Pinkerton National Detective Agency, in a 1862 photo taken during the Battle of Antietam. Pinkerton was asked to provide intelligence and to protect the president during the Civil War in what was a forerunner to the US Secret Service.

Photo by Alexander Gardner and courtesy of the U.S. Library of Congress.

2

Pinkerton's Detectives

Allan Pinkerton lived with his wife and son on the Fox River, "about thirty-eight miles northwest of the city of Chicago" in the "beautiful village of Dundee." Pinkerton was a cooper by trade—the first in his village—crafting barrels, casks, and kegs by hand, and he called himself the "Only and Original Cooper of Dundee."[1] He was well respected for both his craftsmanship and his work ethic, and though Pinkerton was the only cooper around, the villagers were always willing to engage in business with him.

One of the biggest impediments in the 1840s to businesses such as Pinkerton's was the scarcity of ready cash available for exchange, and much of what little money was on hand was counterfeit. This was because of the use of "wildcat" banknotes—currency printed by state and local banks that was, unfortunately, easily counterfeited.[2] Although "counterfeit money did not directly affect Pinkerton's cooperage," according to Pinkerton's biographer Frank Morn, it did harm "those upon whom he depended for business."[3] While this lack of available currency and the dangers inherent with counterfeit dollars provided Pinkerton with an economic excuse for not purchasing his wood from other local vendors, he later admitted, "I was actually too poor to purchase outright a wheel-barrow load of hoop-poles, or staves, and was consequently compelled to cut my own hoop-poles and split my own staves."[4] So Pinkerton often spent days searching for suitable wood to cut, trim, and transport back to his cooperage. And that was exactly what he was doing the day his life changed forever.

According to another Pinkerton biographer, James Mackay, it was "one day in June of 1846" that "Allan poled his raft up the Fox River to a little island a few miles above Dundee and close to the village of Algonquin."[5] While searching for the right kind of wood to make his casks, he had recently found the island to have a good copse of trees for this purpose. While there, Pinkerton found "some smoldering embers and other traces indicating that the little island had been made quite common use of." As Pinkerton noted, it was uncommon at the time for people to picnic or camp in such locations for leisure, so he suspected that, whoever the occupants had been, they were either "coin-counterfeiters" or "horse-thieves."[6] Upon his return to Dundee, Pinkerton informed the local sheriff, Luther Dearborn, of his discovery and suspicions.

Dearborn knew there was indeed a band of counterfeiters operating in and around Dundee and so gathered his deputies, asking Pinkerton to lead them to the location. In order to ensure the legality of Pinkerton's participation, Dundee temporarily deputized him, and he then "led the officers" to the location on the island where, he later wrote, they managed to capture "the entire gang, consisting of men and women." They also managed to secure the implements used in making the counterfeit coins, as well as a "large amount of bogus coin," and because of this thereafter the island was known as "Bogus Island."[7]

In the wake of the capture of the counterfeit ring, Pinkerton found himself constantly cornered by members of his village asking him to retell the exploits of his detection, the courageous manhunt, and the daring capture of the nefarious evildoers. "The arrest and subsequent conviction of the 'cony men' brought Allan a great deal of publicity; every farmer and trader who came to the shop for casks and kegs wanted to hear the story until Allan grew weary of telling it."[8]

Pinkerton's foiling the counterfeit ring had another, unexpected, outcome: people from all over began calling upon him to investigate other potential counterfeiters in the area. He was, reluctant to say yes, however, for he saw such work as a "will-o'-the-wisp piece of business."[9] But in the end, couldn't say no and was prevailed upon to performed a number of these investigations. "The country being new, and great sensations scarce," he later wrote when describing his change of heart, "the affair was in everybody's mouth, and I suddenly found myself called upon, from every quarter, to undertake matters requiring detective skill, until I was soon *forced* to relinquish the honorable, though not over-profitable, occupation of a cooper, for that of a professional detective."[10]

Allan Pinkerton was born in Glasgow, Scotland, on August 25, 1819.[11] His father, William Pinkerton, worked for an early form of a police department in the same city. In 1830, William was injured in a demonstration and subsequently died from those wounds. Allan was only ten years old at the time, but in order to help his family survive financially, he left school and began working for a loom company as an errand boy. He later recalled working "from dawn to dusk for pennies" and soon knew he needed to find some other form of employment.[12] His uncle John had been a cooper, and so Allan decided to learn the trade. He bound himself to William McAuly and on December 26, 1837, after a seven-year apprenticeship, obtained his journeyman's card, becoming an official member of the Coopers of Glasgow. Allan was now a barrel maker.

Although he remembered that day fondly, it wasn't long before Pinkerton grew disillusioned. Working his trade in the waning years of 1830s Scotland was hard: the political climate had grown rather hostile toward the working class, and Scotland was both economically depressed and oppressed. "In my native country," Pinkerton later wrote, "I was free in name, but a slave in fact. I toiled in and out of season, and my labor went to sustain the Government."[13] Pinkerton was so dissatisfied that he joined the Chartist movement, which called for political reform, fought against political corruption, and demanded justice for the working class.[14] He soon became very active in the movement, especially when demand for barrels was low, often touring throughout Scotland and England advocating for Chartist demands. As Pinkerton matured, however, his passionate advocacy was tempered, and he became more attuned to the realities of the Chartist movement—a movement that had become a cause for everyone and anything. That, and he met a woman.

In the summer of 1841, soprano Joan Carfrae sang at a concert Pinkerton had helped organize. As soon as she walked on stage, Allan fell madly in love, and he began attending her every concert. "I got to sort of hanging around her," he later said, "clinging to her, so to speak, and I knew I couldn't live without her." They married on March 13, 1842. Desiring a fresh start, the newlyweds set sail for America on April 9 aboard the *Kent*.[15]

Crossing the Atlantic Ocean in the mid-nineteenth century was a hazardous affair, and the Pinkertons didn't prove to be extraordinarily lucky. On April 19, their ship was spotted by another vessel "listing badly with both pumps going."[16] The *Kent* had been sailing for Montreal via the Gulf of Saint Lawrence, but a hurricane had blown through, forcing the boat 250 miles off course. It had foundered on Sable Island, a thirteen-square-mile sandbar located east of Nova Scotia. The passengers had taken to lifeboats and made it ashore, only to be set upon by a band of natives who had taken advantage of the passengers' plight. Joan was robbed of her wedding ring, but the couple managed to retrieve their luggage from the ship the following day, and soon after their rescue they caught a passing boat bound for Halifax. From there they booked passage to Montreal.

In what was to be their new home, Pinkerton found the Coopers' union and obtained both lodging and work through them. He began his new job making beef barrels, while listening closely to news of the economic situation in Montreal. What he heard was not good: most people were criticizing the city's decline while simultaneously speaking dreamily of the opportunities available in Chicago. Several months later, when the work had all dried up and he still hadn't heard of any good prospects in Montreal, Pinkerton came to a decision: "I all at once made up my mind to jump to that thriving little city of Chicago."[17]

Although he found work almost immediately in a brewery, Pinkerton found Chicago to be more hype than much anything else: it was a dirty, disgusting place, and he wanted no part of it.[18] He also wanted to own his own business and so began looking farther afield, when he found the little town of Dundee, Illinois, surrounded by woods and lacking a cooper. The Pinkertons moved there in the spring of 1843, purchasing a small farm with a house and a workshop for him to hang his sign—"Only and Original Cooper of Dundee."[19] They settled into their new life, and in April 1846, their son William was born. Two months later, Allan spoiled the counterfeit ring on Bogus Island.

After the raid on Bogus Island, Pinkerton had retained his deputy status in Kane County under Sheriff Luther Dearborn and, at the encouragement of his many admirers, continued investigating local counterfeit. But he soon realized that greater opportunities for this new profession would be found in back in Chicago, where he once again moved his small family, thus beginning a series of jobs that eventually led to the creation of his famous detective agency.

It is difficult to follow his career in local law enforcement during this time period, for there are many conflicting narratives. Some suggest he initially capitalized on his position as a Kane County deputy sheriff in order to join the Cook County Sheriff's Office. Others suggest that his first true position in Chicago was in 1847 with the police department and that, after the department reorganized in1849, he was officially named its first detective. What is known, in any case, is that he resigned from that position in late 1850, which he later claimed was "because of political interference."[20] The real reason, however, may have had more to do with Pinkerton's playing fast and loose with the rules: If he worked for the Cook County Sheriff's Department or for the Chicago Police Department, he would not have been authorized to work for another agency or under contract. But this is most likely exactly what he was doing, and any "political interference" he suffered may actually have been his seniors cracking down on his moonlighting.

It is similarly difficult to pin down Pinkerton's creation of his private security agency.[21] Pinkerton Security dates its founding to 1850, and it has been suggested that Pinkerton's National

Detective Agency was created to handle private cases while he was working for the Chicago PD.[22] It has also been suggested that after resigning from the police department Pinkerton went into partnership with Edward A. Rucker, a young Chicago lawyer, creating the North-Western Police Agency. In addition to this private-security venture, over the next five years Pinkerton also took on counterfeiting cases for the US Department of the Treasury, served as a Special United States Mail Agent for the US Post Office, and was deputized by the Cook County Sheriff's Office. As was typical of this time period, all of Pinkerton's early investigative work, it would appear, consisted of private government contracts, save the work he did for the Chicago PD.

The federal government of the 1850s had little in the way of federal law enforcement other than the US Marshals Service, as we discussed in chapter 1. Historian Frank Morn explains that, when not relying on the marshals, "a characteristic trend of federal policing in the first half of the nineteenth century was to hire private persons for police work as occasion arose." Any federal agency, in other words, might contract with a private organization to conduct any investigation. The Department of the Treasury, for example, "had a mandate to investigate and police counterfeiting since the founding of the nation," but "it did not create a detective force to carry out that mandate until after the Civil War."[23] And so Pinkerton and Ruker's North-Western Police Agency filled an important role for both the federal government and local governments like Cook County. The very absence of federal, state, and many local agencies was the very reason Pinkerton became so successful and was also why he could work for so many different agencies while still operating his newly created private-detective agency during the early 1850s: he was operating off of government contracts.

Regardless of the outfit for whom he was working, time and time again Pinkerton proved to be of great value to his clients.[24] He was hired by the Treasury Department on several occasions, first in 1851 and then in 1853, to break up counterfeiting operations and was successful in both cases, making arrests in Chicago in the first case and in Galena, Illinois, in the second. The Cook County Sheriff's Office have him several assignments, including a harrowing kidnapping case: while rescuing two girls from Michigan who had been abducted to Rockford, Illinois, Pinkerton was forced to shoot one of the abductors. And in 1855 he cracked an important case for the US Postal Service, catching two employees, brothers who were related to the Chicago postmaster, who had been stealing cash sent through the US mail. Pinkerton was quickly gaining a reputation as the right person to contract if an agency wanted something done. The local press sang his praises, writing, "As a detective police officer Mr. Pinkerton has no superior, and we doubt if he has any equals in this country."[25]

Despite his success in the first half of the 1850s, Pinkerton was in a precarious financial situation. Government contracts were never consistent, arising as agencies were faced with individual cases and as these agencies found funds in the budget to pursue them. So, while Pinkerton was making a name for himself, he was not yet as successful financially as he would have liked. This was also due in part to the reality that Pinkerton "was a loner, handling all of his cases personally," which would have naturally limited the number of cases he could accept at any given time.[26] All of this changed for him on February 1, 1855.

The rapid rise of the railroads at midcentury brought an abundance of opportunities to not just Chicago but the entire country. However, it also brought an increase in crime. Once again, the lack of a federal or state law-enforcement structure and reliance on local law-enforcement—what little there was of it at the time—often meant that travel on trains posed no guarantee of safety. "Once the train left the city," Morn explains, "it lost all the protections of urban society until it reached its destination."[27] As a result of the industry's growth and its criminal misfortunes, Pinkerton received several contracts to investigate cases of theft on some rail lines. His success in these investigations motivated the owners of six of the Midwestern railroads to pool together ten thousand dollars to contract Pinkerton full-time to provide security and to investigate crimes on their railroad lines. Using the substantial fee—an estimated half-million in today's dollars—Pinkerton hired four employees to assist him in his near-total dedication to the lucrative railroad contract.

On November 6, 1860, Abraham Lincoln was elected the sixteenth president of the United States, much to the chagrin of the Democratic Party and the disgust of the Southern slaveholding states. While the he had received the support of the Northern states and two Western states, the Southern states had been unanimous in their support of his Southern Democratic opponent, John C. Breckenridge. And although Lincoln only managed to win a plurality of the votes, he did win the electoral college quite handily and began preparing for his presidency.[28] But before Lincoln had even had the chance to solemnly swear he would "faithfully execute the Office of President," South Carolina seceded from the Union, and by February 1, 1861, Florida, Mississippi, Alabama, Georgia, Louisiana, and Texas followed suit.[29]

There was little Lincoln could do, for in those pre–Twentieth Amendment days, the inauguration was not held until March 4, so he had to wait another four months before he could use his executive authority to take action. In the interim, Lincoln formed his "team of rivals" and announced plans for a whistle-stop tour in advance of his inauguration, traveling through eight Northern states and stopping in seventy cities on his way to Washington, D.C.[30] He intended to thank his voters at the preplanned train stops, as well as shore up political support in the North as he faced down opposition in the South.

The South's growing rancor was becoming more evident with each passing day leading up to the train's departure from Springfield, Illinois, which had been scheduled for February 11, 1861. It was certainly felt by Samuel Morse Felton, president of the Philadelphia, Wilmington and Baltimore Railroad, whose line Lincoln would be taking to Washington, through Southern-sympathetic Maryland. Felton did not want anything to happen to the new president-elect during the journey, as it would reflect poorly on his railroad. And so when he heard rumors that the lines entering Baltimore were to be destroyed by "Southern sympathizers" in advance of Lincoln's arrival, he sprang into action, seeking the advice of his closest associates and friends.[31] Colonel Bringham of the Adams Express Company—today one of the oldest companies on the New York Stock Exchange—suggested that Felton hire the Pinkertons,[32] to which Felton readily agreed, contracting with the private police for what became Allan Pinkerton's first railroad contract outside of the Chicago area, as well as one of his most lucrative.

Meanwhile, the president-elect's people had come to the same conclusion Felton had: the security situation was too precarious. On the second day of the inaugural train tour alone, Lincoln had given a speech to forty-five thousand onlookers from his balcony in the Bates House, Indianapolis's first hotel. His plans, including his route, was public knowledge, and the newspapers had been widely advertising each stop well in advance so that Americans could turn out to see their future president. While Lincoln was traveling with a large and growing entourage, he had no formal protection. Elmer E. Ellsworth had been charged with seeing Lincoln through the crowds at each stop, and Edwin V. Sumner, the senior military officer on the train, took it upon himself to organize Lincoln's overall security, such as it was. But it was commonly agreed that Lincoln remained too vulnerable.

A solution was found in Ward Hill Lamon, who had been with Lincoln throughout his campaign, serving as a sort of private secretary. The older, more senior men ushered the thirty-one-year-old Lamon into a private room in the hotel, where, as Lamon recorded later, they "proceeded in the most solemn and impressive manner to instruct me as to my duties as the special guardian of Mr. Lincoln's person during the rest of the journey to Washington." After they had finished reviewing all that was expected of him, including laying down his own life for Lincoln's, Jesse Dubois—whom they all called "Uncle Jesse"—attempted to lighten the solemnity of the meeting: "We intrust the sacred life of Mr. Lincoln to your keeping," said Dubois, "and if you don't protect it, never return to Illinois, for we will murder you on sight."[33] The joke, no doubt, brought nary a chuckle from the somber group.

Between February 12 and 14, as Lincoln continued to give speeches to the crowds that massed in Cincinnati, Columbus, Cleveland, and Pittsburgh, Lamon performed his special services as the first unofficial secret-service agent. But even with these improvements, Lincoln was too exposed, as they would discover on February 16, when Lincoln arrived in Buffalo, New York. Despite military escorts and the presence of the police, the crowd of supporters there pushed forward to catch a glimpse of the president-elect, resulting in injuries to some in Lincoln's party. Lincoln himself only narrowly escaped the crush of the crowd, but the vulnerability of the president on the whistle-stop tour became abundantly clear.[34]

Meanwhile, Pinkerton, along with his best operatives, was working undercover, performing the duties of the first unofficial secret-service intelligence-gathering advance party. Pinkerton himself departed Chicago with his five best operatives: Timothy Webster, Harry W. Davies, Charles D. C. Williams, Hattie Lawton, and Kate Warne—the first female detective. The group first traveled to Philadelphia to receive instructions from Samuel Felton. From there they traveled on to Maryland—and Baltimore, a particularly harrowing part of the trip, as it was known that were any attempt to be made on the president-elect's life, it would most likely happen in Baltimore. As a slave state, Maryland was not overly keen on Lincoln, who was believed to harbor abolitionist sentiments. He had won less than 3 percent of the vote in Maryland during the presidential election, coming in fourth there in what was essentially a field of four candidates, and in seven of the state's precincts he had not received a single vote. But it was Baltimore, out of all of Maryland, that was the most sympathetic to the Southern cause, and it was in Baltimore that Pinkerton and his operatives chose to concentrate their energies.[35]

Each of the security operatives approached Baltimore very differently: Kate Warne and Hattie Lawton played the role of Southern belles, putting on clothing and accents to fit the bill, and then infiltrated the many secessionist groups, using their womanly charms to obtain information.[36] Timothy Webster and another of Pinkerton's operatives, Joseph Howard, also infiltrated several secessionist groups as men who wanted to fight for the cause. Pinkerton himself posed as John H. Hutchison, a stockbroker, so he could rub elbows with the more aristocratic Southern sympathizers among Baltimore's elite. Each agent found their own piece of the larger puzzle, which Pinkerton was able to quickly put together to decipher a conspiracy to assassinate the president-elect.

Among the active leaders in Baltimore's secessionist were a barber, Cypriano Ferrandini,[37] and a self-professed soldier of fortune, Otis K. Hillard. They were part of such secret groups as the Knights of the Golden Circle, the National Volunteers, the Palmetto Guard, and the Constitutional Guard, the latter having been formed "to prevent Northern volunteer companies from passing through the State of Maryland . . . to invade the South."[38] Capitalizing on the published schedules of Lincoln's train stops, the conspirators had planned to do the same thing to Lincoln: prevent his passing through Maryland.

One location among the Baltimore stops made Lincoln particularly vulnerable, due to an oddity of railroad construction. On February 23, 1861, Lincoln was to arrive at the city's Calvert Street Station, a stop along the Northern Central Railway; but in order to proceed to the capitol, he would have to disembark there and transfer by carriage to Camden Station on the Baltimore and Ohio Railroad, where another train would be waiting for him to continue his journey to the capital. At the exchange the plotters planned for Lincoln to be surrounded by a crowd of Southern sympathizers, which would give an assassin cover for a deadly assault on the president-elect. Even police protection was complicit in the conspiracy: They were planning to allow physically marked agitators through their lines, thus allowing the assassins to approach the carriage. Once the attack was finished, the assassins could then just disappear back into the crowds, killing Lincoln before he ever took office.[39]

Pinkerton needed to get immediate word to Lincoln and so dispatched a message of urgency through an intermediary. He then consulted Lincoln's scheduled stops, leaving immediately thereafter to intercept him in Philadelphia. The two men had many friends in common, and while "Lincoln had been an attorney for the Illinois Central from 1853 to 1859 . . . his work brought him into occasional contact with Pinkerton's detective activities."[40] When Pinkerton finally caught up with Lincoln, the detective "advised him to leave Philadelphia at once and pass through Baltimore on a night train ahead of schedule to confound the conspirators."[41] As Ward Lamon later wrote, "This he flatly refused to do."[42]

Lamon explained that Lincoln "had engagements with the people" in which he had promised "to raise a flag over Independence Hall in the morning, and to exhibit himself at Harrisburg in the afternoon."[43] Pinkerton pressed upon the president-elect the severity of the situation, but Lincoln, never the reactionary, demurred. He agreed to take Pinkerton's information under advisement, but he believed he could not change his behavior based on what amounted to rumor. Lincoln continued with his monumental tour through the Northern states.

Later that same day, however, Senator William H. Seward, Lincoln's choice for secretary of state, summoned his son Fred to come to him immediately.[44] When Fred met his father, he was handed a note from General Winfield Scott and told to "find Mr. Lincoln, wherever he is. Let no one else know your errand." Fred obeyed his father and immediately boarded a train bound for Philadelphia. He arrived late that same night, traveling by carriage to the Continental Hotel, where Lincoln was staying. As Fred later explained, "I found Chestnut street crowded with people, gay with lights, and echoing with music and hurrahs," thus forcing him to wait several hours before he could have confer with the president-elect.[45] After a quick exchange of pleasantries, Fred handed Lincoln the letter from General Scott.

Lincoln read it slowly, then read it a second time, giving greater consideration to what Pinkerton had told him just that very morning. "If different persons," he thought out loud to Lamon and Seward, "not knowing each other's work, have been pursuing separate clews that led to the same result, why then it shows there may be something in it. But if this is only the same story, filtered through two channels, and reaching me in two ways, then that don't make it any stronger. Don't you see?" Fred Seward, crestfallen at Lincoln's rationalizing, looked glum; but Lincoln added, "You need not think I will not consider it well. I shall think it over carefully, and try to decide it right; and I will let you know in the morning."[46]

The next morning, as promised, Lincoln shared his decision: He believed it prudent to bypass Baltimore and head straight to the nation's capital, but only after his stop that day in Harrisburg, Pennsylvania.[47] That night, on February 22, Pinkerton had the telegraph lines cut between Harrisburg and Baltimore, preventing any advance notice of Lincoln's secret change in plans.[48] All other trains on the line were sidetracked. Accompanied both by his secretary-turned-bodyguard Lamon and by Pinkerton, Lincoln—wearing a felt cap rather than his traditional stovepipe—boarded a special train that passed through Baltimore at 3:30 a.m. and proceeded directly to Washington, D.C. Soon after, Pinkerton sent the vice president of the railroad a message: "Plums delivered nuts." Pinkerton had delivered Lincoln to safety, foiling the first known plot to kill a president-elect.[49]

Lincoln's arrival into the United States' seat of government had been under the cover of darkness and known to only a handful of people.[50] When the newspapers discovered the secret, much of the press criticized his method of entry into Washington, D.C., with one political cartoonist depicting Lincoln wearing a Scottish kilt as a disguise.[51] The Southern newspapers immediately called the possibility of an assassination absurd, while the Northern newspapers were divided: some, like the *New York Times* and the *Chicago Tribune*, believe the threat was real, while others, like the *New York Daily Tribune* and the *Chicago Democrat*, believed the conspiracy had been constructed by Pinkerton to drum up business.[52] The *Chicago Democrat*'s editorial asked, "How much longer will the people of this country be the dupe of these private detectives?" For, the editor explained, "if a man is dependent upon his professor for a living, as these detectives are, they must have cases." As such, "there was no conspiracy at all," he concluded, "save in the brain of the Chicago detective."[53] So critical of the conspiracy were the editorials that famous diarist George Templeton Strong wrote he actually "hoped that the conspiracy can be proved beyond cavil. If it cannot be made manifest and indisputable, this surreptitious nocturnal dodging or sneaking of the President-elect into his capital city, under cloud of night, will be used to damage his moral position and throw ridicule on his Administration."[54]

Lincoln had neither the time nor resources to defend his actions or investigate the matter, but he quickly came to regret having ever listened to Mr. Pinkerton or General Scott.[55] Although in the immediate aftermath it was concluded that the conspiracy was not real by a number of investigations, including a congressional study into the matter, recent scholarship has brought to light that there had indeed been a plot to assassinate President-Elect Lincoln and that Pinkerton was material in exposing and foiling it.[56]

Throughout the Civil War, the government continued to contract Pinkerton's services on a wide range of assignments, from collecting intelligence in the South to protecting the president. But when the war ended, his services no longer considered necessary, Pinkerton was let go. Had he remained under contract to protect the president, history may very well have turned out differently.

Even had Pinkerton created the Baltimore plot in order to drum up more business, after Confederate batteries attacked the federally held Fort Sumter on April 12, 1861, Pinkerton had more work than he could handle. In addition to the Northern railroads that had hired Pinkerton to prevent destruction of the rail lines and track down would-be saboteurs, the federal government also began contracting with Pinkerton's agency to handle a wide array of duties as the United States had no national police force to cope with the problems brought on by the Civil War.

The first to take advantage of Pinkerton's network of detectives was General George McClellan. Prior to the Civil War, in 1857 McClellan had resigned his commission and begun a civilian career as chief engineer and vice present of the Illinois Central Railroad, which was under contract with Pinkerton for its security. McClellan and Pinkerton had become fast friends, and so after the war broke out and McClellan had received his commission as a major general of volunteers and was placed in charge of the Ohio militia, he asked Pinkerton to come work for him under a military contract. He was in need of information and intelligence regarding the enemy operating in and around Ohio, and so "McClellan asked Allan to organise a Secret Service Department for his army."[57] Pinkerton had actually proposed the same thing to President Lincoln, but after receiving no reply,

Pinkerton agreed to McClellan's offer and set up his headquarters in Cincinnati.

Pinkerton and his operatives began gathering intelligence in Ohio on potential plots against the Union, as well as on Confederate strength and positions in the area. Pinkerton himself purchased "a splendid bay" and took off behind enemy lines posing as a "gentleman from Georgia."[58] As always, Pinkerton proved quite adept at gathering information—such as when he boldly forayed in the Kanawha Valley, finding "only fifty soldiers at the Red House" who were "equipped with muskets and poor rifles and with the exception of the Kanawha Rangers (100 strong) were very poor specimens of mortality, many not exceeding fifteen years of age."[59] This intelligence allowed McClellan to precisely target pockets of Confederates and Southern sympathizers. These successes elevated both McClellan and Pinkerton to the highest levels of power.

After General Irvin McDowell's embarrassing defeat at the Battle of Bull Run, Lincoln began looking for a general who showed greater promise of success; that someone was "the man of the hour," George B. McClellan.[60] Lincoln placed McClellan in charge of the Military Division of the Potomac, and McClellan, in turn, brought Pinkerton to Washington, D.C., to head the Secret Service.[61] In that role, "Pinkerton had two wartime duties to perform: investigating suspicious people within the Union territory and gathering information from behind enemy lines."[62] Once again, he proved highly successful. But this time, McClellan did not.

A "Young Napoleon" McClellan was not, having never proven audacious and always overestimating his enemy's strength, which led him to inaction and made him largely ineffective. Lincoln fired "Little Mac" after his failure to pursue General Robert E. Lee in the aftermath of the Battle of Antietam.[63] With McClellan went Pinkerton, who resigned in protest because he "felt McClellan was treated unjustly by conniving politicians."[64] Nevertheless, the federal government continued to contract with Pinkerton through the end of the war, including hiring him for one mission to infiltrate the hotbed of New Orleans.

Even after the Civil War, the federal government continued to issue contracts to Pinkerton's National Detective Agency, often to investigate fraud and other violations of government contracts.[65] These contracts came out of a myriad of departments within the federal government and were issued on as-needed basis. Pinkerton began receiving many of his contracts from the United States Department of Justice after its founding in 1870. In addition to investigating many cases of fraud against the government, Pinkerton was once contracted after Lincoln's assassination to hire detectives to help arrest conspirators who had plotted to steal the president's body, while another contract authorized the hiring of twenty guards for the 1889 inauguration of President Benjamin Harrison.[66]

One of the most common lucrative of Pinkerton's contracts during this time period concerned tensions between businesses and attempts by labor to unionize. The most powerful weapon the labor unions had against the businesses was the strike. And because the strike caused a disruption to production, businesses did everything they could to shut them down as rapidly as they could, often by hiring Pinkerton detectives to do it for them. In fact, a Congressional committee noted that from 1870 to 1892 the "Pinkerton's [sic] had been involved in seventy strikes."[67] Those lucrative contracts, however, all came to an end with the debacle that unfolded during the Homestead Strike.

The Homestead Steel Works was located in Homestead, Pennsylvania, near Pittsburgh.[68] In 1876, the steel workers unionized under the Amalgamated Association of Iron and Steel Workers (AA) in an attempt to negotiate for better pay, improved working conditions, and more reasonable workloads. Andrew Carnegie owned the steel mill, and, although he publically professed he had no problem with the formation of the steel workers' the union, he placed his right-hand man, Henry Clay Frick, in charge of the mill's operations in 1881.[69] Frick was largely known to be Carnegie's strongman, and he had really been placed there to break the back of the union. In a letter to Carnegie, Frick wrote, "The mills have never been able to turn out the product they should, owing to being held back by the Amalgamated men."[70]

As the collective-bargaining agreement that had previously been put into place before Frick's arrival was set to expire on June 30, 1892, new negotiations were opened in February of that year.[71] The union wanted an increase in wages; Frick told them there would be a decrease. Frick had no intention of entering into any agreement with the AA, and after three months of failed "negotiations," Frick announced on April 30, 1892, that he would give negotiations one more month to work themselves out. If they failed, there would be no more union at Homestead.

Frick contacted Andrew Carnegie about the situation, and, after receiving Carnegie's approval, he moved forward with his plan.[72] On June 29, well after the deadline, when no agreement was reached, Frick locked the union out of the Homestead Steel Works. Frick had ordered a solid board fence be built to surround the facility for just this purpose, and on June 29, now newly topped with barbed wire, it was completed. The union members began referring to the Steel Mill as "Fort Frick."[73]

The union members met and decided they would surround the plant and keep it from operating by preventing all employees from entering the steel mill, as well as any replacement-worker "scabs" Frick planned to hire.[74] Frick had been in the process of hiring replacements, placing ads in newspapers up and down the eastern seaboard, in Saint Louis, and as far away as Europe. The problem, however, was getting the new replacement workers into the steel mill, which was now surrounded by Amalgamated men. For that problem, Frick hired three hundred Pinkerton men to break up the strike.

Frick wanted the mill opened with replacement workers on July 6, so on the night of July 5, the Pinkerton men assembled at Davis Island Dam on the Ohio River. Using two barges to travel upriver to the plant, the Pinkerton men began their journey toward Homestead as Winchester rifles were distributed among them. Local Sheriff William H. McCleary was also on hand, specifically to deputize the Pinkerton detectives; but in all the excitement, he forgot: Soon after assembling, McCleary and company had learned that the strikers were armed just as well prepared. They also had their own boats and had intercepted Pinkerton's men on the river, harassing them enough to slow them sufficiently that an alarm could be sounded, which brought thousands of people to their aid—men, women, and children—all in support of the strikers.

The Pinkertons, having been delayed by the union flotilla, did not arrive at the plant until around 4 a.m. There they were met by a crowd outnumbering them at least five to one, at which point they attempted to disembark from the barges. Chaos ensued, and according to reports, the fence was torn down and rocks were thrown at the Pinkertons. Tensions escalated, and finally shots were fired. Who fired the first shot has always been hotly contested, but one of the boatmen hired by the Pinkertons described what happened next: "The armed Pinkerton men commenced to climb up the banks. Then the workmen opened fire on the detectives. The men shot first, and not until three Pinkerton men had fallen did they respond to the fire. I am willing to take an oath that the workmen fired first, and that the Pinkerton men did not shoot until some of their number had been wounded."[75] The workers reported that the Pinkertons had fired first.

Regardless of who fired first, what happened next was not in dispute: A battle ensued. The Pinkertons retreated and then tried again to gain the shore, but more were injured. The workers then tried to dynamite the Pinkerton barge, burn it out by lighting another barge on fire and pushing it toward the Pinkerton men, and finally pouring oil into the river and lighting it on fire. None of these attempts were successful except to keep up the pressure on the detectives. By late that afternoon, thousands of armed workers from nearby mills and the surrounding area had arrived in a show of solidarity with their fellow union members, and by 5 p.m. the Pinkerton detectives, realizing their plight, raised a white flag in surrender.

As the Pinkerton men were rounded up, many were subsequently beaten.[76] After being forced to run a gauntlet through the strikers, they were then marched off to jail. Along the way two more were beaten unmercifully, and it has been said that any "cries for mercy were treated with derision."[77] In the end, the Homestead strike left seven strikers and three Pinkerton men dead, and many more were injured, including nearly every one of the Pinkerton detectives. The state militia was soon sent in to quell the disturbance.

A Congressional investigation into Homestead quickly ensued, and despite the sheriff's failure to deputize the detectives, Pinkerton received the blame. The committee also found it reprehensible that a private detective agency could cross state lines, but they left the final resolution to the states themselves. Keying in on this, the states began proposing anti-Pinkerton legislation, which forbade "armed detectives from entering their states."[78] These laws began passing in 1893, with West Virginia and North Carolina leading the way and Nebraska, Wisconsin, Texas, Pennsylvania, and the District of Columbia following soon thereafter.[79] While Congress had left the issue largely to the states, it did prohibit all executive departments from issuing any further contracts to the Pinkerton National Detective Agency or any other such detective agency.[80] That left the Justice Department and many other departments in the lurch, for they still had no investigators of their own. By this time, Treasury did have some investigative capacity, but they had already taken over most of the investigations into counterfeiting that had once been handled by Pinkerton and they were insufficiently prepared, and staffed, to handle any more investigations.

And so by the second half of the nineteenth century, without adequate federal resources to counter it, one of the most intractable problems facing the US government remained inadequately challenged. The issue that had led Allan Pinkerton into detective work in the first place, that had earned him renown, a career, and a goodly sum of his earnings, continued to plague the federal government for decades. It is to this issue—America's counterfeiting problem—that we now turn.

LOW-DOWN AND ILLEGAL.

Counterfeiters plying their trade in this photomechanical print by Keppler & Schwarzman and which appeared in a 1910 issue of the magazine Puck.

Photo courtesy of the Library of Congress.

3

Counterfeiters

Counterfeiting, the problem that allowed Allan Pinkerton to become a detective and make a living through both private and federal-government contracts, was brought on by the federal government's inability to create a stable currency. This was in spite of the fact it was under their Constitutional purview to do so. Article I not only gave Congress the enumerated power "To coin Money, regulate the Value thereof . . . and fix the Standards of Weights and Measures," it also specified they were "To provide for the Punishment of counterfeiting the Securities and current Coin of the United States."[1] The problem of counterfeiting was so widespread during the Antebellum era that constantly threatened to destabilize the American economy. It was not until the Civil War that Congress finally decided to take some kind of action, largely in response to Southern counterfeiters who were beginning to undermine the Northern economy.

When Adam Smith published *An Inquiry into the Nature and Causes of the Wealth of Nations* in the year America gained independence from England, he explained the origin and use of money in societies around the world. He put forth that "when the division of labour has been once thoroughly established," the laborer most often produces more than he needs, but because he has other needs "every man thus lives by exchanging." Initially, the form of exchange is by way of commodities, be it excess fruits and vegetables or livestock. Eventually, however, a form of value must be fixed for the common exchange of goods, for a bushel of corn is not valued the same as a cow. Early forms of valuation were often based on the common worth of a cow or some quantity of salt. Yet the vagaries of maintaining these commodities as a form of currency is was wrought with danger, for livestock die and fruits and vegetables rot. This is why "in all countries," Smith says, "men seem at last to have been determined by irresistible reasons to give the preference . . . to metals above every other commodity."[2]

"Metals can not only be kept with as little loss as any other commodity," Adams continues, but they can also be "divided into any number of parts" and thus represent the value of both fruits and vegetables, as well as cattle. So, once the division of labor develops into an exchange process, it becomes necessary to have something serve as currency in trade, and that something is usually metals. "Different metals have been made use of by different nations for this purpose," including iron by the ancient Spartans, copper by the ancient Romans, and of course silver and gold among the more developed, rich, and commercial nations.[3]

Only when an economy has achieved some stability and a separation grows between the rich and the poor does the need for a paper currency develop: when someone, such as a merchant, gains so much wealth that the weight of metals—iron, copper, silver, gold—becomes burdensome and it is no longer feasible to carry or exchange large amounts of metals, trading the bullion for paper currency makes sense. And when the need for a more manageable paper currency arises, it is—at least at first—developed to represent some value of the metal—be it copper, silver, or gold. This is done to represent the metals themselves so that the actual metals do not have to be moved and, rather, the paper currency can be exchanged in its place.

This process of moving from products to metals to paper, however, increases the risk for fraudulent crimes. It is difficult to forge commodities, for one cannot make fake cattle or vegetables. Metals can be cheapened with inferior metals, thus making them less valuable than their stated worth, but these alloys still retain some of their original value. Paper currency, however, with the right equipment and skill can be faked to such a dangerous extent that it can flood the market with so much additional money that it undervalues the currency and destabilizes the market.[4]

During the Colonial era in America, commodities were still commonly used in trade, but three additional forms of currency were also exchanged.[5] The first was, of course, British coins, but because so few circulated in the colonies and "the British government limited the export of gold and silver to the colonies," other coins such as pieces of eight, doubloons, and reals—mostly of Spanish and Portuguese origin—freely circulated. These foreign coins were mostly made of silver, and they became a favored currency.[6]

Another form of currency that came into use was commodity money, typically referred to as "bills of credit."[7] These were paper documents, much like a banknote, that represented some value of a specific type of commodity, such as cows, bushels of corn, salt, or tea. They were not true legal tender but were, rather, more like an IOU. They were often used when either coins or paper money were scarce and the actual commodity was too difficult to transfer. These notes proved to be so highly problematic that they were made illegal by the British government in 1684 and later by the US government with the passage of the US Constitution.[8] Commodity money is still used today under dire circumstances, such as when cigarettes become commodity money in prisoner-of-war camps or in modern-day prisons.[9]

The final form of currency was, of course, paper money. Paper money proved to be just as problematic in Colonial America, for it was supposed to be British paper money, in the denominations of pounds, shillings, and pence.[10] The problem, again, however, was the rarity of this paper money in the colonies. Once told they could not print bills of credit, the colonists discovered "a loophole in British regulations" for paper money, which appeared not to "infringe on the home government's monopoly on coinage," so the colonies decided to begin printing their own currency.[11] The first to do so was the government of Massachusetts, which ended up printing "the first authorized paper money issued by any government in the Western World."[12] The problems that soon developed had much to do with the valuation of the currency, which varied from colony to colony, and was not supposed supersede the value of the British currency. Trade in paper money between the colonies also proved problematic generally, creating a loss in value each time the currencies were exchanged. Where the real loss arose was in the exchange between the colonies and Britain— so much so that the British became very reluctant to have colonists pay their debts with the currency, as they always lost value in the exchange. Britain's attempt to control the problem with its Currency Act of 1764 only made things worse, driving many to rely on the Spanish dollar and the colonists toward war.

When the Revolutionary War was won by the rebellious colonies, which became independent states, a monetary system was needed to replace the British one, so the Continental Congress created its own scrip to pay for military expenses. Because this new continental currency was based on neither silver nor gold, it was, in reality nothing more than bills of credit. "Without anything 'hard' to fall back on," notes historian Ben Tarnoff, "paper can become worthless overnight, more useful as wallpaper or kindling than as money."[13] Similarly, each of the colonies produced its own currency, but they too were not based on anything hard. The only colony to base its currency on something hard was Pennsylvania, which based it on land. It allowed people to borrow scrip with their land as collateral at twice its value. Benjamin Franklin, who helped create the Pennsylvania scrip, believed "the utility of this currency became by time and experience so evident as never afterwards to be much disputed."[14] A less interested person, Adam Smith, also agreed.[15]

Despite Pennsylvania's limited success, most Colonial currency ended up devalued because of the need to print more money in order to support the war effort. By the end of the Revolutionary War, the continental currency had collapsed. The money had become, as Tarnoff mentioned, more useful as wallpaper and kindling than as currency. The new nation was in desperate straits and knew that if it was to survive it needed to restore its monetary system and stabilize its economy. So it turned to the "Financier of the Revolution," the man who, next to General George Washington, was "the most powerful man in the world."[16]

Robert Morris was born in Liverpool in 1734 and emigrated to America at age thirteen to live with his father, who traded tobacco in Maryland. Morris proved to be an adept student and was soon sent to Philadelphia to work with a banking firm run by Charles Willing. The following year, Morris's father tragically died when a gunship fired a salute in his honor and the wadding from the ship's gun struck him in the arm. "The bone of his arm was broken a little above the elbow and a large wound and contusion was made in the flesh," and then "the wound began to mortify."[17] He died soon after. One apocryphal story tells of his favorite spaniel dog who refused to leave the sick chamber; when Morris finally succumbed to his wound, the dog died as well.

After his father's funeral, Robert Morris returned to Philadelphia and continued working with the same bank until Willing's death ten years later. Willing's son Thomas inherited his father's wealth, and he and Morris became partners in a prominent shipping and banking firm that lasted until 1779. When the Continental Congress was struggling with British rule, they established a Secret Committee of Trade in 1775 and contracted with Willing, Morris & Co. to devise a means to smuggle in war supplies from France. The following year, Morris, now a congressional delegate from Pennsylvania, voted against declaring independence from Britain. However, seeing the overwhelming support among the other delegates for breaking from England, the next day Morris abstained from voting, and he eventually signed the Declaration of Independence. In explanation of his political change of view he said, "I am not one of those politicians that run testy when my own plans are not adopted. I think it is the duty of a good citizen to follow when he cannot lead."[18]

Not long after, the new Continental Congress came to appreciate of his belief in good citizenship, for they were cash strapped and could not afford to pay their own soldiers in the Continental Army. They turned to Morris for help. Morris agreed to assist in the war effort by personally underwriting the army by paying Washington's soldiers for their service with what became popularly known as "Morris Notes"—paper currency that featured his own portrait on the front of ten-dollar silver certificates. In the end, he contributed the equivalent of ten million pounds' worth of those silver certificates.

In honor of his assistance to the new government, Morris was appointed superintendent of finance. One of his first plans to help salvage the national economy was to create a bank that would essentially serve as the first unofficial national bank of America. The Bank of North America, as it was named, was established in Philadelphia and chartered on May 26, 1781. Its first president—and Morris's old partner—Thomas Willing, saw the bank as nothing more than a "novelty," mainly because he believed banking in America "was a pathless wilderness ground but little known to this side of the Atlantic"; to him it was all just "a mystery."[19]

Despite Willing's skeptical leadership, the bank proved to be the forerunner to the first true bank, the First Bank of the United States, which was established ten years later, in 1791, with the earnest approval of the first secretary of the treasury, Alexander Hamilton. A year later, Congress passed the Coinage Act of 1792, creating the first United States Mint, which was also located in Philadelphia. Now that the US government had both an official bank and a mint, it seemed the next natural step was to create a single monetary system. However, that goal was not achieved until after the Civil War was underway.

The US Mint, under the Coinage Act, was allowed to produce gold, silver, and copper coins—and only coins—ranging in value from a halfpenny up to ten dollars; however, that did not mean that they did. Almost from the beginning the US Mint was slow to produce coins and could not keep up with demand when they did.[20] In November of 1792, to help alleviate the shortage, President Washington ordered the striking of a "half-dime," and the following year a "half-cent" coin.[21] The first gold coins, "half-eagles"—worth five dollars at the time—did not circulated until 1795, followed by the "quarter-eagle" in 1796. Despite these additional coins, there were simply never enough produced in these early years to satisfy the demand, necessitating people to turn elsewhere for currency.

In addition to shortages of coins, there was another reason no single national currency was established in those early years. To put it simply, the people did not trust the government. As Johnson explains, "Most nineteenth-century Americans . . . were deeply suspicious of their federal government and viewed proposals to expand its power with alarm."[22] A proposal to create a national currency would have been met with so much animosity and derision that it most likely would never have passed. What developed instead were many state-chartered banks and even more corporation-run banks across the United States, especially in the northeast in the older, more established cities.

Three years after the Bank of North America opened in 1781, John Hancock chartered the Massachusetts Bank and Alexander Hamilton established the Bank of New York. When George Washington was inaugurated as the first president of the United States, these were the only banks in existence. Despite Hamilton's establishing the First Bank of the United States as the first system of banking, it did not truly amount to a national system of banks and became the focus of much animosity.

As Federalist Representative Fisher Ames predicted in 1791, "the state Banks will become unfriendly to that of the US," and "Causes of hatred & rivalry will abound."[23] He was right. Many people, believing the Bank of the United States to be unconstitutional, saw it as a threat to states' rights to develop their own banks. State bankers realized that it was going to be difficult to compete with a bank that had the backing of the United States government, for it would obviously have more capital to back its loans. And because the national government would want to protect its own interests, it would be able to pass regulations that could curb other banks' abilities to make loans, especially if those loans were to cross state lines. Finally, it would prevent banks from opening to serve the people in their states and their communities, because people willing to open a bank would think twice about doing so knowing they would have to compete against the Bank of the United States. Still, between President Washington's inauguration and 1811, a span of twenty-two years, eighty-five additional banks managed to open, holding a total of forty-three million dollars in capital and circulating approximately twenty-three million dollars between them by that time.[24]

Yet the First Bank of the United States remained controversial, and so in 1808, years before the twenty-year charter was set to expire in 1811, debate started in Congress.[25] It proved to be a volatile debate over the next two years, for the Federalists, who had instituted the bank, were no longer in power. The opposition party, the Democrats, were on top, and they pulled out every argument against the bank, including circulating a number of false rumors—for example, that three-quarters of the bank's stocks were in the hands of foreign investors who were manipulating the appointment of the bank's directors in their favor. On January 24, 1811, the House voted sixty-five to sixty-four against renewal of the bank. In the Senate, the vote was even closer—an even split. On February 17, Vice President George Clinton cast the tie-breaking vote against recharter. The First Bank of the United States had dissolved.

This dissolution of the bank had two major impacts on America. The first was felt almost instantly, with the financial vacuum the dissolution left in America's banking. Ready to fill the void were financial entrepreneurs, who began opening up many new state and corporate banks.[26] It is estimated that between 1811 and 1815, 120 new banks were opened holding 180 million dollars in capital and circulating 110 million dollars.[27] This was certainly good for the economy.

The second impact occurred the year after the dissolution, when America went to war with Britain a second time. Because the United States no longer had a national bank to draw on for loans, it made it very difficult for President James Madison to finance the War of 1812. In order to borrow funds, Madison had to appeal to the other American banks; however, most of them were located in the northeast, and they didn't think much of "Mr. Madison's War."[28] Madison's administration scrambled to find funding from other banks, and, in what is perhaps one of the strangest financial ironies ever to occur, they managed to obtain a loan from Barings Bank, a British merchant bank based out of London.

It was the impediment of obtaining loans for emergencies, such as wars, that motivated many to revisit the chartering of a national bank. In 1816, after the war was over, Congress passed a twenty-year charter for the Second Bank of the United States.[29] Once again, the bank was established in Philadelphia, but this time its holdings were even greater.[30] Almost instantly opposition to the new bank's charter began to foment, and throughout the 1820s that opposition continued to grow. But so did the bank. By the time President Andrew Jackson was inaugurated in 1829, the bank was financially sound, the economy was doing well, and public perception of the bank was positive. Despite all of this, Jackson decided to go to war with the banks.[31] As Jackson told Martin Van Buren, who had just returned from England as foreign minister, "the bank, Mr. Van Buren, is trying to kill me, *but I will kill it*."[32] Nicholas Biddle, then head of the Bank of the United States, is said to have responded, "This worthy President thinks that because he has scalped Indians and imprisoned Judges he is to have his way with the bank; He is mistaken."[33] Jackson mobilized his base, vetoed the early renewal recharter bill, and then—despite Biddle's assertions otherwise—removed all federal deposits from the national bank and disbursed them to twenty-three smaller state banks; in the end, Jackson had his way with the banks.

Not everyone, of course, agreed with Jackson's maneuver, and these twenty-three state banks became derogatorily known as Jackson's "pet banks."[34] This caused, at first, a poorly orchestrated financial crisis by Biddle but was soon followed by a real crisis—the Panic of 1837—which lasted for approximately the next seven years.[35] The problem of financial instability became an all too common problem in the decades leading up to the Civil War as many banks became insolvent and the American economy repeatedly went into recession.

One of greatest problems contributing to the chaotic economy was the fluctuating state of America's currency. The only official currency provided by the federal government were coins, and there were never enough of them. That left the banks to fill the void by creating paper money—banknotes—issued by nearly every bank in the country, including the First and Second Banks of the United States while they existed. Back when President Washington had been inaugurated, this hadn't proved to be much of a problem, for there were only three banks in existence. But by the time the Civil War began, it is estimated there were between 1,500 and 1,600 banks spread across America, and nearly every one of them printed their own banknotes in multiple denominations. That means that in addition to US government coins there were at least seven thousand different bills circulating as currency, if not more. And according to Tarnoff, "by the time the federal government began regulating the money supply, there were more than ten thousand different kinds of notes circulating in the United States."[36] It was only now that the federal government began regulating the money supply.

Prior to the war that pitted the North against the South, each of these seven- to ten-thousand–plus individual banknotes would have the name of the issuing bank featured on the front and the amount due in coin, along with some form of ornamental design. "Unlike a national currency," Craughwell explains, "the banknotes had no uniform design—bankers adopted whatever style they found appealing."[37] The currency served as a promise that the bank would pay in coin the amount shown on the bill, as the banknotes were tied directly to the precious metals in the weights and amounts as determined by the US Mint. The problem arose in paying for goods in one state with banknotes printed from a bank in another state. The recipient of the banknote would only be able to obtain the amount in coin if they traveled to the other state and to the specific bank upon which the note was drawn. This, of course, led to the necessity of dealing with banknote brokers—those individuals who made a living by buying up notes from out of state banks or even those that were just a day's journey away. Once they collected up enough of the notes from a particular bank, the brokers would travel to the bank and collect the amount in coin and then transfer it back to the location in which they worked. The brokers, it should be noted, always purchased their banknotes at increasing discounts the farther away the banks were located, thus making sure their travel expenses were covered and a tidy profit was made. This was clearly not an efficient system, especially as America's economy continued to grow. And although additional conveyances such as the Erie Canal, the early railroads, and steamboats made travel for some easier in the years leading up to the Civil War, most people still traveled primarily by horse and carriage, meaning trips to banks in other states were long and arduous.[38]

The other problem that contributed greatly to the volatility of America's financial system prior to the Civil War was, most assuredly, counterfeiting. By the time "the Civil War erupted," historian David R. Johnson explains, "perhaps as much as half of the paper notes in circulation were counterfeit."[39] The fact that the federal government let America's currency go unregulated for so long is stunning in hindsight, but there are reasons why— reasons that date back to the Colonial era.

Johnson suggests that counterfeiting "is probably one of the oldest crimes in America, dating approximately from the 1680s."[40] It was in that decade that William Penn "was shocked to learn that spurious coin was abundant in Pennsylvania."[41] Early in the Colonial period of American history, when colonists used British coins for all trade beyond the conventional use of commodities. "Coins would have been more convenient," writes Tarnoff, "but the paucity of precious metals in North America made coinage difficult." Yet even when the Massachusetts colony obtained enough silver to mint their own coins in 1652, "by 1684 the British government had ordered the colonists to stop, citing their violation of the royal right of coinage."[42]

It was around this same time that the earliest-known counterfeiting case arose in the colonies, which proved to be the first arrest of career counterfeiter Robert Fenton. As historian Kenneth Scott explains, "Fenton is first heard of in Philadelphia in 1683, when he, Charles Pickering and Samuel Buckley were arrested and charged with coining New England shillings and Spanish silver pieces made of silver alloyed with copper."[43] Fenton had worked as a servant in Philadelphia and was able to produce counterfeit coins because "the necessary skills and materials were widely available" and "anyone with the basic knowledge could produce coins in practically any locality."[44] Despite his conviction and sentence to the stocks for one hour, Fenton was not a reformed man.[45] By the 1690s, Fenton was trying his hand at the alteration of paper bills of credit; once again he was caught and arrested, this time in Boston, in 1691. Although brought to trial, the disposition of the case is unknown. Still, this did not stop Fenton, who then moved to Connecticut where John Potterfield had hired him to make "false bits and pieces of eight."[46] Fenton was once again arrested, but as the new colony had no laws to deal with counterfeiting foreign (Spanish) coins, he was let go.

How successful Fenton was in making a profit from his counterfeiting is also unknown, but his peripatetic lifestyle spread his knowledge of counterfeiting to other colonies. Organized counterfeiting rings began to appear throughout the American colonies and were soon undermining the economy of both the colonies and England. "Whatever the origins of Fenton's knowledge," counterfeiting historian David R. Johnson concludes, "his persistent counterfeiting activities contributed to the diffusion of that knowledge, as well as to the formation of social networks that could, as in his case, cross colonial boundaries by the end of the 1690s."[47]

As America entered the eighteenth century, most of the colonies soon found ways to circumvent the limited amount of British coin circulating and the laws against minting their own coins.[48] It seems "the colonists had discovered a loophole in British regulations"—namely, that "paper money didn't infringe on the home government's monopoly on coinage, and since the Massachusetts bills of credit were not redeemable by the British Crown, they weren't officially considered money."[49] Counterfeiting of both coin and bills of credit began to proliferate. However, as Stephen Mihm explains, "despite the grim promise that adorned many bills—'To Counterfeit is Death,' counterfeiters operated with relative impunity in the future United States."[50] The reasons for this varied greatly.

Counterfeiters enjoyed such free rein in their trade in part because the laws could not keep up. Counterfeiters could ply their trade in new colonies with few laws—as in Connecticut, discussed above—or, if a state did create such laws, the counterfeiter could simply move across state lines. In addition, many counterfeiters simply set up their trade outside of the colonies, either in the French territory, Indian country, or New Spain (Florida).[51] A second reason counterfeiters operated relatively unchecked is that as the number of bills of credit expanded, the number of opportunities for counterfeiting increased while the government had no enforcement mechanism to track down counterfeiters.[52] A third reason counterfeiting proliferated has to do with colonial ambivalence toward counterfeiters: some saw it as a "harmless activity," while others saw it as a benefit for, "Counterfeiters, after all, did a public service by increasing the amount of money in circulation in a part of the world where the demand for money invariably outstripped the supply."[53] Still further, counterfeiting was favored also because it undermined the British government's economy, which was growing more troublesome with time.[54] When British Parliament passed laws prohibiting Colonial banks from issuing bills of credit, it only stoked colonial desire for revolution.

Once the American Revolution was underway, it seems turnabout was fair (unfair?) trade. The Continental Congress, in order to pay for the war, began producing a national paper currency, "popularly known as continentals." In order to now turn around and undermine the rebellious American's economy, the British loaded a printing press onboard the HMS *Phoenix*, docked in New York Harbor, where they began printing fake continentals. It seems the British printed continentals so well that people considered them just as good as if not better than the real thing. By the time America declared its independence, British counterfeiters had established an elaborate system for selling the counterfeit continentals to British loyalists, and it only cost them "the paper it was printed on."[55] Although "the British lost the war," historian Craughwell explains, they had "won the campaign to undermine America's finances," which was left in shambles.[56] It was at this time that Robert Morris stepped in and rescued the foundling nation.[57]

Initially, because there were so few coins and banks issuing notes, most counterfeiters spent their time forging foreign currency. However, once the First Bank of the United States dissolved and new banks were created to fill the void, as more currency began to meet demand, so too did the counterfeiters. It is estimated that "between 1812 and 1819, the circulating medium of the country disintegrated to a condition as bad as that of the Continental days," for "proportionately, there were approximately as many counterfeits as notes on sound banks."[58] It became so bad by 1818 that famed publisher and editor Hezekiah Niles of the much-read *Niles' Weekly Register* lamented how "We can hardly open a newspaper without seemingly hearing a bellowing aloud of *'counterfeiters'*—*'more counterfeiters'*—*'beware of counterfeiters'*—*'forgery'*—*'more forgery,'* and the like."[59]

Then, just as the Second Bank of the United States was getting the economy on solid footing, Jackson implemented his "free banking system," and all hell broke loose. Jackson's dismantling the bank troublesome and then some, for it spawned the creation of "wildcat banks" that "were, as the name implies, unsafe speculative ventures" producing their own "wildcat banknotes."[60] When the banknote brokers traveled to redeem their banknote holdings, they often had trouble finding the banks. Many of these wildcat banks just opened up, as Niles reported, "in inaccessible places, many in the northern wilderness, where white men seldom trod and only an Indian guide could find."[61] The idea behind the remote locations was so they would not be found; that way, they would not have to redeem the banknotes. If they were located, the banks were often nothing more than a shanty with a few pages serving as the bank's ledger, and no coins in sight.

And as if Jackson's free banking system were not trouble enough by itself, adding to it the numerous counterfeiters taking advantage of a system that had no uniformity, little regulatory oversight, and almost no mechanism of enforcement, it was clear to many that a crisis was developing. Fretting over how he could not even go "two days together without having forged notes in my possession," Niles predicted that America was "about to become liable to be called *a nation of counterfeiters!*"[62] As explained by Stephen Mihm, author of a book by that title, *A Nation of Counterfeiters*, "It staggers the imagination to comprehend the extent and ubiquity of counterfeiting during the first half of the nineteenth century."[63] It was because of this very problem that Allan Pinkerton was able to step in, foil a counterfeiting ring, and develop a prosperous career in an entirely new sector of the American economy that he created—private security.[64]

Pinkerton prospered because there was no bona fide mechanism built to address the problem of counterfeiting. The only federal law-enforcement agency in existence at that time was the US Marshals Service.[65] And since marshals were paid mainly through the fees they earned for the services they provided, and as America had no national currency, there was no incentive to pay them for investigating the counterfeiting of state and local banknotes. "Most marshals, therefore, were unconcerned with counterfeiters."[66] Occasionally if citizens—and their Congressmen—complained enough, the federal government might hire a temporary investigator to look into the problem of counterfeiting, with many of those contracts going to Pinkerton himself. This, however, was not a permanent fix and only addressed a small portion of a much larger problem.

As no state police agencies yet existed, the enforcement of counterfeiting laws was largely left to the local police. This also proved to be problematic because prior to the Civil War there were so few modern police departments in the United States; most were still constabularies and watchmen. Only the major cities like Boston, New York, Philadelphia, Chicago, and Baltimore had bona fide police departments.[67] "These officers, however," writes Johnson, "continued the tradition of expending their energies only for rewards, while maintaining the convenient corrupt arrangements that had previously evolved between constables and thieves."[68] Despite citizen demand to address the problem, the reality was that in the years leading up to the Civil War there were no enforcement mechanisms and counterfeiters were pretty much free to ply their illicit trade.

In the end, it took a war to solve the problem.

With South Carolina's secession from the Union on December 20, 1860, and with every state secession that followed, the American economy slipped further into crisis. In the first two months of the Civil War alone, from April to May 1861, the federal government spent 23.5 million dollars but only earned revenue amounting to 5.8 million dollars.[69] In the fall of that year, Salmon P. Chase, who had been appointed the secretary of the Treasury the previous March, lamented to a friend that "the expenditures everywhere are frightful."[70] He told of how in just two weeks the federal government had spent nearly two million dollars. Securing loans from other countries was too slow a process, and because there was no Bank of the United States they could not obtain a loan from themselves. The American economy was about to be destroyed, and Chase knew he had to move, and move quickly. What followed was a flurry of activity that saved America's economy, if not the Union.

Chase first did what he could do at the Treasury by ordering a slowdown in Treasury payments and issuing 414 million
dollars in bonds and treasury notes to raise money for the war
effort. He then went to Congress and encouraged them to raise
custom duties, implement taxes, and sell off some of their public
land holdings. He then "negotiated a loan from a consortium
of New York, Philadelphia, and Boston Banks—$150 million in
gold."[71] The bankers assumed they would issue a line of credit
on the gold, but Chase demanded that all 150 million dollars in
gold be transferred to the Treasury, thus giving him the hard
currency and the banks the paper rather than the other way
around. As all of these were nothing more than stopgap measures, Chase next set about drafting legislative proposals for
Congress to get the Union's finances on solid footing.

First Congress passed the Act of July 17, 1861, which allowed
the Treasury to print fifty million dollars in demand notes—
money not backed by any precious metals, just the good name of
the federal government.[72] These bills came to be popularly known
as "greenbacks" because, unlike the state bank–issued money,
they were printed on both sides and all in a uniform green. The
Legal Tender Act followed the next year, authorizing the Treasury
to issue $150 million in United States notes. Now that the federal
government had a form of currency, the following year Congress
passed the National Bank Act of 1863, which created a new central
bank with a permanent national currency and gave the government the ability to sell war bonds. A second National Bank Act
followed in 1864, giving the federal government control over all of
the commercial banks, and a third National Bank Act in 1865 and
1866 forced these banks to pay a 10 percent tax to the federal government if they wanted to remain in existence. America now had
a national banking system and a national currency. But what it
once again forgot was to create was any enforcement mechanism.

Congress did pass the Revenue Act of 1862, creating the
office of commissioner of Internal Revenue, which passed a
temporary income tax on American citizens and authorized
the new Internal Revenue Service to enforce the tax laws. Yet
"when Congress passed the Legal Tender Act, it neglected to
stipulate an enforcement mechanism for protecting the integrity

of the new currency."[73] Once again, despite the fact that Article 1, Section 8, of the US Constitution gives Congress the power "to provide for the Punishment of counterfeiting the Securities and current Coin of the United States," that body failed to address counterfeiting in any of the acts.[74] The US Marshals Service was the only federal agency that could enforce the laws against counterfeiting, and as historian Johnson has already pointed out, they "had already demonstrated that they had neither the experience nor the incentive to acquaint themselves with the social milieu of the urban underworld."[75] That left the new greenbacks wide open to unfettered counterfeiting.

"The combination of a weak federal government and a multifarious money supply," writes historian Mihm, "proved a liability in the opening months of the crisis between North and South."[76] One of those liabilities was counterfeiting greenbacks, for, "like the rest of the American public," as Craughwell explains, "counterfeiters adjusted to the new national currency quickly."[77] When Congress did finally respond in the summer of 1863, it was to authorize the expenditures of $1,184 to hire contract detectives, like Pinkerton, to investigate counterfeiting.[78] The following year, the secretary of the Treasury would establish a small working force, operating under William P. Wood, warden of the Capitol Prison, which began to address counterfeiting. Wood's success against the counterfeiters led Hugh McCulloch, Lincoln's secretary of the Treasury during his second term, to propose the idea of making the organization more permanent.

On April 14, 1865, Lincoln held a cabinet meeting in which Secretary McCulloch was said to have brought up the problem of counterfeiting. When Lincoln asked how he would handle it, McCulloch proposed an organized force. Lincoln is said to have agreed, adding, "Work it out your own way, Hugh. I believe you have the right idea."[79]

That evening, Lincoln was assassinated.[80] The organization President Lincoln and Secretary of the Treasury Hugh McCulloch had set in motion would one day address not only the threat of America's money supply being counterfeited but also the threat of American presidential assassinations—the subject of the next chapter.

Anarchist Leon Czolgosz shoots President McKinley with a concealed revolver at the Pan-American reception in Buffalo, New York. McKinley's assassination made Theodore Roosevelt the twenty-sixtth president of the United States.

Photo courtesy of the Library of Congress.

4

Assassinations

President Lincoln's assassination was not the first time a president's life was threatened, but it was the first time an assassin successfully managed to murder a sitting president. After Lincoln's death, however, not much changed in the way of protecting the life of America's chief executive. That did not come about until after two additional presidents had been assassinated—Presidents Garfield and McKinley. In order to understand how the national government slowly evolved its protection of serving presidents, it is important to trace the evolution of both assassinations and attempted assassinations on the lives of American presidents.

During the Constitutional Convention, held during the long, hot summer of 1787, one topic that the members never addressed was the protection of the head of the executive branch, the president of the United States.[1] This lack of foresight is not that surprising when considering the Founding Fathers also neglected to consider a means of conveying the national government's laws and acts to the American people and neglected to develop law-enforcement mechanisms for its many specified powers. It is surprising, however, when one takes into consideration the fact that the president of the Constitutional Convention, George Washington, was himself the target of an assassination plot and had previously created a group of bodyguards for his protection while serving as general of the Continental Army.[2]

After the American colonists had already gone to war with Britain, they appointed George Washington to be their commander-in-chief, on June 15, 1775.[3] As Washington settled into the position, he thought of developing his own elite force of personal bodyguards, a "Commander-in-Chief's Guard."[4] As historian Harry M. Ward explains, "The idea of having his own life guard appealed to George Washington." What he wanted was "A life guard, doubling as body and honor guard," which "had been customary in European practice for the purpose of serving sovereigns and commanding generals."[5] So, on March 11, 1776, General Washington issued an order:

> The General being desirous of selecting a particular number of men, as a Guard for himself, and baggage, the Colonel, or commanding Officer, of each of the established Regiments (the Artillery and Rifflemen excepted) will furnish him with four, that the number wanted may be chosen out of them. His Excellency depends upon the Colonels for good Men, such as they can recommend for their sobriety, honesty, and good behaviour; he wishes them to be from five feet, eight Inches high, to five feet, ten Inches; handsomely and well made, and as there is nothing in his eyes more desirable, than Cleanliness in a Soldier, he desires that particular attention may be made, in the choice of such men, as are neat, and spruce.[6]

Two of the men selected to serve on Washington's Life Guard were Sergeant Thomas Hickey and Private Michael Lynch. However, they only served for a short time period: Not long after their appointments they were caught passing counterfeit bills of credit. They were arrested by civilian authorities and confined "to close custody under the Guards at the City-Hall."[7] After being transferred to the custody of the Continental Army, the two soldiers awaited trial.

Despite having been consider "a favorite" by Washington, Hickey had a somewhat-sketchy past, for he had served in the British Army where he had been personal assistant to Major General William Johnson during the Seven Years' War. When the Revolutionary War broke out, Hickey switched sides. Because he met the physical requirements desired by General

Washington and "bore a good character," he became a member of the Life Guard.[8]

After being charged with passing counterfeit bills, while detained at city hall, Hickey met another man with a sketchy past, Isaac Ketchum, who had been accused of being a British loyalist. Hickey and Isaac spoke openly with one another about the current political situation, and Hickey revealed he was part of a conspiracy to assassinate General Washington. Ketchum divulged the secret to the authorities, and word quickly reached the Continental Congress, which in turn issued an arrest warrant for Hickey, citing treason.[9] More specifically, the charges were "exciting and joining in a mutiny and sedition, and of treacherously corresponding with, inlisting among, and receiving pay from enemies of the United American Colonies."[10]

The very thought of a plot to assassinate General Washington so reviled those privy to the secret information that they were left in "amazed disbelief." Army surgeon and future governor of Massachusetts William Eustis described the plot to a colleague as "the greatest and vilest attempt ever made against our country; I mean the *plot*, the infernal *plot* which has been contrived by our enemies."[11] The conspiracy was quickly dismantled: less than two weeks later, Hickey was court-martialed and found guilty, sentenced to "suffer death for said crimes by being hanged by the neck til he is dead."[12] Two days later, on June 28, "some twenty thousand people turned out to witness Hickey's hanging."[13] Washington vetted his Life Guard's members more closely after learning of the plot, and he banned foreign-born men from serving.

The fact that General Washington had been drawn out of military retirement by James Madison to represent Virginia during the Constitutional Convention, and the fact that he had been elected the body's president, meant that he had every opportunity to advocate for some means of protection for the new executive.[14] If Ward is correct—and there is nothing to suggest he is not—that "the idea of having his own life guard appealed to George Washington," one must wonder why he did not consider a Life Guard for the president of the United States.[15] Whatever the reason, as the Warren Commission concluded almost two centuries later, while investigating the assassination of President John F. Kennedy, "In the early days of the Republic, there was remarkably little concern about the safety of Presidents and few measures were taken to protect them."[16]

The presidents of the United States from the Founding Fathers' era were fortunate to never be targeted by assassination attempts while serving. The only real threat to a president's life during that era came when the British entered Washington, D.C., in 1814, during the War of 1812, forcing President Madison and his wife, Dolley, to flee for their lives. It was then that Dolley Madison achieved her greatest fame when she ordered the White House servants to "save that picture if possible! . . . Under no circumstances allow it to fall into the hands of the British."[17] The picture in question was Gilbert Stuart's full-length portrait of George Washington, which had hung prominently in the White House ever since it was painted. Had she not ordered it saved, it most likely would have burned with everything else in the famous house on Pennsylvania Avenue.

It was the first president not associated with the founding fathers, Andrew Jackson, who was the first to face several assassination attempts on his life while in office.[18] As historian Robert V. Remini once wrote, Jackson "was just a little too strong, too controversial, too dominant a character, and therefore an obvious target for the demented in society."[19] The first attack to come from the "demented" occurred on May 6, 1833, when Robert B. Randolph, previously a naval officer who had been drummed out of service for misappropriating funds, approached Jackson onboard a steamboat traveling from Alexandria to Fredericksburg, Virginia. Jackson was seated behind a table when Randolph approached him, reached across the table, and shoved his hand into this face. While Jackson's nose was bloodied, he was otherwise unharmed.[20] Taken into custody upon their arrival in Fredericksburg, Randolph was turned over to the local authorities. Jackson's nephew, Andrew Donelson, who had been present that day, later wrote of the event, "The object of the attack was no doubt assassination, but the ruffian was unnerved by the countenance of Uncle and he could do no more than display his intention."[21] Despite this being, as Donelson believed, the first assassination attempt ever on a sitting president, America's reaction, as the *New York Evening Post* conveyed, was that it was merely "a sign of the times."[22] Later, the Warren Commission came to the odd conclusion that Randolph's assault had not been an assassination attempt, "since Randolph apparently did not intend serious injury."[23]

The second, and more harrowing, assassination attempt on Jackson's life came from Richard Lawrence. Born in England around the turn of the nineteenth century, Lawrence lived and worked in the Georgetown neighborhood of Washington, D.C., at the time Jackson became president. Lawrence fancied himself a great painter, but in reality he was nothing more than a house painter, and even that proved an infrequent occupation.[24] By the winter of 1832, Lawrence had stopped working altogether because of his plans to return to England. Embarking on his great trip, he only managed to get as far as Philadelphia, when, after declaring it too cold, he returned home. He tried a second time, this time with the intention of studying landscape painting in England; but once again, he only made it as far as Philadelphia before returning home. This time he claimed the reason for cutting his trip short was because of a personal attack that had been launched against him in the newspapers. Lawrence, like his father and an aunt before him, was clearly becoming mentally unstable.[25]

Asked how he was going to support himself now that he had stopped working, Lawrence was reported to have told his sister that "he had made claims before the US Congress and that they would soon issue him large sums of money as he was, in fact, King Richard III of England."[26] Lawrence believed that, as royalty, he had the right to several estates that the US government had seized and that, therefore, they would have to pay him under eminent-domain laws.

In keeping with this lunatic belief that he was British aristocracy, Lawrence grew a mustache, began dressing like an "English dandy," and was often seen riding around on horses with women of "loose character."[27] At first his behavior was ebullient and obviously eccentric, but then it took a turn to-

ward the dark. He became irritated with everything and everyone, exploding in bouts of rage and violence, and he was said
to often fall into "fits of uncontrollable laughter and cursing."[28]
At one point he threatened a black maid's life, followed by his
sister's, and, finally, his landlord's when the man had come to
collect Lawrence's rent. The landlord greeted him kindly, but
Lawrence was reported to have fired back, "Go to hell! What's
that to you?" The landlord, bravely—or foolishly—pressed the
issue of the rent, and Lawrence told him, "You mean to warrant me for it, I suppose? If you do, I will put a ball through
your head."[29]

Lawrence took to spending much of his time sitting in his
old paint shop, talking to himself, engaging in wild conversation, screaming, yelling, cursing. He once was overheard
shouting, "Damn him, he does not know his enemy; I will put
a pistol . . . erect a gallows . . . Damn General Jackson! Who's
General Jackson?"[30] On the morning of the assassination attempt, Lawrence was again overheard conversing with himself, and, after a burst of laughter, he chuckled, "I'll be damned
if I don't do it."[31]

As was later learned, Lawrence had come to blame President
Jackson for his financial problems: The US government was not
paying him the money he believed they owed him because Jackson was too busying destroying the national bank. The breakup
had delayed the settlement of Lawrence's claim, leading him
to reason that if he assassinated Jackson, Vice President Martin
Van Buren would become president, which would clear the way
for Lawrence to be paid.[32] Then he could go to England in style,
regardless of the cold weather.

The day of the assassination attempt, January 30, 1835, was
damp and misty.[33] President Jackson, along with nearly every
other politician in Washington, D.C., was at the funeral services
for House Representative Warren R. Davis of South Carolina,
who had died the previous day. To honor Warren's tenure in
Congress, services were held in the House chamber of the US
Capitol. "The president sat stoically listening to the droning
of the chaplain," recalled an English socialite by the name of

Harriet Martineau, who observed, "There sat the gray-haired president, looking scarcely able to go through the ceremonial."[34]

When the services were over, Jackson and his entourage descended to the Rotunda and exited by the east porch of the Capitol building. As Jackson arrived on the porch, there were many attendees milling about, when a slender man with a thick black beard stepped in front of the president, only six feet away. He pointed a pistol at Jackson, squeezing the trigger, and there followed the report of a loud explosion, like an "ordinary cracker," recounted Senator John Tyler.[35] Another observer, Thomas Benton, described how "the explosion of the cap was so loud that many persons thought the pistol had fired."[36] It had not. The pistol had misfired. Lawrence dropped the first pistol to the ground, and then, reaching into his coat, pulled out a second pistol and again fired directly at Jackson. It too misfired.

Jackson had started to move toward Lawrence after the first shot, and by the time the second shot had sounded, Jackson took a swipe at Lawrence with his walking cane. Lawrence, however, "managed to duck and avoid the wrath of the president."[37] Jackson was heard to yell, "Let me alone! Let me alone! I know where this came from."[38] Jackson believed Senator George Poindexter, with whom he strongly disagreed, had put Lawrence, his house painter, up to the act. There was later found to be no connection, but the suspicion ended Poindexter's political career.

Meanwhile, Jackson's secretary of the Treasury Levi Woodbury also attempted a swing at Lawrence, but he too missed. When Lawrence twisted away from Woodbury, he managed to turn right into the path of a lunging Lieutenant Thomas R. Gedney of the US Navy, who knocked Lawrence to the ground, pinning him down. Others then moved in to help subdue Lawrence, as did Senator Davy Crockett from Tennessee, who said of the matter, "I wanted to see the d-mnd-st villain in the world—and now I have seen him."[39] The newspapers remarked that all during this time, "The President pressed after [Lawrence] until he saw he was secured."[40]

Taken to the White House by carriage, Jackson, rather than being shaken by the incident, was just plain mad. When Vice President Martin Van Buren later arrived at the White House, he was surprised to find Jackson in a room full of people, playing with Major Donelson's children on his lap and conversing with Major General Winfield Scott.[41] The vice president later remarked that Jackson was "apparently the least disturbed person in the room."[42]

Lawrence was taken into custody and eventually remanded to the blandly named Government Hospital—later renamed St. Elizabeths—where he remained until his death twenty-six years later, on June 13, 1861.[43] Although it was later revealed that both of Lawrence's pistols had been properly loaded, it is believed the damp, misty air of that morning had caused both pistols to misfire. Nevertheless, popular sentiment held that "the hand of a special Providence" had intervened to spare Jackson's life, enhancing his reputation with the "common man."[44] After serving two terms as president, Jackson retired to his Hermitage plantation in the year of the great Panic of 1837, which he had triggered during his war against the national bank.[45] Andrew Jackson died there on June 8, 1845, at the age of seventy-eight.

Despite President Jackson's having endured two attempts on his life, little was undertaken in the official manner of protecting the president.[46] While earlier James Monroe had erected an iron fence around the White House perimeter "with a series of heavily locked gates," the only change in the wake of the Lawrence attempt on Jackson's life was the installation of a watch box at the south-side gate leading into the presidential gardens. The box was manned by "a lone sentry," and after Martin Van Buren became president it, "was manned infrequently." As Oliver and Marion conclude, in the aftermath of the attempts on Jackson's life, "There seemed little concern for future assassination attempts, much less an actual assassination."[47]

Although history records Abraham Lincoln's 1865 murder as the first presidential assassination, suspicions have always lingered regarding the strange death of President Zachary Taylor. The story generally told is that on the hot July 4th of 1850 in Washington, D.C., President Taylor attended Independence Day celebrations, where he ate cherries and drank cold milk. Upon returning to the White House, he grew violently ill, and several days later, he died. "Cherries and milk," as it has been noted, "do not usually cause death," so questions over Taylor's rapid decline and death have remained.[48] His symptoms of nausea, diarrhea, and vomiting, along with the shakes, were thought at the time to have been cholera, but cholera occurs in the water supply, and there was no reported outbreak of the disease that summer in Washington, D.C.

It has been suggested that President Taylor's actual cause of death may have been arsenic poisoning, but many attempts to test the theory have proven futile. It was only recently, in 1991, that the president's body was exhumed and a test conducted. However, the results were not made available to the public— only the physician's statement, concluding that he had died from "gastroenteritis."[49] When the medical examiner's report was finally obtained years later, it was reported that Taylor's arsenic levels were five to fifteen times higher than today's normal range, once again calling into question the circumstances of his death. Yet in fairness it should be noted that most Americans of the mid-nineteenth century would have had levels of arsenic in their bodies much higher than would be acceptable by today's standards.[50]

Taylor was the second American president to have died in office—the first being William Henry Harrison, who had spoken too long at his inauguration in the snow, caught cold, and died a month later. Though Taylor was from the South and himself owned slaves, he did not support expanding the institution of slavery. His vice president, Millard Fillmore, however, did. Some have suggested that Taylor was assassinated by poisoning precisely to elevate Fillmore to the Oval Office, allowing for the Compromise of 1850, which brought California into the Union as a free state but allowed New Mexico and Utah to enter as slave states. Despite this possible motive for murder, however, "there is no definitive proof that Taylor was assassinated, nor would it appear that there is definitive proof that he was not."[51] And because any conspiracy was unknown at the time of his death, nothing was done to further protect sitting presidents.

On November 6, 1860, ten years after the death of President Taylor, Abraham Lincoln was elected the sixteenth president of the United States. Before his first term had even started, he managed to outmaneuver an assassination plot in Baltimore. In the first four years of his presidency, from Washington he deftly led the nation through a bloodying civil war. And barely a month after a landslide reelection to a second term, at Appomattox Court House he saw that war end in victory for the Union.[52] Five days later, on April 14, Good Friday, Abraham Lincoln was jubilantly happy, and he told everyone how he felt. Even the dream he'd had the previous night—that he was "in some singular, indescribable vessel, and that he was moving with great rapidity towards an indefinite shore," the same dream that had proceeded numerous disasters during the war—could not dampen his spirits.[53] Even the lengthy cabinet meeting—the one in which he advised Secretary Hugh McCulloch to work out the details for the creation of an agency to enforce the laws against counterfeiting—did not detract from his joy.[54] Everyone was taken aback at just how happy he was, including Mary, his wife. "Dear Husband," she admitted to him, "you almost startle me by your great cheerfulness."[55] "I may well feel so, Mary," Lincoln replied. "I consider *this day*, the war, has come to a close," adding, "We must *both*, be more cheerful in the future—between the war & the loss of our darling Willie—we have both, been very miserable."[56] To celebrate, Lincoln planned to take his wife to Ford's Theatre to see *Our American Cousin*.

General Ulysses S. Grant and his wife, Julia, had been invited to attend the play with the Lincolns but had graciously declined. So had several others when the invitation was extended. And after Mary came down with one of her headaches, she advised her husband she could not go. But Lincoln told her "that he must attend," for "the evening newspapers had carried an announcement that he would be present and tickets had been sold on the basis of that expectation."[57] Feeling better by that evening, Mary relented, and in any case they had finally found a couple that would attend with them—Major Henry Rathbone and his fiancée, Clara Harris, daughter of a New York Senator.

By the time the Lincolns were supposed to depart, the president appeared to be experiencing a change of heart. "I supposed it's time to go," he reluctantly told Speaker of the House Schuyler Colfax, "though I would rather stay."[58] It was then that Lincoln's personal bodyguard, William H. Crook, advised him not to go to the theater. A second time that day Lincoln insisted, "It has been advertised that we will be there and I cannot disappoint the people."[59] Crook had a bad feeling about the evening: He'd already worked from 8 a.m. until some time around 6 p.m. that day and ought to have been relieved at 4 p.m. But his replacement, John Frederick Parker of the Metropolitan Police, was late.[60] This was typical of Parker; though he was one of the original police officers at the founding of the department in 1861, his record was riddled with charges of dereliction of duty and conduct unbecoming an officer; he was often drunk on duty.[61]

When Lincoln left for the theater, he called out, "Goodbye, Crook," who was now off-duty for the night. "Good night, Crook"—that was what the bodyguard later recalled Lincoln always said to him, never just "Goodbye."[62]

The Lincolns and their guests arrived late for the play, but after making their way to the box seats, they took their places. Seeing their arrival, the company suddenly stopped the play, and the musicians played "Hail to the Chief," while everyone in the theater stood.[63] Once the play resumed, Lincoln settled into the rocking chair in his box seat and, by all accounts, appeared to be enjoying himself. At intermission, the foursome spoke thoughtfully of the play, until it once again resumed. Absorbed again by the play, Lincoln did not know that the night's bodyguard, Officer John Frederick Parker, had left his post: after finally showing up for duty, he had slipped out to a local tavern across the street.[64]

About 10:25 that night, with Parker still absent from his post, actor John Wilkes Booth made his way to the president's box.[65]

Nothing was unusual about that; he was, after all, a recognized actor, in a theater, going to pay his respects to the president. Positioned outside the box seat door, Booth waited for a certain line to be delivered on stage—one that had received uproarious laughter every night it was delivered. On cue, the laughter drowning out any noise, he opened the door, stepped forward, and shot Lincoln in the back of the head at point-blank range. Booth was part of a conspiracy to topple the Northern government and reignite the Southern cause.

The conspirators' plans had been for Lewis Powell and David Herold to assassinate Secretary of State Seward, for George Atzerodt to shoot Vice President Andrew Johnson at his hotel, and for Booth to kill the president, all at 10:15 p.m. that evening. The mass confusion that would ensue would present the opportunity needed for the South to rise again and continue the fight, but it was not meant to be: Herold drove Powell to Seward's house, where the secretary was laid up from a carriage accident. But when Seward unexpectedly put up a struggle, Herold rode quickly away, and Powell had to escape on his own. Seward survived.

Atzerodt, waiting in a bar near Johnson's hotel, got cold feet at about 10 p.m. and fled. Johnson survived.

Sadly, Booth—alone among the conspirators—managed to accomplish what he set out to do. But after a scuffle with Major Rathbone, he leaped from the box onto the stage, catching his boot spur on the ceremonial drapings. Upon landing on stage awkwardly, he weakly shouted, *"Sic semper tyrannis"*—"Thus Always to Tyrants," Virgina's motto.[66] His actions confused the theater audience, who, thinking it was a part of the play, remained seated. That momentary disorientation was enough for Booth to escape out the back door and into the night. But, after a twelve-day manhunt, he was discovered, shot, and killed.

Despite the fact that "Lincoln's assassination revealed the total inadequacy of Presidential protection," the congressional investigating committee "called for no action to provide better protection for the President in the future." The Warren Commission later concluded that "this lack of concern for the protection of the President may have derived from the tendency of the time to regard Lincoln's assassination as part of a unique crisis that was not likely to happen to a future Chief Executive." Still, some military guards remained on duty at the White House until the end of Reconstruction, and the Metropolitan Police provided some protection, but usually only on special occasions.[67]

The next president assassinated in office was James A. Garfield, who hailed from the mother of presidents," the State of Ohio.[68] Garfield had received a commission in the Union Army at the beginning of the Civil War and rose to the rank of brigadier general.[69] He exceled both on the battlefield and as chief of staff for General William Rosecrans, which inspired some, noting his political acumen, to call on him to run for Congress. Garfield won election in the fall of 1862, and, after being seated as a member of the Thirty-Eighth Congress, he served through the Civil War, through Reconstruction, and up to his election as a dark-horse candidate in 1880. Garfield took office on March 4, 1881; four months later he was shot by Charles J. Guiteau, and after lingering for two months more, he was dead.[70]

In a day and age when every position in the federal government was filled through political patronage, Guiteau was a sycophant. He had first supported reelection for Ulysses S. Grant before pledging his allegiance to Garfield. Guiteau had even written a speech for Garfield, and, after sending it to the candidate, he "seriously believed that his speech would tip the election for Garfield."[71] Although Garfield never used the speech, Guiteau felt he had played a role in Garfield's election and so went to Washington to accept the president's gratitude and collect his political patronage position with the government. Like thousands of other people hoping to meet the president, Guiteau stood in a long line and managed to meet Garfield face-to-face for a few minutes. But of course Garfield had no idea who he was and did not consider him for any of the coveted government positions. Afterward, when Guiteau heard nothing from the president, he began contemplating his murder.[72]

As Guiteau began planning the assassination, he knew he needed a gun, so he stopped at O'Meara's gun shop where he "bought a relatively expensive .44-caliber snub-nose British Bulldog revolver with a white bone handle." A version of the same gun with a wooden handle sold for a dollar cheaper, "but Guiteau wanted the white one because it would show better on display in a museum once he killed Garfield."[73] Now armed, he began following the president around.

A month of stalking presented little opportunity to assassinate Garfield. Then, on July 2, planning to join his wife on vacation up in New England, Garfield had a train to catch at the Baltimore and Potomac Railroad station in Washington, D.C. When his carriage arrived at the train station, he was met by Metropolitan Police Officer Patrick Kearney, who walked in front of him, clearing the way into the station. "When Garfield walked in, Guiteau was standing right behind him" and realized that this "was his chance to kill the president."[74] Garfield was only three steps away when Guiteau pulled the trigger, hitting the president in the right arm. Garfield threw up his arm and shouted, "My God! What is this?"[75] When he turned to see what was happening, Guiteau shot him again, striking him in the back. The president slumped to the floor.

Garfield was rushed back to the White House, where he lingered through the rest of July, all of August, and well into September. He finally succumbed to his wounds—or, more likely, from infection spread him from the many unsanitary fingers probing into his wounds in search of bullets—on Monday, September 19. He was two months shy of his fiftieth birthday.

Guiteau was immediately arrested and later tried, convicted, and sentenced to death. He was hung the following year. "At least one newspaper, the *New York Tribune*, predicted that the assault on Garfield would lead to the President becoming 'the slave of his office, the prisoner of forms and restrictions.'" As the Warren Commission later noted, however, "the prediction of the *Tribune* did not come to pass," for "although the Nation was shocked by this deed," the president did not become a prisoner of the White House and Congress "took no steps to provide the President with personal protection."[76] It took the assassination of William McKinley—the third president murdered in office—for them to finally act.

The United States Secret Service was created the summer after Lincoln's death not to serve the commander-in-chief but to protect America's money supply from counterfeiters. In 1894, the service began providing security for the president, but only on an informal and case-by-case basis.[77] As a result, there were actually three Secret Service agents assigned to McKinley at the time he was assassinated, but only one was standing immediately next to the president, and under the circumstances he was able to do very little to protect him.

Like Garfield, William McKinley was born in Ohio and after serving in the Civil War found himself involved in home-state politics. He rose to the governorship before being elected to the presidency in 1896. He enjoyed a successful first term, becoming very popular after reluctantly entering and winning that "splendid little war"—the Spanish-American War.[78] When he bid for reelection in 1900, he ran alongside Spanish-American War hero Theodore Roosevelt, who had been nominated to serve as McKinley's vice president. They won both the popular vote and the electoral college, and McKinley was inaugurated to serve his second term on March 4, 1901. He and his wife, Ida, began a six-week celebratory tour of the nation, partly as a vacation, partly as a thank-you to the voters, and partly as a means of shoring up political support for his expansion of US trade, which had stalled in Congress.

As part of this American tour, McKinley was to appear at the Pan-American Exposition in Buffalo, New York.[79] The exposition was a world's fair ushering in the new century, the perfect opportunity for the president to talk about trade, which did, on September 5, before a crowd of some fifty thousand people. The next day, in the Temple of Music, McKinley stood to receive a long line of well-wishers, eager meet the president and shake his hand.[80] One of the people standing in line was an anarchist by the name of Leon Czolgosz.

Czolgosz was a poor factory worker who had become a devoted follower of Emma Goldman, a popular speaker and anarchist of the day. The assassination the summer before of Umberto I, King of Italy, got Czolgosz thinking: He didn't enjoy much popularity or respect in his political circle, but, he reasoned, "if he shot McKinley, it would prove something to the anarchists and they would finally accept him."[81] So he purchased a .32-caliber Iver Johnson revolver from the Sears, Roebuck catalog—the same model used to assassinate Umberto—and he began tracking the president.

Standing in line at the Temple of Music on September 6, 1901, Czolgosz had concealed the gun in his right hand, having wrapped a handkerchief around it to appear as if he were injured. When it was finally his turn, he approached the president, reached out his left hand to take the president's hand, and then, drawing McKinley toward him, pushed the gun into his chest and fired twice. McKinley raised up on his toe, and then fell back into the hands of a Secret Service agent. The first shot had ricocheted off a button on his coat, but the second bullet "passed through the stomach, nipped the top of the left kidney, and lodged in the pancreas."[82] McKinley lingered for a week before finally succumbing to his wounds on September 14, at 2:15 in the morning.

Immediately after he'd fired the gun, Czolgosz had been seized by McKinley's entourage, which included Secret Service agents George Foster and Albert Gallagher, and had been heard to have said simply, "I done my duty."[83] Like Guiteau before him, Czolgosz was tried, found guilty, and sentenced to death. But unlike Guiteau, rather than languishing in prison for a year, he was executed only a month after his conviction. Although Czolgosz got his wish, his notoriety as an anarchist did not improve their cause; on the contrary, it brought the wrath of government down upon these groups for the next twenty years.[84]

After the assassination of President McKinley—the third president murdered within a thirty-six-year span—the government finally decided to take action and get serious about security. This is when "the US Secret Service began to provide full-time protection for the president."[85] Not only had McKinley's assassination solidified the twofold mission of the United States Secret Service, it also elevated Theodore Roosevelt to the White House. As the first president to receive permanent, full-time protection from the Secret Service, Roosevelt soon came to fully appreciate the usefulness of federal law-enforcement agents—which sparked ideas about forming another federal law-enforcement agency. Understanding the evolution of the Secret Service from its origins to Roosevelt's presidency is the subject of the next chapter.

John E. Wilkie, the Chicago Times *reporter who became the Chief of the United States Secret Service, was a controversial figure at the center of the Secret Service controversy between President Roosevelt and Congress.*
Photo courtesy of the Library of Congress.

5

The Secret Service

The United States Secret Service is widely known today as the agency that protects the life of the American president. What is not as widely known is that it also continues to protect America's money supply. When the service was originally created in the summer of 1865, addressing the problem of counterfeiting was the organization's only concern, and it was only over time, with the assassination of three presidents, that it picked up the responsibility of its more popularly known mission. Like its name, the origins of the agency, originally housed under the Department of the Treasury and today a part of the Department of Homeland Security, are somewhat shrouded in mystery. That is because during the Civil War there were no less than three agencies that bore that title at one time or another.

The first agency called the Secret Service actually originated before the Civil War. "The Secret Service traces its origins to the year 1857," writes historian Willard B. Gatewood Jr., "when the Treasury Department received an appropriation for use in detecting counterfeiters; but the formal Secret Service Division was not created within the department until eight years later."[1] While it is true there was an appropriation for the Treasury Department to address the problem of counterfeiting, today's banknotes are nothing like the banknotes of the mid-nineteenth century, issued by the various state banks, and the counterfeit issues surrounding them were particular.[2] The appropriations did not create a unit within the Treasury Department that was called the Secret Service; that came eight years later in 1865.

The first of the actual agencies bearing the name Secret Service derived from Allan Pinkerton's friendship with General George B. McClellan. At the start of the Civil War, McClellan had contracted with his friend to set up a spy network and gather intelligence for his Army of the Ohio.[3] Pinkerton agreed, and he "called his spy network the Secret Service."[4] Although one aspect of Pinkerton's intelligence did pertain to the problem of Southern counterfeiters undermining the Northern economy with counterfeit bills, it was not the main purpose of this Secret Service entity. Rather, Pinkerton moved into both pockets of Southern sympathizers in the North and into Confederate-controlled states in order to gather intelligence on troop size and movement.

In 1862, as the federal government began to organize and fight the Civil War, Pinkerton's Secret Service underwent an administrative transfer into the War Department, and the leadership of the organization went to General Lafayette C. Baker.[5] Baker was an exuberant man, often reckless, who ran his Secret Service agency more like the vigilante group he had been a part of in San Francisco before the war. One biographer's description of him conveys the outsized impression some say Baker made: "His name struck terror in the hearts of his embattled, divided countrymen. He was red-bearded, ferret-eyed Lafayette C. Baker, the man who created the Secret Service, a frightening oppressive organization."[6] Baker's autobiography was no less flamboyant, often including ego-filled passages, like when he described General Walbridge begging him to take on the Secret Service: "Baker," the man himself wrote of that incident, "you are the man of all others to go into the secret service; you have the ability and courage."[7] As if this were not enough, Baker created a badge to be worn by all of his agents reading "Death to Traitors."[8] His Secret Service was much more about exacting revenge on the South than collecting intelligence.

Not surprisingly, then, Baker's recklessness and insatiable ego rubbed Secretary of War Edwin M. Stanton the wrong way. So as to undercut Baker, Stanton encouraged the creation of yet another Secret Service agency—this time, however, under the Treasury Department, with the focus of addressing war-time counterfeiting. Stanton then placed his own man, William P. Wood, in charge. Wood, however, was not much better than Baker: both men were ego-driven, yet where Baker was flamboyant, Wood was shady.

Secret Service historians Walter S. Bowen and Harry Edward Neal described Wood as a "swashbuckler, spy, a man without fear, without a complete stock of scruples, and sometimes without good judgement." They were perhaps too kind. Physically, Wood was described to be "tall, stocky, with a Dick Tracy–ish granite face and piercing eyes, a mop of dark brown hair parted on the left, and he had a deep, furry voice," not to mention that, "contrary to the fashion of the day, Wood wore no mustache, no beard."[9] The lack of facial hair was indicative of the man who made it a habit to do things differently and to boast of it later.

Other people had less kind things to say about him, but all acknowledged he was good at being shady. The service's provost marshal once described Wood as "short, ugly, and slovenly in his dress; in manner affecting stupidity and humility, but at bottom the craftiest of men."[10] But perhaps the best description of Wood came from those who had closely followed his exploits, such as the *Evening Star*, which noted in his obituary that "Col. Wood's life was a continuous melodrama, bordering on the tragic."[11] While Wood certainly faced more than his share of adversity, he was also the type of man who manufactured his own melodrama.

William P. Wood had become connected to Edwin M. Stanton long before the Civil War. In 1855, Cyrus McCormick, inventor of the mechanical reaper, sued a man named John Henry Manny for patent infringement. McCormick hired some high-powered lawyers of the time, so Manny hired Edwin M. Stanton, then an attorney with a Pittsburgh practice. "Wood was brought in as a consultant" on the case by Stanton and, according to historian Craughwell, "thanks to [Wood's] expertise, Stanton's firm won the case." It was "whispered around town that Wood had doctored the evidence in Stanton's favor," his "reputation as a shady character" already well established.[12] The entire complicated lawsuit "rested on the shape of a divider blade on a reaper that had originally been bought from McCormick and had been in use for fifteen years"; so, "if the divider was straight, McCormick would lose the suit," but "if it was curved, he would win." When the reaper was entered into evidence in court, the divider was found to be straight, meaning McCormick lost the suit, Manny was not liable, and Edwin Stanton achieved a major professional victory. Stanton was so indebted to Wood because, as historians Bowen and Neal explain, "the divider was straight because it had been straightened by William P. Wood!"[13]

In that particular case, Manny had also hired three additional lawyers to assist him—George Harding, P. H. Watson, and Abraham Lincoln. Manny had hired the future president because he'd needed a lawyer out of Springfield, Illinois, in hopes of influencing the judge in the case, Thomas Drummond. Manny had mostly exhausted his funds on the other lawyers in the case, so he needed a lawyer he could hire on the cheap, and since Lincoln was in debt over his failed 1854 Senate campaign—among many early political failures—he was selected. When Lincoln became president about five years later, Stanton became Lincoln's secretary of war, and when Stanton was looking to fill posts, he thought of Wood. At the time of his hire, Wood had already serving in the Union Army as a corporal, but after Stanton made his pay commensurate to a colonel's, ever after, Wood preferred to be titled according to his military pay grade: "Colonel Wood."[14]

"I first won and ever after have enjoyed the confidence of Mr. Stanton," the colonel later said.[15] And Stanton's confidence meant that when he needed someone to run the federal prison located in the nation's capital, "Wood was appointed by Secretary Stanton to be keeper of the Old Capitol Prisons."[16] It was through the wide array of prisoners held at the prison that Wood first began the practice of gathering useful intelligence by interrogation. Many of the prisoners were either Southerners or Southern sympathizers, and the information they held proved useful to the Union cause.

Wood, finding his success addictive, became ever more aggressive with his interrogations and intelligence operations, even going so far as to set up his own personal incursions into the South to the Confederate capital in Richmond, Virginia. There he posed as a Confederate soldier with money—which was most likely counterfeit—in order to purchase Confederate documents and negotiate prisoner exchanges. One Union officer, who knew what Wood was doing, attempted to notify Washington of Wood's shenanigans, wiring, "Mr. Wood is doing the most absurd things in Richmond."[17] Yet Wood's brash use of his role as warden was tolerated because he obtained results. He took some enormous risks, but they were so bold that most people believed he knew what he was doing. Perhaps the best summation of William P. Wood's tenure as warden of the prison came from a contemporary, Baltimore resident Catherine V. Baxley: "Thus old infidel Wm. P. Wood fooled and trifled with us all, he was indeed a strange compound, a perfect mass of contradictions."[18]

Wood's various antics caught the attention of Secretary of the Treasury William P. Fessenden, who was dealing with counterfeiting of the nation's new currency. Knowing Wood had foiled several counterfeiting operations, he asked Secretary Stanton to loan this perfect mass of contradictions to Treasury so he could take charge of their anticounterfeiting operations. So it was that Wood was made a Treasury operative in December of 1864.[19] As Wood later recalled, it was Lincoln, Stanton, and Fessenden, who appointed him "to give the counterfeiters a shaking up, which I proceeded to do under an order from the War Department."[20] Once again, despite much criticism for the way he performed his new role, Wood enjoyed a fair bit of latitude. "At that time it was currently reported that about half the money in circulation was counterfeit," he later recalled, and "I was permitted to use my own methods and I determined to capture the engravers and principals active in the counterfeiting business."[21]

As when he was warden, Wood employed his own methods as head of this new Secret Service. "It was also my purpose," he explained, "to convince such characters that it would be no longer healthy for them to ply their vocation without being handled roughly, a fact they soon discovered." And handling them roughly he did, for he used his intelligence to locate the counterfeiting operations and then conducted raids that "were swift and unexpected."[22] He refused to have anything to do with civilian authorities, knowing that most were probably on the take from the counterfeiters, and he refused to use military assets so as to better conceal his movements. His raids proved highly successful, and for the first time Wood was putting prisoners in the Old Capitol Prison rather than receiving them as warden.

It was then on Good Friday, April 15, 1865, not long before the president was to depart for an evening at Ford's Theatre, that he was said to have met with Secretary McCulloch to discuss establishing within Treasury the anticounterfeiting agency that would later become the security mechanism for all future presidents of the United States.[23] This story, historian Mihm explains, "with its tragic anticipation of the agency's later mission (the Secret Service did not begin protecting the president until century's end) is probably apocryphal." "More likely," he continues, "McCulloch and Jordan acted independently in the political chaos that followed Lincoln's assassination."[24] In fact, there is no evidence in the Congressional Record that Congress ever approved the creation of the Secret Service or that the president signed a bill into law authorizing the agency. It is rather more likely, as historian Johnson suggests, that the agency was created by "bureaucratic entrepreneurs."[25]

Regardless, today the United States Secret Service proudly declares itself one of the "oldest federal law enforcement agencies in the country" and marks its birth as July 5, 1865.[26] As for who would run the new agency, Wood was the most obvious choice; and so on that date, "Treasury moved to make his posting more permanent, naming him the chief of a new departmental anticounterfeiting force called the US Secret Service."[27] The best documentation for this action came in a letter from Secretary McCulloch, formally advising Secretary of War Edwin Stanton that William P. Wood "has been designated as the Chief of the detective force to act under the direction of the Solicitor of the Treasury in detecting and bringing to punishment persons engaged in counterfeiting. There is an urgent necessity that he should enter at once upon the discharge of his duty."[28]

That Congress itself did not create the US Secret Service that summer posed several problems: One originated in the Constitutional requirement that all appropriation bills originate in the House and then be passed by Congress. This meant that the Secret Service had no appropriation budget but had to be funded out of existing Treasury funds. Still further, "Since the Treasury, not Congress, created the Secret Service, its operatives didn't have the power to make arrests or obtain search warrants."[29] That forced agents to be deputized by the US marshals, work with the local police, or make "citizen's arrests,"[30] which posed its own set of problems: Marshals were "not obligated," and neither did they have any incentive, to deputize Treasury agents.[31] Many local police were likely on the take from the very counterfeiters Wood was trying to take down, making them inappropriate collaborators, and they had no incentive to cooperate with the Secret Service agents. This meant that in most instances Secret Service operatives, as they were called then, were forced to invoke citizen's arrests.[32]

Once Wood was officially established as chief of the Secret Service, he set about immediately creating his new agency. The first thing he needed to do was hire operatives to work for him, and he turned to people who knew about counterfeiting—the counterfeiters themselves. Wood "didn't just recruit counterfeiters as informants, he hired them as full-time employees." Of Wood's initial hires, "almost half of the original Secret Service team had criminal records." Wood's attitude was that "it takes a thief to catch a thief"—counterfeiting thieves, to be precise. And "despite his men's questionable methods, Wood delivered results."[33]

As historian Mihm explains, in those wild early years of the Secret Service, "Wood and his operatives dealt several blows to the counterfeit economy of the western states," and "the Secret Service also put away hundreds of less important figures, mostly petty dealers, shovers, and boodle carriers." These latter three were people who bought and sold counterfeit dollars, those who "shoved" the money into circulation, and those who transported the counterfeit notes (the "boodle"). Although arresting these types of criminals helped Wood achieve his mission, in reality, "Much of Wood's success depended on finding ways to circumvent local law enforcement officials, many of whom colluded with counterfeiters."[34] Wood essentially had to find ways to go after the counterfeiters without running into local police with a vested interest in the counterfeiters going unharassed so they could earn their graft.

Perhaps the greatest example of Wood's successful tactics that still managed to land him in hot water is the case of notorious "King of the Counterfeiters," William E. Brockway.[35] Allan Pinkerton himself once called Brockway "the most successful counterfeiter known to modern times."[36] One reason for Brockway's exceptional success was that he had in his possession forged plates that had been so expertly crafted, it was "difficult to tell the difference between the real notes and the forgeries."[37] The Treasury Department was so concerned that it issued a twenty thousand dollar reward for the recovery of the plates. Wood asked if he, as chief of the Secret Service, was eligible for the reward. When told that, yes, he was, Wood immediately sought out Brockway to strike a deal. When he finally caught up with Brockway, the criminal balked, and Wood arrested him. When the case finally went to trial, Wood was supposed to testify against him but instead testified on Brockway's behalf. After Brockway was convicted, he escaped, only to be hired by Wood several days later through a government contract.

The *New York Times* pointed out the problem: "the dealings of the Government with *counterfeiters* have long been a mystery to the common mind," they wrote, especially when counterfeiters like Brockway quickly "turned up *in the employ of the Government*."[38] The judge in Brockway's case, William Davis Shipman, explained his own grievance: "We have thus had the unseemly spectacle before this Court of an officer of the Treasury Department encouraging the defense of a prisoner, while the regular prosecuting officers were presenting proofs of his guilt." Shipman, like the *New York Times*, was left to ask, "Can the Government punish them in no other way than by taking them into partnership?"[39]

Wood's antics had been seen as bold and brave during a time of national crisis, but now, during peacetime, they were seen as reckless and downright criminal. The truth of the matter was, as historian Tarnoff explains, "With the Civil War over, people had less patience for Wood's heavy-handed style."[40] After three years of this reckless behavior, even Wood himself saw the writing on the wall. Despite attempts to appear reformed and professional, including issuing "the Service's first handbook of rules and regulations on 1 August 1868," it wasn't enough for him to keep his job.[41]

In 1869, upon being elected to the presidency, Ulysses S. Grant installed a new secretary of the Treasury, George S. Boutwell, who sent word that there would be a change in the head of the Secret Service. Wood resigned, reflecting that "Being a Republican I disclaim all hereditary right to continue in office."[42] It was also probably a good thing for, at the time, he was under indictment in a false-imprisonment case in New York.[43]

Under its new chief, Hiram C. Whitley, the Secret Service began moving in a different direction. Whitley himself was an imposing figure, towering to a height of six feet, ten inches; but it was his implementation of new policies that made him a most formidable chief.[44] Whitley began hiring new recruits "because of their civilian and military experiences," and "he adapted their behavior to bureaucratic routine." These new middle-class operatives "represented an important change in the Service's recruiting patterns," moving from the hiring of thieves to the hiring of bureaucrats.[45]

Things had certainly changed, and as one historian has commented, "The Secret Service was no longer very obliging, now that Wood was gone."[46] It certainly was no longer obliging to the counterfeiters, but like any good bureaucracy, it wasn't obliging to anyone, which was exactly how Whitley wanted it to be. As historian Johnson concluded of Whitley's tenure as chief, "Within four short years Whitley had shaped the Service into a general policing force for the federal government."[47]

Although the Secret Service was still hamstrung by their inability to effect an arrest, their budgetary situation was looking up. Beginning in 1871, Congress began issuing "lump-sum appropriations" for "the detection and prosecution of crimes" against the United States. Out of this lump sum, the Secret Service had to pay for its operatives and investigations, but because the number of available operatives was so low, the government "at first relied primarily upon private detectives, especially those from the Pinkerton Agency" for most counterfeit investigations.[48] They had little choice, for the number of operatives in the Secret Service remained low. During the late nineteenth century, the average number of operatives was twenty-five, "and for sixteen years, 1878 to 1893, the number of employees classified as operatives remained well below that average."[49] It also didn't help matters when in 1880 "Congress cut the Service's budget from $100,000 to $60,000" and added a "rider to the budget appropriation that restricted the Service to performing only one mission—investigating counterfeiting and forging."[50] This would not have been a problem were the Secret Service truly relegated to only counterfeiting operations; however, as early as 1869, other agencies had begun calling upon their operatives to provide investigatory services.

Historian Johnson has explained that "early in 1869 the IRS apparently asked for help in uncovering fraud," and "in 1870, when the second auditor of the Treasury found himself inundated with claims from veterans or their relatives for pensions and bounties, he turned to the Service for help in verifying the claims." This set a precedent for other agencies to call upon the Secret Service whenever they needed something investigated, and "for the remainder of the century it performed a wide range of investigations for its parent organization, including cases of embezzlement, robbery, smuggling, fraud, and illegal aliens."[51] Again, it only managed to conduct all of these investigations, including those involving counterfeiting, by issuing contracts to private agencies like the Pinkertons. However, after the Pinkerton riots, in 1892 Congress prohibited the contracting of private agencies, meaning the Secret Service could no longer rely on contract agents.[52]

This problem was somewhat ameliorated by the fact "things had begun to turn around on Capitol Hill for the Service, whose annual appropriations for the agency were on the rise and whose duties were broadened a bit to include the investigation of fraudulent pension claims and the management of national banks."[53] With so few agents and so many responsibilities, however, the Secret Service was stretched extremely thin. The solution the agency came up with was to rely on temporary agents for assistance.

Unlike the external contracts with the likes of the Pinkertons, these temporary agents were actually government-approved operatives who were referred to as per diem agents.[54] The names of these agents were kept on an approved list of men who could be called upon to work for the Secret Service piecemeal and were only paid out of per diem funds—funds that were designed to pay for expenses such as food and lodging. These per diem agents were a form of internal contract agents rather than the external contracts that had long existed but were now no longer legal.

Despite being assigned so many investigations outside of their Congress-directed mission to focus on counterfeiting and forgery, and despite the fact that they could no longer hire private contractors, the Secret Service truly did appear to have a handle on the problem of counterfeiting by the end of the 1800s. In historian Johnson's study of the Secret Service of that era, he concluded that "in one of the most successful, though little noticed, campaigns in the history of law enforcement, the Service essentially destroyed counterfeiting as a major criminal activity by the end of the nineteenth century." It also did not hurt that "by the 1890s the Service had also developed a reputation within the underworld as an organization that was dangerous to provoke."[55] That proved to be a good thing, because in 1894 the Secret Service began to provide informal protection for the American president, a job that would task their resources and once again place them on a steep learning curve.[56]

It is almost shocking to realize that as late as 1894 Congress had not yet authorized the Secret Service to provide protective services to the president, despite the Lincoln and Garfield assassinations. Although Secret Service agents had occasionally been loaned to the White House for special occasions, it was not until that year that, "for the first time in the agency's history, Chief William P. Hazen assigned two of his men to the White House to protect President Grover Cleveland."[57] In addition to the two men who generally accompanied the president when he traveled, there were also "two or three men assigned as personal guards at his summer residence at Gray Gables on Buzzards

Bay in Massachusetts."[58] And though he had no authority to do so, but when McKinley replaced Cleveland as president, Hazen kept the agents on the protective detail. That choice, however, created problems for him.

Hazen had called these loaned out agents "special policemen" in order to mask their specific duties and to conceal who they actually were. However, in 1898, when Treasury was conducting a routine investigation of monetary expenditures by its agencies, it discovered that the Secret Service had been providing protection at both Cleveland's and McKinley's private homes. What happened next would be bizarre by today's standards. "Legislators and other officials railed against Hazen," historians Philip H. Melanson and Peter F. Stevens explain, "because the Service had no formal protective mission at all and the guarding of a president's home was perceived as reeking of monarchy." Hazen was demoted for what was deemed "shocking administrative mismanagement."[59] John E. Wilkie was called in to replace him.

While Wilkie has been described as "a polished civil servant," for most of his life he had been a reporter, financial editor, and city editor for the *Chicago Tribune*.[60] Although in all fairness, it should be noted that "Wilkie possessed a wide reputation as a crime reporter on the Chicago *Tribune*."[61] More importantly, however, Wilkie was a good friend of President McKinley, which is how he really was appointed chief of the United States Secret Service. That is not to say he did not perform well in the role: in actuality, by all accounts he performed admirably and was well respected in the position.

When President McKinley chose engage in the Spanish-American War, the Secret Service was called upon to once again renew its role in counterespionage and intelligence gathering, a role for which it still did not have Congressional authority. Yet the service went ahead, "proving more adept at counterintelligence work than at producing effective intelligence."[62] Of course, agents still had no statutory authority to provide presidential protection, but because it was wartime Wilkie still assigned agents both to the White House and to accompany McKinley on his travels.[63] One biographer explained that Wilkie "had no legal warrant to pay these men out of the funds allocated to his bureau. Yet they had to be paid. So it came about that he was forced to commit technical perjury."[64] He did this by sending the Secret Service agents to guard the president knowing he was "risking official censure" when he "charged the cost to counterfeiting."[65]

These problems remained even after the war and despite McKinley's assassination, so that even into the twentieth century the Secret Service was still spread thin and had no legal right to use agents for any duty other than investigating counterfeiting. The actual number of agents remained small, numbering less than twenty in field offices across the country. In order to try and compensate, "Wilkie recruited primarily young men with experience as policemen or as claims agents for railroads." At least agents with experience knew what to do and how to investigate; but even with all the expertise, the service's numbers were too low to observe their mandate. In order to operate the service, "there were per diem agents whose names were on the eligible list of the Civil Service Commission," and, "as the need arose, such individual were called into service." Yet again, the practice of loaning Secret Service agents, including per diem agents, to other agencies was tasking both manpower and the budget and was legally questionable. "Technically," of course, "there were no Secret Service agents in any federal department except the Treasury." Even after the Department of Justice was created in 1871, if that department needed a case investigated, it relied on the use of contracted agents. However, when that practice ceased in 1892, everyone looked to the Secret Service to loan them agents when the need arose. So, "by the beginning of the twentieth century the detailing of agents from the Secret Service Division for use by other departments was a well-established practice."[66] Still, this and the protection of the president remained technically illegal, as these duties were outside of the Secret Service's Congressional mandate, and there were no Congressional appropriations for these additional duties.[67]

Yet for truly the first time, after the assassination of McKinley the Secret Service agents protected the president not on an as-needed basis but as a permanent, around-the-clock force. Or, as Roosevelt would come to think of it, "a full-time nuisance." Roosevelt found the agents to be "inexorable"; "they checked their watches when he went upstairs, stared at his window while he slept, and hung yawning around the kitchen at break-fast time. They webbed the estate with trip wires, and treated all visitors as potential anarchists, even a party of dowagers from the Oyster Bay Needlework Guild."[68]

After McKinley's assassination at the hands of Leon Czol-gosz, Theodore Roosevelt became president of the United States on September 14, 1901. He was truly the first president to receive the constant Secret Service protection that is taken for granted today. And although as a thoroughly self-sufficient outdoors-man he considered them as a nuisance, he found ways to have fun with them. Roosevelt enjoyed leaving the White House for Rock Creek Park to play Point to Point. The game only had one rule: You started off on your march through the woods, and you went from one point to another in a straight line. "If a creek got in the way, you forded it. If there was a river, you swam it. If there was a rock, you scaled it, and if you came to a precipice you let yourself down over it."[69] If he didn't have friends, gener-als, ambassadors, or cabinet officers to play the game with him, he always had the Secret Service, and he loved to see if he could lose them on these fast-paced marches or see what they would do with their guns when he would strip down naked to swim the rivers.

After having served for one year in office, in advance of the midterm elections of 1902, Roosevelt began touring the New England states. Accompanying Roosevelt on the trip was Secret Service operative William Craig. Born in Scotland, Craig had "previously served for twelve years in the British Army" and, after moving to America, joined the Secret Service. He was a large man, coming in at "six feet, four inches tall and weighing 260 pounds."[70] Though he had only "served with the agency for less than one year," Roosevelt had already become fond of him.[71]

On September 1, 1902, Craig granted a reporter from the *Worcester Telegram* an interview about what it was like being a Secret Service operative, protecting the life of the president. When asked about the inherent peril in being the president, Craig explained, "The danger lies in some fanatic getting up to the president and shooting or stabbing so quietly that it cannot be prevented. If no outsiders are allowed within 10 feet of the presidents—and 25 feet is still better—the danger is greatly lessened."[72] Little did he or anyone know, this would be Craig's final interview, ever.

The following day, which was also the final day of Roosevelt's tour, "a speeding trolley car crashed headlong into the open carriage carrying Roosevelt and his party from Pittsfield, Massachusetts, to Stockbridge." The force of the impact overturned the car, throwing Roosevelt, his private secretary George Cortelyou, and Massachusetts governor Winthrop Murray Crane clear of the wreck. However, "Roosevelt's favorite Secret Service agent, William Craig, was caught under the wheels of the rushing trolley car and torn apart."[73] When Roosevelt saw what had happened, he sadly lamented, "Poor Craig," and he was overheard despondently saying over and over, "Too bad, too bad."[74] Roosevelt pressed ahead with the final legs of his tour, but he asked his aides to "gallop ahead" and "tell the people everywhere along the line that Craig has been killed and I wish no cheering."[75] Roosevelt also pondered, "how my children will feel," for "Craig had become almost a part of the Roosevelt family."[76] William Craig had the unfortunate distinction of becoming the first Secret Service agent to die in the line of duty.

In the aftermath now of both McKinley's assassination and Craig's death, the protection of the president had become a well-established practice. "Although Wilkie still had no official power to guard the president," Secret Service historians Melanson and Stevens explain, "no one questioned him when the Secret Service assumed full-time responsibility for President Roosevelt's safety."[77] In the wake of McKinley's assassination, Congress had wrestled with a measure for presidential protection, but it failed to make it to the floor for a vote.[78] This reality meant that no appropriation was made for this added duty of the Secret Service, so the agency again had to absorb the costs from its counterfeiting budget. It was not until 1906, when Congress passed the Sundry Civil Expenses Act of 1907, that they authorize funds, but funds "for no other purpose whatever, except in the protection of the person of the President of the United States, one hundred and twenty-five thousand dollars."[79]

Stipulating that the funders were "for no other purpose" had a history. In an 1879 budget for the Treasury Department, Congress had used the same limiting language because, as historian Richard B. Sherman explains, "of the alleged misdeeds of some Secret Service operatives in investigating the conduct of a United States senator."[80] It was this clause that allocated every Secret Service dollar to counterfeiting and forgery investigations—and was also what had made the service's presidential detail an inherent violation of federal law. And so it was with the 1907 act that the Secret Service's express and actual missions finally were funded and legalized.

If there ever was a president for whom facing death was nothing new, that was assuredly Theodore Roosevelt. His entire life had been fraught with life-threatening perils, from his early hunting expeditions to his service in Cuba as the head of the Rough Riders during the Spanish-American War. It is said that once, while serving as McKinley's vice president, he was wintering in Colorado when a cougar attacked some of his hounds, whereupon Roosevelt leaped off his horse, kicked the hounds aside, and fought the cougar to death with a knife.[81] Even after his time in the White House, when he voyaged to Brazil to explore the River of Doubt, he faced enormous hardships, contracted malaria, and almost died. Roosevelt, however, never allowed himself to fear death, for as he once wrote, "Only those fit to live who do not fear to die."[82] And it was because Roosevelt was no stranger to danger that, as his biographer Edmund Morris stated, "Roosevelt was not worried about assassination."[83]

Yet if any president ought have been worried about assassination, it was Theodore Roosevelt, for he had assumed office because of an assassin. He was also quite cognizant of America's history of presidential assassination, for when he was a mere six years old, he had hung out the window of his grandfather's Union Square mansion in New York City to watch Lincoln's funeral procession pass by. And after Garfield's assassination he had written in his diary, "Frightful calamity for America."[84] In addition to the tragic trolley incident in September of 1902 that had killed his favorite Secret Service agent, the following year, on September 1, while working late in his library, Roosevelt heard a scuffle outside. He immediately stepped outdoors and heard someone shout, "There he is!" upon which Secret Service agents pursued and caught a young man whom, after brandishing a firearm, they'd knocked to the ground. The man was then handcuffed and turned over to the police. Later, when upon questioning, he admitted, "I came to kill the President."[85] And if that weren't enough, during Roosevelt's second term in office another man managed to walked into Roosevelt's office with a "needle-sharp blade up his sleeve" before being apprehended by the Secret Service.[86] Despite all of these close calls, however, the reality was that "Theodore Roosevelt remained officially unprotected."[87]

But despite the fact that President Theodore Roosevelt was better protected than any sitting president before him, he still required the assistance of investigators outside of the Secret Service. Roosevelt understood the agency was stretched thin with too many mandates, some of which were unofficial, and was budgetarily constrained. Through a series of actions while president, based largely in part on beliefs he had formed prior to taking office, Roosevelt championed the formation of a special bureau of investigation comprised of general investigators who could be called upon whenever the need arose. In order to understand the relationship between today's Secret Service and the Federal Bureau of Investigation, it is important to understand the man who proposed and politically fought for the creation of what many call the world's premier law-enforcement agency. Theodore Roosevelt is, therefore, the subject of the next chapter.

Theodore Roosevelt, shown here with his horse Manitou on his ranch, was a lover of the "vigorous life" who established a conservation policy as president, fought against land fraud, and was instrumental in establishing America's National Park system.
Photo courtesy of the Theodore Roosevelt Center.

6

The Making of President Theodore Roosevelt

Although we often think of controversial presidents as a modern-day American conundrum, one of the most controversial presidents ever to sit in the White House took office at the beginning of the twentieth century. Theodore Roosevelt was, according to historian Kathleen Dalton, "remembered as both an honored political leader and one of the most picturesque personalities who has ever enlivened the landscape."[1] In his own time Roosevelt was both hated and loved. Some people agreed with Mark Twain that he was "clearly insane," while Woodrow Wilson thought him "the most dangerous man of the age." Still others who knew him from the beginning of his career, such as New York Assemblyman Newton M. Curtis, saw him as "a brilliant madman born a century too soon."[2] This range of opinions is typical of how most people responded to Theodore Roosevelt: they either loved him or hated him; he was polarizing. Even Roosevelt himself recognized his effect on people. "If a man has a very decided character, has a strongly accentuated career," he explained, "it is normally the case of course that he makes ardent friends and bitter enemies."[3] That was most certainly the case throughout Roosevelt's career, including his creation of the Federal Bureau of Investigation. In order to understand Roosevelt's involvement in the birth of the world's foremost law-enforcement agency, it is important to understand the man himself and his "strongly accentuated career."

Theodore Roosevelt was born on October 27, 1858, in Manhattan. His father, Theodore Roosevelt Sr.—referred to in family circles as "Thee"—took to calling Roosevelt Jr. "Teedie," to distinguish between senior and junior. The nickname stuck.[4] Roosevelt was fine when the sobriquet was used by family and friends, but in later years, when people began referring to him as "Teddy," he came to abhor it.[5]

Teedie had been born with a poor constitution and suffered from a number of ailments in his early years, the worst of which was asthma. As his younger sister Corinne later remarked, "Theodore Roosevelt, whose name later became the synonym of virile health and vigor, was a fragile patient sufferer in those early days of the nursery."[6] "Nobody seemed to think I would live," Roosevelt himself explained, because he was "a sickly and timid boy" and "a wretched mite."[7]

Growing up, Teedie's father hired the best tutors to educate the young boy, and his sister recalled that, "from the very fact that he was not able originally to enter into the most vigorous activities, he was always reading or writing."[8] He read voraciously and was soon personally cataloging the many flora and fauna he encountered, as well as writing stories and keeping what became a lifelong diary. It was on a family vacation to Europe that his father noticed how truly unbalanced his son's intellectual and physical gifts had become. He told his son, "Theodore, you have the mind but you have not the body, and without the help of the body the mind cannot go as far as it should." "You *must* make your body," his father insisted. "It is hard drudgery to make one's body, but I know you will do it." And Teedie did, placing himself on a rigorous regiment of exercise designed to increase his strength and endurance, and, most importantly, to increase the capacity of his asthmatic lungs. Ever after, Roosevelt led what he referred to as "the strenuous life."[9]

Roosevelt's years as autodidact and homeschool pupil prepared him well for his entry into Harvard University. As he wrote his older sister Bamie, "Is it not splendid about my examinations, I passed well on all the eight subjects I tried."[10] Roosevelt capitalized on his time at Harvard and managed to enhance his already stellar education and solidify his physical development.

But more importantly, it yielded a social confidence he had never before enjoyed. As his sister Corrine recalled, "His college life broadened every interest and did for him what had hitherto not been done, which was go give him confidence in his relationship with young men of his own age."[11]

While Teedie was away at college, Roosevelt's father became ill, and the doctors diagnosed him with cancer. It spread quickly, and Theodore Sr. suffered incredibly. The family, however, had decided to keep Teedie in the dark about his father's condition, believing this would allow him to concentrate on his studies. When it looked like end was near, they finally summoned Theodore Jr. But after "he raced to catch the overnight train," explains historian Goodwin, he "reached New York on Sunday morning to find his father had died late Saturday night."[12]

The loss of his beloved father struck Roosevelt hard. "I felt as if I had been stunned," he wrote in his diary, "or as if part of my life had been taken away."[13] He continued to feel the loss acutely—until he finally found someone to help replace it. Alice Hathaway Lee was introduced to Theodore Roosevelt through a friend at Harvard, and not more than a month after meeting, Teedie was determined "to win her."[14] Roosevelt decidedly "made everything subordinate to win her," and with this solitary focus and determination, he won her hand, and they were married on October 27, 1880.[15]

By this time, Roosevelt had graduated from Harvard and gone on to Columbia Law School to earn his law degree. At the beginning of his senior year at Harvard, Theodore had begun writing his first book, mostly as a personal exercise. *The Naval War of 1812* ended up being published in 1882 to much acclaim, the *New York Times* even noting "The volume is an excellent one in every aspect."[16]

During this period, in addition to sending off his manuscript and going on a European vacation with his wife, Roosevelt had also found time to engage in politics, becoming acquainted with the various members of the New York Republican Party. He was not an overnight sensation, for Roosevelt was different—Roosevelt was always different—and as one member of the party recalled, "He looked like a dude, side whiskers an' all, y' know."[17] In little time, however, "he won over his comrades with the warmth, unabashed intensity, and pluck of his personality."[18] So when a seat in New York's twenty-fifth district became available, Roosevelt was chosen to run for the position on the Republican ticket. In the fall of 1881, Theodore Roosevelt was elected as the youngest member of the New York State Assembly, launching the beginning of what was truly an unprecedented political career.

It was in the New York assembly that Roosevelt first publically displayed elements of the bravery that historian H. W. Brands believes essential to understanding both Roosevelt's image and force of will for affecting change. "What makes the hero a hero," writes Brands, "is the romantic notion that he stands above the tawdry give and take of everyday politics, occupying an ethereal realm where partisanship gives way to patriotism, and division to unity, and where the nation regains its lost innocence, and the people their shared sense of purpose."[19]

This part of Roosevelt's personality came out when he began to fight the corrupt elements of New York's Democratic-controlled Tammany Hall political machine. They saw Roosevelt as an outsider elite who was nothing more than a young upstart, born with the proverbial silver spoon in his mouth. Even worse was the fact that almost from the beginning Roosevelt had "pushed for an investigation of corruption in the New York city government," angering the Tammany machine, because they were the ones being investigated.[20] When Tammany lieutenant John McManus threatened to toss this young troublemaker in a blanket, Roosevelt responded with a pugilist's flair: "By God! If you try anything like that, I'll kick you, I'll bite you, I'll kick you in the balls. I'll do anything to you—you'd better let me alone."[21] It worked. McManus and the others left him alone.

Still, the pressure continued to mount, for Roosevelt's focus on political corruption was seen as a threat, and his enemies believed—wrongly—that he would cave.[22] This drama continued to unfold until one late-winter afternoon when Roosevelt had gone to Hurst's Roadhouse, a saloon just outside of Albany, frequented by New York's assemblymen. When Roosevelt entered without a coat on that cold day, "one Tammany Tiger taunted him by asking, 'Why don't your mother buy you an overcoat? Won't Mama's boy catch cold?'" Two others joined in throwing insults, which, as a reporter noted, Roosevelt simply ignored. When they came over to him and one shouted in his face, "You—little dude," Roosevelt had had quite enough. Little did they know, this "little dude" had been a boxer during his college days. "Quick as lightning, Roosevelt slipped his glasses into his side pocket," as the reporter described it, "and in another second he had laid out two of the trio on the floor. The third quit cold."[23] Although quickly dispatching his two assailants won him fame, what endeared himself to so many, including the three Tammany thugs, was the fact that immediately afterward he offered to buy each of them a beer.

Assemblyman Roosevelt proved as feisty in his floor debates in the New York legislature as he had been in the roadhouse, and despite his often irritating ways, he had an ingratiating manner. So much so that in his second elected term in Albany, he "rose like a rocket," as he himself later recalled.[24] He had become one of the Republican party leaders and, despite losing his run for speaker of the assembly, proved a successful legislator, writing more bills than anyone else during his time in the legislature.[25]

Things were going exceptionally well for Roosevelt at this early point of his career, for he was having much success in the assembly, he had just taken a much-anticipated vacation hunting in the Badlands, and his wife was about to give birth to their first child. Alice Lee Roosevelt came into the world on February 12, 1884—Abraham Lincoln's birthday. "I shall never forget when the news came and we congratulated him on the birth of his daughter," recalled Ike Hunt, one of Roosevelt's closest allies. "He was full of life and happiness—and the news came of a sudden turn and he took his departure."[26]

Even before the baby's birth, Alice had not been feeling well; she had been having difficulties with water retention, had been "crampy," and generally just felt poorly.[27] But after the baby was born, her condition grew precipitously worse. In addition, under the same roof, Roosevelt's mother had fallen ill and been diagnosed with typhoid fever.[28] On February 14—Valentine's Day—Roosevelt could do nothing but lament his situation, cry-ing, "There is a curse on this house! Mother is dying, and Alice is dying, too."[29] Tragically, at 3 that very morning, only hours after he had rushed home from the assembly, his mother succumbed to typhoid fever; she was only forty-nine. Eleven hours later, Roosevelt lost his wife; she had died of what was then known as Bright's disease—kidney failure that had gone undiagnosed because of her pregnancy. In a single day Theodore Roosevelt had lost both his mother and his wife to diseases he could not fight; he was absolutely devastated.[30] The only entry in his diary that day was a large X, under which he wrote, "The light has gone out of my life."[31]

After the double funeral, Roosevelt did the only thing he knew how to do: he threw himself back into his work. But even that proved to be insufficiently cathartic. So, after the presidential convention of 1884, Roosevelt retired from politics, and, having already placed baby Alice into the care of his sister Bamie, fled West into the Badlands of North Dakota. There he took to ranching and living the life of a cowboy and turned his writing to the topics of hunting and frontier life. This was his life for the better part of the next two years, though he occasionally drifted back east. But after the horrible winter of late 1886, in which he lost more than half his herd, he once again became a fixture of New York City.

Upon his return to New York, Roosevelt began courting his childhood friend Edith Kermit Carow, and they were soon married, on December 2, 1886. They settled into Sagamore Hill, their estate on Oyster Bay, on the northern side of Long Island. He and Edith had taken in young Alice, and the couple went on to have five children of their own: Theodore "Ted" III in 1887, Kermit in 1889, Ethel in 1891, Archibald in 1894, and Quentin in 1897.

Before long, Roosevelt decided to return to politics, and his first foray back was running in the mayoral race of New York City, which he lost. Unsure of his future, he turned back to his frontier writing, which he soon began publishing in 1889 as a six-volume series, titled *The Winning of the West*. The book was a runaway best-seller and quickly gained critical acclaim, including the praise of the historian whose name became synonymous with the history of the West, Frederick Jackson Turner, who called it "a wonderful story, most entertainingly told."[32]

Prior to the publication of Roosevelt's first volume, events had already been set in motion that would change the direction of his life. In the fall presidential election of 1888, the man who managed to interrupt President Grover Cleveland's two terms in office, Benjamin Harrison, was elected president. One of his key campaign issues had been advocating for good governance through the establishment of a merit system for government employees, rather than maintaining the corrupt spoils system. Roosevelt supported these efforts and wrote to his friend Henry Cabot Lodge, then representing the state of Massachusetts in the House, "I do hope the President will appoint good Civil Service Commissioners."[33] Lodge got to work and managed to secure from President Harrison one of three positions for Roosevelt. Roosevelt seized the opportunity and was soon racing off to the nation's capital.

There he faced a tough task, for Americans were not ready to eliminate the spoils system. As one of his biographers, Henry F. Pringle, explains, "Until he began to roar, the merit system had been a subject that interested a small fraction of the intelligent minority."[34] What Roosevelt had to do, as he put it, was "change the average citizen's mental attitude toward the question."[35] He rose to the challenge and began to roar.

Recalling the extensive corruption that had existed in the New York government, Roosevelt made the assumption, correctly, that the federal government faced a similar problem. He immediately set about conducting his own investigation into the extent of the corruption and soon found that the Indianapolis postmaster, William Wallace—a friend of the president's—was making appointments that violated civil-service rules. Roosevelt took action immediately, explaining to Lodge, "We stirred things up well, but I think we have administered a galvanic shock that will reinforce his virtue for the future."[36] Roosevelt proved to be right, and problems with Wallace ceased.

But this was only the start. Roosevelt proved to be a whirlwind of activity, and anywhere he sensed corruption, he ferreted it out and exposed it. He had become the face of the Civil Service Commission, and many often wondered if he was their only member. For this he was vilified by the press: to them he was altering the way things had always been done. The *Washington Post* was especially brutal:

> He came into official life with a blare of trumpets and a beat-
> ing of gongs, blared and beat by himself. He immediately an-
> nounced himself the one man competent to take charge of the
> entire business of Government. To his mind every department
> of the Government was under the management of incompetent
> and bad men. He said to himself, to his barber, to his laundry-
> man, and to all others who would listen to his incoherent gib-
> berish: "I am Roosevelt; stop work and look at me." For a short
> time he had clear sailing. As he sailed he took in wind. As he
> took in wind he became more puffed up. As he became more
> puffed up he became insolent, arrogant, and more conceited.[37]

All in all, this was probably a pretty fair assessment, except perhaps for the charge of speaking gibberish: even if he was a feisty
public speaker, Roosevelt was eloquent, too.

Roosevelt received public support from the one man that
mattered—President Harrison—if always with great reserve. In
private, however, Harrison said "Roosevelt seemed to feel that
everything ought to be done before sundown."[38] Publicly, Roosevelt himself believed that it was "to Harrison's credit, all we
are doing in enforcing the law." Still, Roosevelt also sensed Harrison's true feelings, privately writing his sister Bamie, "I have
been continuing my civil service fight, battling with everybody.
The little gray man in the White House looking on with cold and
hesitating disapproval."[39] But "Harrison dared not take action,"
notes historian Doris Kearns Goodwin, while action was the
only thing Roosevelt knew.[40]

Still, in the end, Roosevelt posed a significant problem for
Harrison's bid for reelection in 1892. The race had split three
ways, with Harrison the incumbent, Grover Cleveland trying
to obtain a second term after four years out of elected office,
and populist candidate James B. Weaver gaining some ground.
After Cleveland won his second term in the end, Roosevelt,
belonging to the opposing party, offered his resignation from
the Civil Service Commission. But Cleveland encouraged
him to stay on "for a year or two," which he did. There he

continued to fight against government corruption, and, as his biographer Nathan Miller asserts, he "won the admiration of ordinary Americans for taking on the spoilsmen." Yet Miller also believes Roosevelt faced a greater problem than ferreting out corruption: figuring out "how to promote efficiency among government workers and make them responsive to the needs of the people they are supposed to serve."[41] And that is exactly what he set out to learn when he accepted an appointment on the New York City Board of Police Commissioners under reform-minded Mayor William Lafayette Strong. With Roosevelt's resignation from the Civil Service Commission, President Cleveland is said to have commented, "There goes the best politician in Washington."[42]

Roosevelt's trajectory at this point in his career had decidedly been toward national office, so it seemed rather odd for him to step down to a city-level position. But he recalled in his autobiography why Mayor Strong's offer had been so appealing: "I was appointed with the distinct understanding that I was to administer the Police Department with entire disregard of partisan politics, and only from the standpoint of a good citizen interested in promoting the welfare of all good citizens."[43] Rather than running counter to Roosevelt's trajectory, in many ways this move was the perfect next step in his anticorruption campaign—an appointment in one of the day's most corrupt organizations of governance.

On the morning of May 6, 1895, Theodore Roosevelt marched up Mulberry Street to report for his first day on the job at New York City Police Headquarters. Watching from across the street, as newspapermen often did trying to catch a story, reporters Lincoln Steffens of the *Evening Post* and Jacob Riis of the *Evening Sun* watched his progression. Roosevelt already knew Steffens from his time in the legislature, and Riis, as Roosevelt noted in his autobiography, he already knew "because his book 'How the Other Half Lives' had been to me both an enlightenment and an inspiration for which I could never be too grateful."[44] Knowing of Roosevelt's strong personality, the two reporters knew there would be a story in his first day on the job. Riis observed to Steffens, "I don't care who the other Commissioners are. TR is enough."[45]

As Roosevelt approached the police headquarters with the other board members at about half past ten that morning, he saw Steffens and Riis watching from their usual stoop across the street. Spying him, they crossed the street to meet him. Steffens recalled that morning fondly: "He came on ahead down the street; he yelled, 'Hello, Jake,' to Riis, and running up the stairs to the front of Police Headquarters, he waved us reporters to follow. We did. With the police officials standing around watching, the new Board went up to the second story." They were heading for the police commissioner's boardroom. On the way, "still running, he asked questions; 'Where are our offices? Where is the Board Room? What do we do first?' Out of the half-heard answers," Steffens recalled, "he gathered the way to the Board Room, where the three old Commissioners waited, like three of the new Commissioners, stiff, formal and dignified." But of course, "Not TR."[46] He enthusiastically went around introducing himself, shaking hands vigorously, entirely exuberant and ready for the task at hand.

The first task was to convene the meeting and then vote on a president of the board—which nomination Theodore Roosevelt readily accepted, because no one else wanted it. Effectively, at the time, this made him the new police commissioner—head of the New York City Police Department. Roosevelt then adjourned the meeting, went to the president's office, pulling Steffens and Riis along with him, and, closing the door, asked them, "Now, then, what'll we do?"[47] It was not What will I do or What will the *commission* do—rather, it was What would Steffens, Riis, and Roosevelt do. And this is how Roosevelt began his tenure as head of the almost wholly corrupt New York City Police Department.

In order to mark the fact his tenure would be different from his predecessors', in the first statement Roosevelt released as president of the commission, he said, "The public may rest assured that so far as I am concerned, there will be no politics in the department, and I know that I voice the sentiment of my colleagues in that respect. We are all activated by the desire to so regulate this department that It will earn the respect and confidence of the community."[48] This was unprecedented for the time, as the police department had always served the political machine, which, until the recent election of Mayor Strong, had been the corrupt Tammany Hall machine. In 1894 public hearings by the Lexow Committee exposed police corruption, which led to the Tammany machine's losing the 1894 mayoral election. This put in a reform-minded mayor, who in turn appointed Theodore Roosevelt to the commission.

Roosevelt as police commissioner generally divided people, as usual, into two camps: they either loved him or hated him. Anyone who benefitted from Tammany, the police corruption, and the Tammany politicians themselves hated him. Most reformed-minded Republicans loved him. Yet even many of the people who should have supported him did not. His strong personality often rubbed people the wrong way; his fellow board member Andrew D. Parker lamented to Steffens that Roosevelt "thinks he's the whole board."[49] In many ways, at least in that first year, Roosevelt truly was the whole board. Or, perhaps more accurately, Roosevelt, Steffens, and Riis were, because Theodore did not trust the insiders of the police department— many of whom also came to despise Roosevelt—but he did trust the two newspapermen. From them Roosevelt obtained information about what was really going on in the department, and together the three developed ways the department could be reformed. "It was," as Steffens recounted, "just as if we three were the police board."[50]

In addition to Steffens and Riis, many who had been victimized by the Tammany machine and the corrupt police department with its graft and brutality, and many of the reform-minded citizens, found Roosevelt as a breath of fresh air and began to think he might finally end police corruption. Shortly after Roosevelt's election by the board, *New York World* reporter Arthur Brisbane wrote, "We have a real Police Commissioner. His teeth are big and white, his eyes are small and piercing, his voice is rasping," and, more importantly, "his heart is full of reform." He was, Brisbane concluded, "the man to reform the force."[51]

As Roosevelt set about his duties, he understood "there were two sides to the work." The first was "the actual handling of the Police Department," the day-in and day-out administrative duties for managing the police department's business. The second side, Roosevelt wrote in his autobiography, was "using my position to help in making the city a better place in which to live and work for those to whom the conditions of life and labor were hardest." He also recognized that these two sides were connected: "for one thing never to be forgotten in striving to better the conditions of the New York police force is the connection between the standard of morals and behavior in that force and the general standard of morals and behavior in the city at large."[52]

Roosevelt knew he was going to have to go after police corruption, something he strongly believed he had the experience to accomplish. As he wrote his friend Henry Cabot Lodge, who had grown concerned that Roosevelt was forgetting about national politics, "In a couple of years or less I shall have finished the work here for which I am specially fitted, and in which I take a special interest. After that there will remain only the ordinary problem of decent administration of the Department, which will be already in good running order." Roosevelt was going to defeat the corruption that had been endemic and entrenched in the New York Police Department for fifty years, and he was going to accomplish all of it in a mere "couple of years."[53]

In turning to the problem of police corruption, Roosevelt first began looking at the evidence brought forth by the Lexow Committee. Several years before, the newly elected state senator, Clarence Lexow, had put forth a bill to create a committee to look into the numerous allegations Pastor Charles Henry Parkhurst's Vigilance League had made against the New York City Police Department.[54] The bill passed, and Lexow had been selected to chair the committee. "By the summer of 1894," writes Mike Dash, "Lexow's commission had turned into a real crusade against police corruption—one that would run for the best part of a year, produce more than 10,500 printed pages of evidence, and examine nearly 680 witnesses."[55]

One witnesses to appear before the committee had been the notorious police officer Alexander "Clubber" Williams, who was aptly nicknamed and had once remarked, "There is more law in the end of a policeman's night stick than a Supreme Court decision."[56] The Lexow Committee had found that on a policeman's salary Clubber had somehow managed to purchase and maintain "a house on East Tenth Street; a seventeen-room mansion in Cos Cob, Connecticut, a small steam yacht; and a jetty, extending 160 yards out of sea, that had cost, him $39,000 to build." When asked how he had accumulated such wealth on only a few thousand a year, Williams had shrugged and said it was from "real-estate investments years earlier in northern Japan."[57]

After his testimony, Clubber had gone on vacation. By the time he returned, Roosevelt was acting as police commissioner, and, with Steffens in his office, he summoned the cop. The plan had been to fire him, but Williams was savvy enough to ask to retire. Roosevelt went out to the reporters and told them, "Inspector Williams has asked for retirement. The law is mandatory, and his request was unanimously granted by the board." He paused before adding, "Notice, I say he asked for a retirement, and that the law is mandatory."[58] Roosevelt was assuring the news reporters that Williams was not fired, even though it was clear Roosevelt had made it a choice to either be fired or retire.

Roosevelt had other targets: one officer who had built a reputation for good detective work was Superintendent Thomas Byrnes. Although the Lexow Committee had not managed to find anyone willing to testify against the head of New York's detectives, it was well known that Byrnes was on the take and was at odds with the new reforms. As Roosevelt wrote to his friend Lodge, "I think I shall move against Byrnes at once. I thoroughly distrust him, and cannot do any thorough work while he remains." Unlike Clubber, however, Byrnes resisted, so confident in his power, warning Roosevelt, "I will break you. You will yield. You are but human."[59] The fight was on. At first, it looked like Byrnes might have to stay, but he was soon caught in a situation where there was evidence against him and, after being dragged before the police commissioners, he realized the end had come. He retired.

Having removed the two most corrupt men in the police department, Roosevelt hoped he had sent a signal to the rest of the department. If not, he reasoned, the targeting of derelicts in the ranks would surely do the trick. In order to ensure his police officers were doing their duty, Roosevelt instituted his "midnight rambles."[60] He went out late at night or early in the morning and looked to see if officers were at their assigned posts. Roosevelt discovered most of the officers were either absent from their posts or sleeping. Coming across one officer, Patrolman Mahoney, standing in front of a saloon, Roosevelt, "What are you doing here?" Failing to recognize his new police commissioner, Mahoney smartly replied, "Why, I'm standing, of course." Roosevelt ordered Mahoney and three other officers he'd caught off-post to report later that morning for trial. Finding all of the officers guilty, Roosevelt merely issued them warnings. But he had achieved his intended purpose: getting the word out to the rest of the department about the new commissioner's expectations. And it worked. Jacob Riis later wrote, "the police force woke up."[61]

As the police department began to understand that things were going to be different under the new police commissioner, Roosevelt then turned his sights to political corruption. "The first fight I made was to keep politics absolutely out of the force," explained Roosevelt, which included "every kind of improper favoritism." Of the many instances of corruption Roosevelt faced, the most egregious was perhaps the Sunday law. "When I was Police Commissioner," Roosevelt later recalled in his autobiography, "New York was a city with twelve or fifteen thousand saloons, with a State law which said they should be closed on Sundays." The problem was "a local sentiment which put a premium on violating the law by making Sunday the most profitable day in the week to the saloon-keeper who was willing to take chances. It was this willingness to take chances that furnished to the corrupt politicians and the corrupt police officer their opportunities."[62]

The problem had developed out of the immigrant community in New York who came from the Old World, where one worked hard six days a week and then, as the good Lord commanded, relaxed on Sundays. To the Irish, Czechs, and Germans, "relaxing" meant gathering in the afternoons in the biergartens with family and friends to enjoy a drink. The immigrant arrivals, however, found that this tradition clashed with American Protestant ethics, which directed one to work hard throughout the week and then abstain from alcohol, especially on Sundays.

And because the Protestants in the legislature trumped the immigrants, New York had a Sunday law.

But Sunday was the most profitable day for saloonkeepers, whose clientele were largely immigrants. So in order to remain open in violation of the law, all they had to do was pay the police for the privilege—the privilege of not seeing their patrons arrested or their saloons closed down on Sundays. As this graft also found its way into the pockets of the politicians, there was simply no incentive for anyone to disrupt the lucrative arrangement. At least, not until Roosevelt became police commissioner.

Roosevelt believed in the law and felt that if the politicians wanted to keep the saloons open on Sundays they should repeal the law that was supposed to keep them closed. Still, in directing his officers to enforce the law, Roosevelt faced an enormous backlash. And everyone was in on the fight—the police, their supervisors, the politicians, the saloonkeepers, and their patrons. As Roosevelt confided to Lodge, "It is an awkward and ugly fight, yet I am sure I am right in my position and I think there is an even chance of our winning on it."[63]

In the opening months of Roosevelt's campaign to enforce the Sunday law, the fight appeared to be going poorly. Nearly everyone except the prohibitionists and Protestant clergymen were against him. But then Roosevelt did what Roosevelt did best: he gave a speech. Before a packed hall at the Good Government Club, Roosevelt claimed to speak not as the police commissioner but as a "fellow-American." He spoke of the corrupting influence the Sunday law had on the police department and the city and argued that, "For an official to permit violation of law whenever he thinks that the sentiment of a particular locality does not favor its enforcement inevitably leads to anarchy and violence."[64] The speech gave renewed life to the enforcement of the Sunday laws, and Roosevelt achieved his victory. As he later recalled in his autobiography, "I had been told that it was not possible to close the saloons on Sunday and that I could not succeed. However, I did succeed."[65]

By certain metrics, he was successful: as historian Edward P. Kohn explains, "Roosevelt had succeeded in closing 97 percent of the saloons on Sunday in accordance with the law."[66] Yet in the end it was a pyrrhic victory: the unpopular saloon closings meant that in the fall elections, Democrat-controlled Tammany Hall was reinstated, and Roosevelt soon found his attempts to effect any additional change at a complete standstill. However, when the great Heat Wave of 1896 broke out, Roosevelt's humanitarian efforts increased his popularity and undergirded his eventual rise to the presidency.[67]

It also did not hurt that in the fall of 1896 Republican William McKinley held the White House. During a visit with one who had the ear of the new president, Roosevelt made it known that "I should like to be Assistant Secretary of the Navy."[68] Roosevelt got his wish the following year and, after the USS *Maine* exploded in Havana Harbor, America went to war with Spain.[69] Wanting to see action, Roosevelt formed his famous cavalry regiment, the Rough Riders, and charged up San Juan Hill (actually Kettle Hill). He earned the title he held in highest esteem for the rest of his life: Colonel Roosevelt.[70] His popularity and fame continued to reach new heights, and in the fall of 1898 he was elected governor of the State of New York.

In November 1899, Vice President Garret Hobart died while in office, which cleared the way for McKinley, preparing to campaign for a second term, to select a new vice presidential running mate. Not only did Roosevelt's popularity among Republicans ensure he would become McKinley's pick, but many saw the powerless office of the vice president as the perfect position in which to control Roosevelt. Leon Czolgosz and his .32-caliber Iver Johnson revolver, however, ensured that Roosevelt wouldn't remain powerlessness for long.[71]

After McKinley was shot, writes historian Miller, "no one yet knew the severity of McKinley's wounds, but the vice president was requested to come to Buffalo immediately."[72] Roosevelt rushed to the president, who was resting in the private home where he had been staying during his fateful New York trip. The bullet, Roosevelt learned, had gone through McKinley's stomach, damaging both the pancreas and liver, before finally lodging in his back. After surgery, the president appeared to be rallying, and there was no evidence that the doctors' greatest fear—gangrene—had set in. "The President is coming along splendidly," Roosevelt wrote to his sister Bamie. "Awful though this crime was against the President it was a thousand-fold worse crime against the Republic and against free government all over the world."[73]

Four days later, with McKinley apparently out of danger, Roosevelt was advised it would be best for him to go about his normal duties, thus signaling to the world that the president was in stable health. Roosevelt joined Edith and the children at their vacation cabin in the Adirondack Mountains. He was hiking up Mount Marcy when he received a telegram: "The President is critically ill; His condition is grave; Oxygen is being given; Absolutely no hope." Gangrene, as the doctors had originally feared, was spreading throughout his internal organs. Just prior to setting off once again for the McKinley's side, Roosevelt received one more telegram: "The president appears to be dying and members of the cabinet in Buffalo think you should lose no time coming."[74]

Roosevelt was loaded up in a buckboard, and they began racing down the mountainside. It was September 14, 1901. Although he did not learn of it 'til later, as of 2:15 that morning, unofficially, Theodore Roosevelt had become president. The carriage reached the Aiden Lair Lodge at about 3:30 a.m., but still no word had been received on the president's demise. Roosevelt raced off again heading for the North Creek station, where he would catch a train to Albany and then another on to Buffalo. Upon his arrival at the station, Roosevelt was handed another telegram: "The president died at two-fifteen this morning."[75]

When Roosevelt arrived in Buffalo at 1:30 in the afternoon, he quickly stopped for lunch at the Wilcox Mansion, where he— along with some of the cabinet members—began making the necessary arrangements. From his first decision, Roosevelt showed that he was his own man and that the cabinet would have to bend to his will, not the other way around. The cabinet informed him that they had already arranged for the inauguration to take place in the Milburn House, where McKinley's body lay, but Roosevelt said no—they would hold it there in the Wilcox Mansion. Ansley Wilcox himself protested, asking Roosevelt, "Don't you think it would be far better to do as the Cabinet has decided?" Roosevelt's reply was telling: "No. It would be far worse."[76]

Roosevelt paid his respects to McKinley at the Milburn House, and then, returning to the Wilcox Mansion, was sworn in as the twenty-sixth president of the United States. He was the youngest man ever to ascend to the presidency. He was forty-two.

Roosevelt then made his way to Washington, D.C., and on his very first day as president in the White House, he invited the press into his office. Unlike in modern times, this was an unusual break with past precedent. The result, however, was the birth of the presidential press corps. He promised them he would keep them up to date on his activities, but he also communicated something else to them—also unprecedented. "I am President," he boldly stated, "and shall act in every word and deed precisely as if I and not McKinley had been the candidate for whom the electors cast the vote for President."[77] He was signaling changes coming to the presidency and that his agenda, not McKinley's, would be at the fore from that point forward.

Were one to reflect on the wide range of experiences Theodore Roosevelt lived in the first four decades of his life, it might seem as if right from the beginning he was being prepared to become the president. His time in the New York State legislature, fighting corruption, led to his tenure fighting corruption with the Civil Service Commission and the New York Police Department. Both of these positions prepared him well for his fight against corruption as president, a role that ultimately led to the birth of the FBI. His leadership in the NYPD, the Rough Riders, and as governor of New York all gave him the administrative experience he needed for the White House. His publication of *The Naval War of 1812* helped prepare him for his service as assistant secretary of the Navy, which, when combined with his tenure as Colonel Roosevelt, led him naturally to assume the role of commander-in-chief. Roosevelt was assuredly one of the most prepared men for the office of the president, ever.

This preparation also naturally led Roosevelt to certain areas that landed on his presidential policy agenda—ranging from corruption, prosecutorial misconduct, trustbusting, and regulations, especially in such areas as pure food and drugs. This concern for fighting corruption is what led him to consider creating the Bureau of Investigation. Oddly enough, however, it was yet another area of Roosevelt's experience that ultimately led to the creation of the FBI—his concern for conservation. In order to understand this strange connection, it is important to understand how Roosevelt's love of the outdoors led to his focus on conservation in America, which in turn led him to create the FBI, all of which is the subject of the next chapter.

President Roosevelt with naturalist John Muir at Glacier Point in the Yosemite National Park. Muir was a conservation advocate, but it was Roosevelt who made it part of his national policy while in the White House.

Photo courtesy of the Theodore Roosevelt Center.

7

Conservation

President Theodore Roosevelt entered the White House with the same mentality that President Harrison had lamented in him when he said, "Roosevelt seemed to feel that everything ought to be done before sundown."[1] The first things to be done were to settle the issues he had inherited from McKinley, many of which stemmed from the Spanish-American War, the need for military reform, and America's relations with Britain and many of the Latin and South American countries. Much of this also led to Roosevelt's desire to see the Atlantic and Pacific Oceans united by the Panama Canal, which, after the ratification of the necessary treaty, began construction in 1903.[2] Also of concern during his first term was the Russo-Japanese War, which, after his mediation in the conflict, led to Roosevelt's being awarded the Nobel Peace Prize in 1906. Despite the attention given to America's foreign interests, Roosevelt's tenure as president is mostly remembered for his attention to domestic policies.

Roosevelt's domestic agenda was certainly full, and it was filled with many of the policies he had already dealt with at the state level and in the various positions he had held within the federal government. Much of his time and attention was focused on trustbusting, breaking up the corporate monopolies and regulating their activities with the goal of improving American lives. This took on many forms, including his focus on food safety through the Pure Food and Drug Act of 1906, regulating the nation's railroads, and negotiating an end to the anthracite coal mine strike in 1902. And, as he had done in the New York assembly, with the Civil Service Commission, and as NYPD commissioner, he moved quickly to stamp out corruption in government. But even in addition to all of this, one of the central themes of his presidency, predominately in the area of domestic policy, but to some degree also in his foreign policy, Roosevelt filled much of his agenda with the issues centered on conservation. Because conservation was the underpinning of Roosevelt's need for the creation of a bureau of investigation, understanding Roosevelt's lifelong passion for nature, his conservation policies, and his determination to see them enforced is the focus of this chapter.

As the National Park Service hedges on their website, "Theodore Roosevelt is often considered the 'conservationist president.'" They explain that, "after becoming president in 1901, Roosevelt used his authority to protect wildlife and public lands by creating the United States Forest Service . . . and establishing 150 national forests, 51 federal bird reserves, 4 national game preserves, 5 national parks, and 18 national monuments by enabling the 1906 American Antiquities Act. During his presidency, Theodore Roosevelt protected approximately 230 million acres of public land."[3]

Roosevelt's conservation policies had added lands to Yosemite National Park and created such national treasures as Crater Lake and Mesa Verde National Parks. Among the national monuments he established were Devils Tower, Jewel Cave, the Petrified Forest, and the Grand Canyon—the later two later being upgraded to national parks. Highlighting the importance of preservation, Roosevelt once wrote, "In the Grand Canyon, Arizona has a natural wonder which is in kind absolutely unparalleled throughout the rest of the world. I want to ask you to keep this great wonder of nature as it now is. I hope you will not have a building of any kind, not a summer cottage, a hotel or anything else, to mar the wonderful grandeur, the sublimity, the great loneliness and beauty of the canyon. Leave it as it is. You cannot improve on it. The ages have been at work on it, and man can only mar it."[4] This is what led historian Douglas Brinkley to write of Roosevelt, "had he done nothing else as president, his advocacy on behalf of preserving the canyon might well have put him in the top ranks of American presidents."[5]

Roosevelt's love of nature traced back to his earliest childhood days. Despite being raised a city boy, Roosevelt says he and his siblings, "of course, loved the country beyond anything. We disliked the city. We were always wildly eager to get to the country when spring came."[6] Tales from his earliest age show Roosevelt was always fascinated with the outdoors and nature, even inside the constraints of the city. A Mrs. Hamilton Fish told the story of meeting a young Teedie on a streetcar; while playing the young gentleman and politely lifting his hat to her, "several frogs leaped to the floor."[7]

Roosevelt's fascination with nature went far beyond simple boyish pranks involving proper ladies and frogs: he was focused on the rudimentary science of nature. On another occasion, Teedie managed to kill a mouse and placed it in the icebox for proper scientific preservation. When the Roosevelt cooks discovered the mouse, they threw it away, causing Teedie to lament, "Oh, the loss to science." This is not to say he did not enjoy his boyish surprises. On yet another occasion, he proudly "alarmed the entire female contingent by producing a dead bat from his pocket."[8]

His serious interest in nature is evident in a letter he wrote his mother when he was ten years old and she was visiting relatives in Savannah. She had written to Teedie telling him she had seen and heard the cry of the mocking bird. In response, he wrote, "I jumped with delight when I found you heard the mocking-bird," imploring her to "get some of its feathers if you can."[9]

He was also compassionate toward the animals he encountered. "My triumphs," he once wrote of his childhood, "consisted in such things as bringing home and raising—by the aid of milk and a syringe—a family of very young gray squirrels, in fruitlessly endeavoring to tame an excessively unamiable woodchuck and in making friends with a gentle, pretty, trustful white-footed mouse which reared her family in an empty flower pot."[10] Despite the fact many people were taken aback by his peculiar behaviors, his parents encouraged him, Roosevelt later recalled, "as they always did in anything that could give me wholesome pleasure or help develop me."[11]

He firmly believed, however, that it was one particular incident that changed his life. One day, upon coming across a dead seal displayed in a New York City market square, Teedie was fascinated and needed to channel that energy somewhere. So began measuring the seal and "carefully made a record of the utterly useless measurements, and at once began to write a natural history of my own, on the strength of that seal."[12] Feeling such strong interest in preserving the seal's story and the story of nature, as naturalist Darrin Lunde writes, his "life changed forever in that encounter."[13] His "subsequent natural histories," he notes, "were written down in blank books in simplified spelling, wholly unpremeditated and unscientific."[14] In time, his natural-history efforts grew more sophisticated, and the desire to chronicle nature became a lifelong passion.

In addition to making him want to chronicle nature, the seal experience, Roosevelt explains, was also the motivating force behind his desire to collect nature as well. After somehow managing to recover the seal's skull, he set about establishing what he dubbed the "Roosevelt Museum of Natural History," assuredly named after the museum his father had helped create—the American Museum of Natural History.[15] "The collections were at first kept in my room," he recalled, "until a rebellion on the part of the chambermaid received the approval of the higher authorities of the household and the collection was moved up to a kind of bookcase in the back hall upstairs." In time, young Teedie was allowed "to take lessons in taxidermy from a Mr. Bell," which, in Roosevelt's words, "spurred and directed my interest in collecting specimens for mounting and preservation."[16]

In time, the young Roosevelt began a serious study of birds, which greatly improved by the realization that he was badly in need of spectacles. "Quite unknown to myself, I was while a boy, under a hopeless disadvantage in studying nature," Roosevelt explained. "I was very near-sighted, so that the only things that I could study were those I ran against or stumbled over." His new glasses "literally opened an entirely new world for me," he wrote. "I had no idea how beautiful the world was until I got those spectacles."

And as Historian David McCullough writes, "It was the world of birds—birds, above all—that burst upon him now, upstaging all else in his eyes now that he could actually see them in colors and in numbers beyond anything he had ever imagined."[17] Blessed with his newfound vision, Roosevelt soon "had a good working knowledge of American bird life from the superficially scientific standpoint."[18] From a naturalist perspective, naturalist Jonathan Rosen explains, this was important, eventually making Roosevelt "a part of a generation of men who helped mark the transition from the nature-collecting frenzy that followed the Civil War to what we today recognize as bird-watching."[19] And this importance is further underscored considering Roosevelt's eventual political rise and the power he would one day yield from his bully pulpit.

But most of his boyhood exploration of the natural world, however, was dealing with the superficial. It was on a trip to Egypt as a teenager that he took his first forays into the truly scientific, assembling a collection of birds caught along the Nile and in Palestine, properly preserved through his new found skills in taxidermy. "Some years afterward," Roosevelt wrote, "I gave them, together with other ornithological specimens I had gathered, to the Smithsonian Institution in Washington, and I think some of them also to the American Museum of Natural History in New York."[20] According to the Theodore Roosevelt Association, "several of these animals—displayed for many years in the Smithsonian—became widely known as iconic pieces of taxidermy."[21]

After visiting Greece and Syria, followed by a lengthy stay in Germany, Roosevelt returned home and launched into preparations for his entry into Harvard. At this time in his life, Roosevelt's father had taken over the summer home at Oyster Bay, and it was there that young Roosevelt "carried on the work of a practical student of natural history."[22] During his stays there, especially during the summer months, writes Brinkley, "Roosevelt sometimes worked eight or nine hours a day on ornithological pursuits."[23] The time proved productive, for it was there in Oyster Bay that Roosevelt finished his first published work, "The Summer Birds of the Adirondacks in Franklin County, N.Y.," which "was reviewed favorably in a leading ornithological journal." Emboldened, the following year, in 1879, he published "Notes on Some of the Birds of Oyster Bay, Long Island."[24]

Throughout his naturalist adventures, Roosevelt had also been "fond of walking and climbing," and he "used to go to the north woods, in Maine, both in fall and winter," where he canoed, tramped through the woods, and often went hunting with several life-long friends.[25] On one excursion to the summit of Mount Katahdin, he recalled that, though "as usual it rained," he would not let the elements deter him and boasted, "I am enjoying myself exceedingly, am in superb health and as tough as a pine knot."[26] Whether as exercise or on some adventure, Roosevelt experienced pure joy when he was out hiking through the woods, communing with nature.

Hunting had also become a passion early on, and throughout his life Roosevelt went on many hunting vacations and safaris to Africa. In his lifetime, he proudly explained he had shot five kinds of animals that "can fairly be called dangerous game— this is, the lion, elephant, rhinoceros, and buffalo in Africa, and the big grizzly bear . . . in the Rockies."[27] During his time in the Badlands of North Dakota, in addition to writing about the American West, Roosevelt found time to write a trilogy of books and numerous articles on hunting. *Hunting Trips of a Ranchman*, *Ranch Life and the Hunting Trail*, and *The Wilderness Hunter* were all "well-received books" in both the United States and Europe.[28]

Today conservation and hunting are generally considered to be diametrically opposed to one another. This was not so in Roosevelt's time, when many saw the two as complementary. Describing Roosevelt's earliest experience with hunting, Brinkley writes that, "by shooting finches in Egypt, for example, carefully studying their eye bands and plumage, taking careful notes of their demeanor, and lovingly stuffing them so as not to damage their plumage, Roosevelt believed he was *honoring* the species." Conversely, Brinkley writes, "Most other men would simply shoot birds," but "Roosevelt, by contrast, shot and collected them for scientific scrutiny."[29] Hunting and conserving, if done with the proper intent, could be entirely complementary to one another, Roosevelt believed.

Toward this end, in December of 1887 Roosevelt hosted a dinner for "a dozen wealthy and influential animal-lovers."[30] One of the attendees was George Bird Grinnell, editor of *Forest and Stream*, a popular magazine dedicated to hunting, fishing, and conservation. During the meal, Roosevelt spoke of their united love of the "manly sport with the rifle" as well as their shared love of preserving nature. The reason he had selectively gathered this group was to advocate for the creation of a new club, to be named in honor his two heroes, American icons Daniel Boone and Davy Crockett. The purpose of the club would to be not only to advocate for hunting but also to "work for the preservation of the large game of this country, further legislation for that purpose, and to assist in enforcing the existing laws."[31]

Roosevelt's proposal was well received by the dinner party, and in January of the following year, the Boone and Crockett Club was formed with Theodore Roosevelt seated as its first president. "Among his first acts" as president of the club, writes Roosevelt biographer Edmund Morris, "was to appoint a Committee on Parks, which was instrumental in the creation of the National Zoo in Washington." More importantly, however, was the club's "determined lobbying on Capitol Hill, in concert with other environmental groups," that resulted in passage of the Forest Reserve Act of 1891, which "empowered the President to set aside at will any wooded or partly wooded country, 'whether of commercial value or not.'" "The time would come," remarks Morris, "when Theodore Roosevelt joyfully inherited this very power as President of the United States."[32] In the meantime, Roosevelt had to be satisfied with his presidency of the Boone and Crockett club, a position from which he stepped down in 1894. His influence, however, had a lasting effect, and the Boone and Crockett Club remains in existence to this day.

As Roosevelt stepped down from the club presidency he was stepping up to serve as NYPD commissioner. His time as both police commissioner and then assistant secretary of the Navy— not to mention his leadership of the Rough Riders—left Roosevelt with little time to concentrate on issues of conservation.

That, however, changed when he became governor of the State of New York. His tenure helped set the stage for his eventual conservation presidency, for as Roosevelt explained in his autobiography, "All that late I strove for in the Nation in connection with Conservation was foreshadowed by what I strove to obtain for New York State when I was Governor." In fact, Roosevelt dedicates an entire chapter of his autobiography to "The Natural Resources of the Nation," and much of it covers his time as governor. Indeed, in the chapter's appendix he provides a lengthy excerpt from his second (and last) Annual Message as the New York Governor.[33] Historian Douglas Brinkley refers to this as "the most important speech about conservation ever delivered by a serious American politician up to that time."[34]

The speech contained a nearly complete agenda for the establishment of conservation policy, covering "everything from illegal hunting to forest fire protection and watersheds."[35] In the speech, Roosevelt argued that the laws of New York were "defective" in all of these areas, ranging from lumbering to the protection of birds, "especially song birds." He also lamented the lax enforcement of those laws. Game wardens and game protectors, Roosevelt explained, were often appointed for political purposes rather than for their expertise as woodsmen. Roosevelt described how he believed that men in those law-enforcement roles should be "men of courage, resolution, and hardihood, who can handle the rifle, ax, and paddle; who can camp out in summer and winter; who can go on snow-shoes, if necessary; who can go through the woods by day or by night without regard to trails."[36]

Still further, he believed there was a "destructive influence" brought about by "unrestrained greed" that cannot be stopped by the disconnected system of laws and their equally disconnected enforcement. "Ultimately," he said, "the administration of the State lands must be so centralized as to enable us definitely to place responsibility in respect to everything concerning them, and to demand the highest degree of trained intelligence in their use."[37] Roosevelt was clearly forecasting not only his plans for a conservation agenda as the New York's governor, he was also forecasting his presidential conservation policy. When the opportunity to become president came faster than he had anticipated, Roosevelt did not hesitate and was soon implementing that conservation agenda at the national level.

Historian Douglas Brinkley begins his description of the president's early tenure with an anecdote that is very telling of Roosevelt's honesty about his love of nature. In February of 1903, the president's cabinet members were assembled in the White House for a meeting, patiently awaiting Roosevelt's arrival. When he finally entered in typical Roosevelt fashion, with frenetic energy, he asked them in serious tones, "Gentlemen, do you know what has happened this morning?" A question like that, of course, coming from the president could only mean trouble of the greatest magnitude—natural tragedy, war, or some other major calamity—so they all nervously awaited the answer to Roosevelt's rhetorical question. "Just now I saw a chestnut-sided warbler," he informed them, adding with genuine surprise, "and this is only February!"[38] One can only imagine the collective sigh of relief coming from the president's cabinet, but the anecdote goes a long way in demonstrating Roosevelt's sincere love of nature, and it is truly why he became widely known as the conservation president.

His love of and concern for nature was important, but what was assuredly more important, especially when it comes to policy, was his knowledge of nature. No one in the room knew more about nature then he did, which made him more powerful and more formidable than any of his opposition. "By the time he was in the White House," writes historian Candice Millard, "Roosevelt was not merely the most powerful elected official in the country, but one of its most knowledgeable and experienced naturalists."[39]

This was acknowledged not only by those who surrounded him or by the public at large but also by the very people of the day who were considered the leading authorities on nature. During one presidential foray, Roosevelt spent time camping in Yellowstone National Park with naturalist John Burroughs. The two men had already spent time there, with Burroughs recalling the president on that visit as "a great boy" and describing how "he climbed everything on the place" and shimmied "up tree after tree, running his arms into every high-hole's and wood-pecker's nest."[40] Their two-week return vacation in 1903 found Roosevelt much the same, for as Burroughs later recalled in his memoir *Camping and Tramping with Roosevelt*, the president was "a man of such abounding energy and ceaseless activity that he sets everything in motion around him where he goes." Burroughs also noted that, when it came to nature, "nothing escaped him, from bears to mice, from wild geese to chickadees, from elk to red squirrels; he took it all in, and he took it in as only an alert, vigorous mind can take it in." Burroughs was also noticeably impressed, writing of their time in Yellowstone, "I was able to help him identify only one new bird . . . all the other birds he recognized as quickly as I did."[41]

When a person is armed with both knowledge and passion for their subject, they make either a formidable friend or foe, and so it was with Roosevelt and his conservation agenda. "The first work I took up when I became President," Roosevelt recalls, "was the work of reclamation." It is telling that his first presidential initiative was conservation, but also telling was the issue. The problem, as Roosevelt saw it from his time spent out West, was America's inability to irrigate the arid lands of the West, because irrigation was typically blocked by petty politics. Roosevelt explained that, "through the General Land Office and other Government bureaus, the public resources were being handled and disposed of in accordance with the small considerations of petty legal formalities, instead of for the large purposes of constructive development, and the habit of deciding, whenever possible, in favor of private interests against the public welfare was firmly fixed."[42]

Matters were made worse by the various state laws that favored builders and by a national government that did not seem to care and could neither see the bigger, long-term effects that might be achieved through irrigation. Rather, as Roosevelt wrote, the national government saw the issue "as a disconnected series of pork-barrel problems, whose only real interest was in their effect on the reelection or defeat of a Congressman here and there."[43] So as to not waste time addressing the issue, in his first message to Congress, delivered on December 3, 1901, President Roosevelt wrote that, "the Forest and water problems are perhaps the most vital internal problems of the United States."[44] Reclamation had moved to the forefront of his agenda.

Roosevelt was in such earnest to have the reclamation bill passed that he took to lobbying Congress himself for its passage, something not frequently done in those days. "I do not believe that I have ever written to an individual legislator in favor of an individual bill," he wrote Speaker of the House Joseph G. Cannon, "yet I feel from acquaintance with the far West that it would be a genuine and ranking injustice . . . to kill the measure."[45] Despite his attempts to "Uncle Joe" Cannon over, the endeavor failed. "Everything is all right out West," Cannon was fond of observing. "The country don't need any legislation."[46] In time, Cannon's anticonservation rallying cry became, "Not one cent for scenery!"[47]

Despite Cannon's opposition, Roosevelt eventually succeeded in obtaining congressional approval for the Reclamation Act of 1902, and he was exuberant. As historian Doris Kearns Goodwin explains, "In speech after speech, Roosevelt lauded the passage of the 1902 Reclamation Act, which, for the first time, made substantial federal funds available to construct dams, reservoirs, and other irrigational projects in the West."[48] The act had set aside money from the sale of public lands in order to fund the reclamation of the arid West through irrigation. There were those who lamented how Forest Service bureaucrats would "sit within their marble halls and theorize and dram about forests conserved," and many newspapers condemned these actions, with one noting that if Washington "continued to create reserves there would be little ground left to bury folks on." Still, while there was much criticism over the waste, fraud, and abuse that did result from the quick implementation of the bill, there can be little doubt it had an impact on improving and preserving Western lands that became "Theodore Roosevelt's great legacy to the American people."[49]

In addition to irrigating the West, another of Roosevelt's grand movements was to achieve the consolidation and centralization of the national forests, which was being overseen by Gifford Pinchot, head of the US Forest Service.[50] "He was already in the Government serving as head of the Forestry Bureau when I became President," recalled Roosevelt, and "he continued throughout my term, not only as head of the Forest service, but as the moving and directing spirit in most of the conservation work, and as counsellor and assistant on most of the other work connected with the internal affairs of the country."[51] Roosevelt spoke fondly of Pinchot, giving him most of the credit for the successful implementation of his conservation agenda. In fact, it was Pinchot who had coined the term *conservation* as it relates to the preservation of natural resources.[52] Roosevelt was so laudatory of this man that in his autobiography he wrote, "Gifford Pinchot is the man to whom the nation owes most for what has been accomplished as regards the preservation of the natural resources of our country. He led, and indeed during its most vital period embodied, the fight for the preservation through use of our forests."[53]

Gifford Pinchot had been born the summer after the Civil War had ended and, ironically, grew up in a family whose fortunes were made from lumbering and land speculation.[54] When his father had a change of heart, forestry became the family's focus, and particularly Gifford's, who went on to study forestry. Pinchot was the type of person who thought big and acted on the passions of his convictions. Author Owen Wister said of Pinchot, "The eyes do not look as if they read books, but as if they gazed upon a cause."[55] And saving of America's forestlands had become Pinchot's cause. Placed in charge of the Forest Service, he was able to do much to preserve America's lands, but it was Roosevelt's elevation to the presidency and their shared cause that enabled Pinochet to succeed. And succeed he did, for it is estimated that by 1907 more than forty-three million acres of forestland were being overseen by the US Forest Service.

Pinchot was able to achieve this, it has been said, tongue-in-cheek, because he "had stretched the meaning of the word *forest* so much, that some westerners wondered when the Great Salt Lake was going to need his urgent protection."[56] In fact the government's constant protection of lands and their oversight by the US Forest Service drew the ire of many, who saw the securing of forestland not as a gain for the country but a loss of power for those who could have profited from land deals. Roosevelt excoriated these people in his autobiography: "The opposition of the servants of the special interests in Congress to the Forest Service had become strongly developed, and more time appeared to be spent in the yearly attacks upon it during the passage of the appropriation bills than on all other Government Bureaus put together. Every year the Forest Service had to fight for its life."[57] Yet Roosevelt had confidence in Pinchot, whose "killer instinct" he liked; and the president especially approved of the fact that Pinchot "fought cleanly," making "him all the more dangerous, because he was invulnerable to charges of corruption."[58]

In addition to the continuous fight to justify its existence, the US Forest Service had to fight along with Roosevelt's administration to ameliorate conservation laws as well. Roosevelt recounted how "the laws were often insufficient, and it became well nigh impossible to get them amended in the public interest when once the representatives of privilege in Congress grasped the fact that I would sign no amendment that contained anything not in the public interest." Unable to either change or amend the laws, Roosevelt believed "it was necessary to use what law was already in existence, and then further to supplement it by Executive action."[59]

The sum of Roosevelt's conservation action garnered serious opposition from groups that had once profited from the land. Roosevelt historian George E. Mowry points out how a wide array of workers, including "ranchers, mine operators, lumbermen, and power companies all protested against this limitation of the right to exploit the nation domain." These men had made both their living and their fortunes off the land, and they were not overly sympathetic to the notion that these lands should be removed from exploitation in order to preserve the very natural resources from which they made their living. Things grew even more heated and "the administration incurred further opposition by its strict enforcement of existing land laws and the grazing, mining, and lumbering regulations prescribed for the new reserves."[60]

As Roosevelt's presidency progressed, Congress became ever more combative. Eventually, toward the end of his administration, after he announced he would not seek another term in office, Congress began curtailing Roosevelt's executive actions. The most sweeping of these actions meant to rein in Roosevelt's power was proposed by Oregon Senator Charles William Fulton at the beginning of 1907. Fulton proposed an amendment to the Agricultural Appropriation Act of 1905 that would effectively end the president's power to designate lands as national forests. Because there was enough opposition to Roosevelt in Congress, the amendment was included in the final passage of the bill on February 27, 1907.

The dilemma now facing Roosevelt was that if he signed the bill into law, only Congress—not the president—would have the power to create a forest reserve, but vetoing the bill meant sacrificing the many things in it that he favored. Working with Gifford Pinchot, Roosevelt developed an end run around Congress—something that was becoming all too common in his last few years as president.

Together with the Forest Service, Roosevelt and Pinchot began an around-the-clock issuance of proclamations followed by presidential executive orders withdrawing those forests from future development. The whole process left Roosevelt exuberant, who shouted, "Oh, this is bully!" and then asked Pinchot, "Have you put in the North Fork of the Flathead? Up there once I saw the biggest herd of black-tailed deer." In the chaos and excitement, "the floor of an entire room in the White House" was said to have been "covered with maps," and "Roosevelt, on his knees with Pinchot, went over individual sections, recalling hikes and hunting trips on land where he had mended a broken soul."[61]

This whirlwind action in the six days before the bill needed to be signed placed sixteen million acres into forestlands and created dozens of new national forest reserves in the West. "Only after the last acre was reserved," writes Roosevelt biographer Morris, "did Roosevelt sign the Agricultural Appropriations Act."[62] As Roosevelt himself proudly noted in his autobiography, "The opponents of the Forest Service turned handsprings in their wrath."[63] Mowry confirms that "cries of executive 'impudence,' 'arrogance,' and 'dictatorship' rang through the capital."[64] Although Congress had thought they'd run roughshod over Roosevelt, as Pinchot claimed, "the joke was on them."[65]

In his last year of office, the president's political abilities were largely constrained, and the focus had largely shifted toward the fall election. Roosevelt, however, developed a new strategy in advancing presidential policy: On May 13, 1908, Roosevelt hosted a White House conference, which he called the National Conservation Congress. Nearly every governor in the nation attended, along with some five hundred political leaders and experts in the conservation field. Roosevelt personally opened the conference with a speech on "Conservation as a National Duty." He opened by saying they had come together "to consider the question of the conservation and use of the great fundamental sources of wealth of this Nation." As Professor Dorsey explains, part of Roosevelt's motivation for the conservation movement, and particularly his hosting the 1908 conference, came out of the complexity of conservation laws and their enforcement. Dorsey states that in the late nineteenth century, "State and local governments attempted to set guidelines for natural resource use, but their ignorance of what constituted valid legislation—coupled with pressure from business interests to maintain their own unfettered access to nature—led to a contradictory jumble of laws and enforcement that made conservation almost impossible." Roosevelt was bringing the governors together to work out these contradictions in order to make the laws both uniform and enforceable. As Dorsey further explains, "Roosevelt's moral crusade readied the government to"—in Roosevelt's own words—"'enforce the laws in aggressive fashion' against unscrupulous foes who abused them."[66]

Roosevelt's administration used the law and executive action to examine every public land claim before it passed into private ownership. This practice of administrative review proved beneficial, for "enormous areas of valuable public timberland were thereby saved from fraudulent acquisition," and in one exceptionally egregious land grab "more than 250,000 acres were thus saved in a single case."[67] Land fraud had become such an extensive problem that Roosevelt was directing many of the federal government's resources toward this problem, including the investigatory powers of the Secret Service.

In the fall of 1908, Roosevelt's vice president, William Howard Taft, won the presidential election against the perennial presidential loser, three-time candidate William Jennings Bryan. With Taft installed as president, Roosevelt believed, wrongly, that his policies and legacy would be protected by his successor. Despite stepping down from the presidency in March of 1909, Roosevelt continued to embrace his love of nature and advance conservation through political channels. And he did so in pure Roosevelt fashion: He went on safari to Africa where he hunted for new specimens for the Smithsonian Institution and the American Museum of Natural History. He also took pen to paper again, writing of his African exploits, detailing his adventures, recalling the people he met, and describing the flora and fauna he had collected, all in the name of science. And in addition to producing material for various newspaper and magazine articles, his adventure also yielded yet another book, *African Game Trails*.[68]

For the popular magazine *Outlook*, Roosevelt also penned the article "Our Vanishing Wildlife," which dealt with social and political issues. He wrote of his fears that based on America's present course at the time, his children's children would not have the pleasure of looking upon America's majestic beauties of nature. He lamented that "we are, as a whole, still in that low state of civilization where we do not understand that it is also vandalism wantonly to destroy or to permit the destruction of what is beautiful in nature, whether it be a cliff, a forest, or a species of mammal or bird. Here in the United States we turn our rivers and streams into sewers and dumping-grounds, we pollute the air, we destroy forests, and exterminate fishes, birds, and mammals—not to speak of vulgarizing charming landscapes with hideous advertisements."[69]

Even out of office Roosevelt continued to fight for the conservation policy that had come to define his presidency. His fight and his legacy is best summed up by historian Douglas Brinkley, who wrote that "Roosevelt's stout resoluteness to protect our environment is a strong reminder of our national wilderness heritage."[70]

President Roosevelt worked to conserve the environment in part through protecting the land and the manner in which it was negotiated and sold by the government to the people. He felt a strong desire not only to protect American land but also, after years fighting corruption in the statehouse, police department, and Civil Service Commission, to fight against criminals who violated American law. Those cases in which environmental concerns and corruption intersected—the land-fraud cases he faced during his presidency—inspired in him a strong personal desire to see justice served. And so to win his fight, he borrowed agents from the United States Secret Service to investigate and enforce the law. In the end, borrowing Treasury agents for non-Treasury-related cases created problems and exposed the political corruption within Congress itself. It is to these cases involving land theft that the next chapter turns.

President Roosevelt and Chief Forester Gifford Pinchot on the river steamer Missis-
sippi in 1907. The Roosevelt and Pinchot team were instrumental in addressing the
problems of land fraud extending from the Homestead Act.
Photo by the U.S. Forest Service and courtesy of the Library of Congress.

8

Land Thieves

As President Theodore Roosevelt had made conservation one of his administration's key concerns, the biggest threat facing this new public-policy issue came from the land thieves. While of great benefit to the people and the national economy, the Homestead Acts, which signed government lands over to private ownership, also proved a great benefit to those willing to commit fraud. As Secret Service historians Bowen and Neal explain, "President Roosevelt had received reports that thousands, perhaps millions, of acres of government-owned land in the West were being stolen and misused."[1] Land was being transferred from the intended homeowners to large companies, such as logging and mining companies, for a tidy profit. The land was usually flipped through intermediaries who made a profit by buying the land from homeowners and then selling it to the various companies. In the end, regardless of how it was acquired, the land was stripped of its natural resources.

Roosevelt knew this was occurring, writing in his autobiography, "Throughout the early part of my Administration the public land policy was chiefly directed to the defense of the public lands against fraud and theft." He knew he had to do something to stop the fraud and theft, so with the help of Gifford Pinchot, his man at the head of the newly created US Forest Service, he developed a plan to address the problem. "I acted on a theory that the President could at any time in his discretion withdraw from entry any of the public lands of the United States and reserve the same for forestry, for water-power sites, for irrigation, and other public purposes," Roosevelt explained. While he fully believed it was within his right as president, even if it weren't he also firmly believed that "without such action it would have been impossible to stop the activity of the land thieves."[2]

Lands transferred into public purposes were in fact save from fraudulent and criminal use, becoming America's national forests, reserves, and parks. However, transferring them did nothing to abate the thefts and frauds occurring with lands that went to homeowners through the Homestead Acts and then on to shady land speculators, thieves, and robber barons.[3] Therefore, Roosevelt saw it necessity to take action against those violating the law out West. However, he faced a problem: the federal government really had no investigatory agency that could address the problem. So, like the presidents before him, he came to rely on the United States Secret Service to conduct these investigations.

Roosevelt fully believed that "the action taken thereon by the Administration" was both necessary and "strengthened the hands of those administrative officers who in the various departments, and especially in the Secret Service, were proceeding against land thieves and other corrupt wrong-doers."[4] This move started a chain of events that soon placed Roosevelt and his administration in an unprecedented political fight with Congress and ultimately led to the creation of the Federal Bureau of Investigation.

Homestead Claims

The idea of transferring government land to private ownership had been considered long before President Lincoln ever signed the Homestead Act on May 20, 1862. The problem with passing such a bill, however, was closely tied to the issue of slavery. Northern Republicans had proposed the idea of a land-grant law but on three occasions had been blocked by Southern Democrats who wanted those Western lands to be open to slave owners for purchase in order to expand their operations. A Homestead Act bill finally managed to be passed by Congress in 1860 but was vetoed by President James Buchanan, a Democrat, siding with the proslavery advocates who feared that if the act were passed the West would be populated by "free soilers." Yet once Lincoln became president and the South seceded from the Union, there was little opposition left, and the act became law.[5]

The act was set to go into effect on January 1, 1863. Daniel Freeman, a Union Army scout who was scheduled to report to Saint Louis from his current assignment in Gage County, Nebraska, was at a New Year's Eve party the night before, where he began talking with a couple of people from the local Land Office. Knowing the act went into effect as of midnight, he talked them into opening their office immediately after welcoming in the New Year. Not long after, Freeman was filing a land claim—the first person to do so under the new law.[6]

The Homestead Act of 1862 established a threefold homestead acquisition process: "filing an application, improving the land, and filing for deed of title." The law was open to any US citizen, or intended citizen, who had never borne arms against the US government. The individual could file an application laying claim to 160 acres of surveyed government land. The only requirement was that for next five years the homesteader had to live on the land and improve it by building a twelve-by-fourteen dwelling and by growing crops. On the five-year anniversary, the homesteader could file for the deed to the land by submitting proof of residency and of the required improvements to a local Land Office. The local Land Office was then supposed to forward the paperwork to the General Land Office in Washington, D.C., along with a final certificate of eligibility. Finally, after the case files were examined to ensure they were bona fide claims, the homesteaders would be granted the deed to their land "free and clear."[7]

Many of the claims filed were fraudulent right from the beginning—as in, there was no real homesteader—while in other cases a phony claimant was hired by a land speculator with the full intention of defrauding the government. The General Land Office was undermanned, underfunded, and unable to hire a sufficient number of investigators for its widely scattered offices.

As a result, overworked and underpaid investigators were often susceptible to bribery themselves.[8]

Some of the earliest fraud committed by land speculators took advantage of a legislative loophole in the language Congress used in the act. The law said the homesteader had to create improvements on the land, including a twelve-by-fourteen building. The only problem was that the language did not specify whether that was to be measured in feet or inches. So some speculators simply crafted a little twelve-by-fourteen-inch building and placed the doll-sized houses on the property, claiming they had met the letter of the law, if not quite the spirit.[9] When that little trick was exposed for what it was, some began building real cabins in accordance with the size in feet, but they placed them on wheels. They then wheeled these "portable cabins from claim to claim and hired witnesses to swear they had seen a dwelling on the property, omitting the fact the 'dwelling' would be on a neighbor's homestead the next day."[10]

Land fraud was extensive during the Civil War, in part because of the war itself. There were little money and few employees within the General Land Office. After the war ended, however, it failed to get any better. "Land fraud became so bad," according to historian Greg Bradsher, "that Congress in 1879 created the first Public Lands Commission to look into revising land laws." The commission did its job, but as Bradsher concluded, Congress "paid little attention to its recommendations." By 1885, William A. J. Sparks, head of the General Land Office, was left to declare that "the public domain was being made the prey of unscrupulous speculation and the worst forms of land monopoly through systematic frauds carried on and consummated under the public land laws."[11]

One kind of the fraud among land speculators emerged in the coal and lumber industries. As Bowen and Neal explain, "Coal and lumber companies were bribing war veterans and others to file claims for homesteads, which would require that the homesteaders build houses and cultivate the land." Veterans of the Civil War were especially sought after by the land speculators because they helped speed up the process: their time in service was deducted from the five-year requirement. Regardless of who filed these claims from bribes, "when the claimants received their ownership papers, the coal and timber interests paid them off, grabbed the land and denuded it of its big trees, or sunk shafts to dig coal."[12] It was the sheer overwhelming amount of fraud and the numerous innovative means by which the frauds were perpetrated that left reporter Henry S. Brown to lament, "There seemed to be no limit to the rapacity of the land sharks."[13]

Oregon Fraud Cases

Land-fraud cases had become so prevalent out West by the time Roosevelt was president that one newspaper, trying to report the full scope of the problem, wrote, "The land grabbers have been men in high positions; they have employed perjury, bribery and forgery, to say nothing of more forceful crimes to defraud their country." The article also highlighted how many of those involved were "backed by wealthy and influential men and included members of the legislatures, United States Commissioners, special land agents, notaries, etc.," and that "the trail led to the head of the General Land Office, into the national House of Representatives and into the United States Senate."[14] Many of these high-level cases originated in the state of Oregon.

Roosevelt, reflecting in his autobiography, wrote that through his administration, "I was prosecuting men who were implicated in a vast conspiracy against the laws in connection with the theft of public lands in Oregon."[15] Of the numerous cases of land fraud being committed in that state, two were high-profile cases involving members of Congress.[16] One came to light from an investigation conducted by the office of the secretary of the interior. Ethan A. Hitchcock had originally been an appointment out of President McKinley's tenure—first as an ambassador to Russia and then as secretary of the interior. Theodore Roosevelt had decided to retain Hitchcock in that position, and it was his office that found the evidence implicating Congressman Binger Hermann of Oregon.[17]

Described by Oregon governor Theodore Geer as "one of the smoothest politicians Oregon ever produced," Binger Hermann had been elected to the House of Representatives in 1884.[18] He first served in Oregon's at-large district before being elected to its first district in 1893. After Hermann had been appointed by President McKinley to a commission in the General Land Office, it became increasingly clear that he was involved in a series of shady land deals, which caused him to continually clash with Secretary Hitchcock. When Thomas H. Tongue, Hermann's successor in Congress, died in office in 1903, Hermann returned to the House through a special election and was then reelected to office in 1904. Eventually, after enough evidence of his involvement in fraudulent land deals had been amassed, Hermann was charged with destroying public documents and collusion in the land deals. Although found guilty of the former in 1907, the charges for collusion ended in a mistrial in 1910. The scandal, however, had contributed to the loss of his congressional seat in 1907, so after the mistrial had occurred in 1910 there was no longer much incentive for the prosecution to refile the charges; he had, some believed, already been punished enough.

Secretary Hitchcock's efforts "in the Oregon land fraud cases," Roosevelt proudly recalled in his autobiography, also "led to the conviction of Senator Mitchell."[19] Senator John M. Mitchell has the distinction of being one of only twelve sitting US senators ever indicted for a crime, and he holds the more dubious distinction of being only one of five ever actually convicted. Mitchell had apparently exhibited loose moral character from an early age: when serving as a schoolteacher, he seduced one of his students and, after getting her pregnant, was forced to marry her. He was soon having an affair with another schoolteacher and, abandoning his first wife, moved with her to California, where they married without his ever divorcing his first wife. He eventually abandoned her too, fleeing to Oregon, where he changed his name. There, he fashioned himself a lawyer, and, having quickly developed numerous political connections, within two years was elected to the Oregon State Senate. Hermann then ran for the US Senate in 1872, when it finally came out during the campaign that he was a bigamist and had deserted his wife and mistress both. Despite the sensation it caused, he won election, but once seated that greatest of deliberative bodies filed ethical charges against him. A Senate committee was formed to look at the allegations, which after their review, were dropped. It seemed bigamy and abandonment were not of great concern to that deliberative body. Mitchell was afforded the opportunity to move forward with his senatorial career.

Secretary Hitchcock, fully aware of the land frauds occurring in Oregon, was becoming suspicious that US attorneys were complicit in the illegal land deals. Hitchcock asked for and received an outside prosecutor, Francis J. Heney, to lead the investigation, and US Secret Service operatives were assigned to assist him. Heney was an advocate for justice and not someone to be trifled with. While serving as an attorney for a wife in an abuse case, Heney had been viciously attacked by the husband. In response to the attack, Heney pulled a gun and shot his attacker dead. Needless to say, Heney's reputation as a tough attorney was at least partially deserved.

Once appointed special prosecutor, Heney began investigating a man by the name of Stephen A. Douglas Puter, "who styled himself chief of the Oregon 'land grabbers.'"[20] The investigation into Puter showed he was indeed a central figure in the land frauds occurring in Oregon, and the investigation eventually uncovered his ties to Representative Hermann and Senator Mitchell. On January 1, 1905, Heney secured an indictment against Senator Mitchell. Working with Hitchcock, Heney agreed that, in order to ensure any possibility of gaining a conviction, he must seek the dismissal of US Attorney John H. Hall, whom the two suspected was in cahoots with Mitchell.

Not only did Heney manage to orchestrate that dismissal, he was also named Hall's replacement. Proving to be not only legally adept but also politically astute, Heney was able to cleared the way for an honest trial of Senator Mitchell. Heney once again achieved the near impossible when on July 5, 1905, he obtained the conviction of a sitting Senator. Mitchell was sentenced to six months in jail, along with a thousand-dollar fine.[21] The case was naturally appealed by Mitchell's attorneys, but it all came to an abrupt end when Mitchell died six months later "from complications of a tooth extraction."[22]

Many saw Mitchell's conviction and sentence to prison as justice served. Others saw it as something downright criminal in its own right. Historian Jerry A. O'Callaghan believed that "Mitchell belonged to a passing generation which did not comprehend a change in public temper" and that Mitchell had simply been "caught in a shift in public mores, which" he adds, can be "a cruel thing."[23] Congress saw what Roosevelt did to Mitchell as cruel: as historian Timothy Egan explains, "Not only had the president done the unthinkable—putting Senator Mitchell, a twenty-two-year veteran of Washington's power corridors, away to rot in prison—but he also was moving far too quickly with the conservation business."[24] They wanted revenge on this arrogant president, but they were patient. "Congress amended the land laws and transferred control of the nation's forests from the General Land Office to the US Forest Service," which was led by Roosevelt's right-hand man, Gifford Pinchot.[25] Attacking Roosevelt for this transfer of power would look like sour grapes; for now, those in Congress who had grown to despise this president would have to bide their time.

The Walker Case

The Oregon land frauds were so high-profile primarily because of who was involved. There was another case of land fraud, however, that had a much farther-reaching impact than those in Oregon, which Secret Service historians Melanson and Stevens detail: "The political furor caused by the Service's land-fraud investigation, which had ensnared two congressmen, overshadowed another episode out West."[26] On Sunday morning, November 3, 1907, four men made their way to a homestead claim near Hesperus, Colorado, about ten miles west of Durango—two from the Secret Service and two working for the government under contracts.

The lead Secret Service operative was Joseph "Joe" A. Walker, who was in charge of the Denver district. Those who knew him considered him "as kindly a soul as ever lived, a brave man and one of the smartest operatives the Service ever knew."[27] The local papers remembered him "as a gentleman in every sense," recalling how "no officer could extend greater courtesy to those under investigation than he did." This was because he always, "bore the reputation of being exceedingly fair." He was, however, considered a threat, with a local paper nothing that "he possessed volumes of information that some people down in this neck of the woods wish had not been dug up."[28] Indeed, in his time in Durango investigating land frauds, Walker had managed to produce as many as "1,400 indictments."[29] And so when Operative Walker paid a visit to a homestead claim it was considered—at least by those involved in the land thefts—a serious threat.

Assisting Walker in the case was Secret Service Operative Thomas J. Callaghan, who was described as a "big husky fellow."[30] There were also two contractors with him—the first a man by the name of Tom Harper, in his early forties, who was a rancher and former miner. He had been hired as a government contractor for the Secret Service investigation because of his knowledge of the local mines. The other gentlemen with them was John E. Chapson, he was a local civil engineer and geologist approaching the half-century mark who was already working on a government contract for the Department of the Interior. Since Walker and Callaghan had been borrowed from the Secret Service by the Department of the Interior, the men were all technically working for the same government agency. Chapson had agreed to assist the two Secret Service operatives and Tom Harper with the investigation of the homestead claim in light of what Walker believed they were going to find there.

Their purpose in going to the homestead claim was to investigate the Porter Fuel Company in Colorado, "one of the largest coal-mining interests in that section of the country."[31] Walker was investigating them because, as Melanson and Stevens explain, "The business's owners were allegedly filing false claims for homes and the cultivation of land, and the company was amassing vast tracts of rich timberland and coal veins for the partners' own use and profits."[32] More specifically, "The men had come to investigate an unexplained air shaft—something that made no sense on a farmer's homestead claim."[33] Except it was not a farmer's homestead: the land just so "happened to belong to William R. Mason, superintendent of the Porter Fuel Company."[34] Based on Walker's suspicions, the four men "set out from Durango to investigate."[35]

The group "drove seventeen miles from the town" and "hitched their team in a ravine," which was referred to rather ominously by the locals as Dead Man's Gulch.[36] Walker, being rather along in years and asthmatic, rode horseback onto the property while the other men walked. Once on the property, it took them little time to locate the air shaft, which they believed would lead to a suspected mining tunnel. "The shaft was perhaps 4 feet square and 65 feet deep," write Secret Service historians Bowen and Neal, and it was "lined with heavy logs."[37] The reinforcement of the shaft essentially ruled any suggestion that it might be a natural shaft or a water well.

The four men conferred about the evidence they had found so far and, realizing they needed more, "decided to climb down and investigate further."[38] Because of Walker's advanced age and health, it was decided he would remain aboveground as a lookout, while the other three would descend to the bottom of the shaft.[39] They then set about figuring out how to safely lower themselves. They had brought along a strong rope, knowing they were likely to have to climb down the air shaft to investigate. Looking around, they found a number of railroad ties piled off to the side. As both railroad ties were stout—seven inches by nine inches—and long—eight feet or so—two of the men "laid a thick railroad tie across the top of the hole and looped a rope over it."[40]

Now ready to descend, Tom Harper mentioned that a person should never descend into a mine without knowing the air was safe. Out of abundant precaution, "to test for air," writes local Colorado historian Carol Turner, "they lowered a candle. Within five feet of the top, a draft extinguished the flame."[41] There was air moving through the mine below and blowing out the air shaft; the men were in no danger of being exposed to poisonous air.

Next, one after the other, "Callaghan, Harper and Chapson lowered themselves down the rope, hand over hand." Their estimates had been fairly accurate: the shaft was sixty-five feet deep, but with their one hundred–foot coil of rope, they were safe. Upon reaching the bottom, the three men had difficulty keeping their candles lit because of the rush of air, but there was enough light for them to see "an opening, or tunnel, about 3 feet high." So "on hands and knees the trio crawled into the dark hole."[42]

The three-foot-high tunnel went back a distance of some twenty-five feet before, as Callaghan later wrote, "We were very much surprised to find ourselves in the main workings of a large coal mine."[43] Had they come any other day, there probably would have been men working down in those mines, which was why they had chosen to descend on Sunday, when the mine was deserted. Now it was time for John Chapson, the engineer, to go to work. He began taking careful measurements with a tapeline "of the size of the 'room' of coal," and "about a half hour later," after securing the evidentiary details they needed, "the three men crawled back through the small tunnel to the bottom of the shaft."[44] It was then, for the first time, they realized they were in trouble.

When they exited the narrow tunnel and entered the bottom of the air shaft, "To their horror, they could see no daylight above." As Don Wilkie explains, "The opening had been shut off. The rope, cut at the knot that had bound it to the tie, lay at their feet."[45] Someone had placed more of the railroad ties over the opening. They began shouting for Joe Walker, but he did not reply. They then realized that not only were they in deep trouble, so was Walker.

Discussing how to proceed, Tom Harper volunteered to climb to the top, but Callaghan offered, "We could draw straws to see who tries it." Harper asked, "You ever climbed a shaft before, son?"[46] Callaghan had not, and neither had Chapson. Harper was clearly the most logical man to attempt the climb; he had done it before. Chapson handed Harper his tapeline.

Chapson, however, did offer up one good idea: "We can't be sure we're getting out of here," he explained to the other two. "And if we do get out, we don't know what's waiting for us up there. I think we ought to write a report of what we found and what happened down here. If anything happens to us, maybe somebody will find it."[47] They all agreed it was a good idea, and so using the candle to see by, Chapson began writing a quick synopsis of what had transpired up to that point in time alongside his measurements. He then tucked it under his undershirt, and, with that done, Harper began his ascent; the others could only watch, hope, and pray.

Harper had clearly done this before, for, rather than climbing with his hands forward, he climbed with his legs and his back against the wall. Because of the timbers used to reinforce the shaft, the climb was relatively easy. The hard part was at the top: In order to lift the heavy railroad crossties while maintaining his position in the shaft, Harper pushed his shoulder up against the underside of one of the beams and pushed upward with his legs. It was then that the inside of the shaft upon which he was bracing himself "suddenly gave way and a shower of earth and rock hurled him down the shaft."[48] Had the walls been smooth, he would have plummeted to his death, but because they were reinforced with timbers, he was able to slow his descent. Still, crashing to the ground, he was fairly sure he had broken a few ribs.

He tried two more times before finally making it to the top, where he was able to push the timbers aside and create a hole large enough to crawl through. He then moved aside the ends of several railroad ties to enlarge the hole and to allow more light into the air shaft. He then lowered the tapeline down to Callaghan and Chapson and, after tying one end of the rope to it, pulled the rope up. He tied it off to one of the timbers laid across the shaft, and Callaghan and Chapson made their way up and out of the earth.

The men then began searching for Joe Walker. They quickly found him, lying in the brush near the shaft opening. He was dead. He had at least a dozen bullet holes in his back, while his revolver remained holstered. As Wilkie explains, "Walker had been shot from behind and at no great distance, as was proved by the fact that almost the entire charge of a shell of buckshot had penetrated his back between waist and shoulders."[49]

The three men realized their situation was still dire, especially if the assailant remained in the area, possibly watching them. They decided their best chance of getting help was to split up. Callaghan took Walker's horse, still tethered nearby, and rode to Durango to find the sheriff. Harper knew of a nearby farmhouse from which he could summon help by telephone, and Chapson stayed behind to guard Walker's body, armed with Walker's revolver.

As Callaghan rode for Durango, he came across "two men in a buggy on the main road, about 5 miles from the shaft. When he saw that one of the men carried a shotgun, he ordered them to halt and identified himself." He asked them who they were, and one of the men said he was William R. Mason, the superintendent of the Porter Fuel Company and owner of the homestead where the shaft was located. The other man, he learned, was Joseph Vanderweide, a local miner. When asked what they were doing out on a Sunday, they replied, "Hunting rabbits."[50]

Believing these were the men who killed Walker, Callaghan seized the shotgun and placed the two men under arrest. He ordered them to proceed with him to Durango. About five miles outside of town, two men approached him on horseback and informed Callaghan they were the sheriff and county coroner, on their way to Hesperus due to an anonymous tip that there had been a shooting. Accompanied by the sheriff and coroner, the three men escorted the two suspects to the Durango jail, where they were questioned.

At first they denied any knowledge of Walker's killing.[51] Eventually, Vanderweide "admitted under questioning that he had shot Joseph Walker."[52] The story he gave was that, while he and Mason were out hunting rabbits, they came across a man— Joseph Walker—who was sitting near the shaft. When they approached him, Walker pulled his revolver, threatening them, at which point an argument followed. Vanderweide then stated that, fearing for his life, he brought his shotgun up and shot Walker while facing him from a distance of about ten feet. Although his story had many problems, the two glaring issues that disproved his story was that Walker had been shot in the back and his revolver was still holstered. In addition, the distance of the shotgun blast could not have been ten feet, otherwise Walker probably would not have died, because the buckshot would not have been concentrated in only an eight-inch spread of his back and neck. Moreover, as any hunter will attest, people hunting rabbits generally do not use buckshot.[53]

Although William Craig had been the first Secret Service operative killed in the line of duty, Joseph Walker became the first Secret Service operative to be murdered in the line of duty.[54]

The newspapers were quick to pick up the story, most having to rely on the Porter Fuel Company's lawyer, C. C. Dorsey, for their information, so they mostly cited the self-defense version of the story. For instance, under the headline "SECRET SERVICE AGENT KILLED BY A MINER," the *San Francisco Call* reported that "self-defense is plea." Dorsey's "report of the affair, which he says is trustworthy," the paper wrote, "clearly justifies the shooting." The article ends repeating Dorsey's insistence that "there was no reason for the secret service men entering the Hesperus mine as the title to the property was not questioned and their act was simple trespass."[55]

Upon learning of Walker's murder, President Roosevelt wrote a letter to Attorney General Charles Joseph Bonaparte and Secretary of the Interior James R. Garfield, son of the assassinated president, who had succeeded Ethan A. Hitchcock to that position. It read: "My attention has been called to the dispatches in reference to the murder of Secret Service Agent Walker while in the performance of his duty investigating certain coal land frauds in Colorado. I trust every effort will be exerted by your department to prosecute vigorously every violation of the land laws which Walker was investigating."[56] When the president wanted something done—especially this president—it was done. The attorney general quickly dispatched Secret Service chief John E. Wilkie to Colorado to personally assume Walker's duties, to move Walker's land-fraud cases forward, and to oversee the investigation into Walker's death. As the murder had occurred in Colorado, however, the state took precedence in prosecuting the case. Indictments were handed down for first-degree murder, and both men who were arraigned that Friday, November 8, pleaded not guilty.

Two days later, Joseph Walker was cremated, and his ashes were buried in the Fairmount Cemetery. He left behind a grieving but pensionless widow, Alida Tunstall Walker, and an adult son by the name of Robert. No pensions existed at that time for the spouses of agents killed in the line of duty. She had enough money to cremate and bury her husband but not enough for a headstone. The funeral for Operative Walker was well attended, and there were many tributes in his honor. One came from noted author Damon Runyon, who wrote, "As a friend he stood 'four-square to all the winds that blow.' He was always to be found with the word of sympathy for the suffering, and he never refused to aid with his substance a friend who had fallen on life's highway."[57]

Three days after the funeral, after having been granted and having paid a twenty-thousand-dollar bail each, both men were set free. They awaited their day in court.

Meanwhile, Wilkie was busy reviewing the evidence Walker had amassed before his murder. After the evidence was organized, it was "presented in Denver and indictments were returned by the Federal Grand Jury."[58] Of the 1,400 indictments that went before Judge R. E. Lewis, all but one were dropped. The sole remaining case was put off to a later date on a continuance and was eventually dismissed for lack of evidence. A federal grand jury, however, hand down two additional indictments against Mason and Vanderweide for conspiracy to assassinate Walker, but Judge Lewis ordered that no arrests be made in the case until the state trial was concluded. So all eyes turned to the murder trial.

The state's case against Mason and Vanderweide commenced on April 20, 1908, and the defense rested on May 1. The case then went into summation, which lasted through the next day. Late on the afternoon of May 2, 1908, at approximately 4 p.m., the jury began to deliberate. After little more than four hours, they returned with their decision: both defendants were found not guilty. Callaghan, having followed the trial in his official capacity, wrote a report concluding, "The acquittal was no doubt due to the intense feeling against all Government agents in that region at the time, caused by the scores of indictments which had been returned by the Government against individuals who had been used as dummies by the big lumber and coal companies in the filing of false claims."[59]

Perhaps even more chilling was what Callaghan added from a confidential source who refused to testify in the case: "It was afterwards learned from a confidential source close to William R. Mason that their purpose in dropping the rope to the bottom of the shaft and making us prisoners was to keep us there until they could return to Hesperus, procure some dynamite, and return to blow up the shaft, obliterating all traces of Harper, Chapson, and myself, and claiming that whoever had descended the shaft had encountered a gas pocket which, through carelessness, was exploded by candles."[60] There is little doubt that the body of Secret Service Operative Walker would have also been dropped down the shaft before the dynamite, eliminating nearly all evidence of murder.

Before Mason and Vanderweide could leave the courtroom, however, the arrest warrants for conspiracy to commit murder were executed. Shortly thereafter, the men were again released on bond, and once again the case took a number of twists and turns.

In November of 1908, a federal judge ruled that the conspiracy charge was limited to the two defendants violating Walker's civil rights; no evidence of murder could be introduced. The US attorneys balked at that and filed an appeal. The case wound its way to the US Supreme Court, which eventually ruled that the attempt to charge the two defendants for conspiracy to commit murder was the equivalent of "double jeopardy"; the case was dismissed.[61]

Then, in August of 1910, there was one last glimmer of hope that a conviction could still be won when the two men were rearrested and "charged with interfering with officers engaged in the performance of their duty."[62] In late October of that year, those charges, however, were also dismissed. In the end, no one was ever held culpable for Walker's death, and perhaps because of the lack of a conviction Secret Service Operative Joseph Walker was not officially recognized as the first Secret Service Operative murdered while conducting an investigation.[63] And because he had no headstone to mark his grave, no one was even sure where he was buried. One day in 2010, his son, Robert Walker, at the age of eighty-nine, lamented this to his two daughters, Sharon Stackhouse and Robynn Thomas.[64] These two ladies most assuredly inherited their grandfather's investigatory skills, for not only did they locate the grave, upon which a headstone has now been placed by the Association of Former Agents of the US Secret Service, but Walker's death is now widely recognized as the first investigatory death in that agency's history.

Outcomes of Walker's Death

Operative Joseph Walker died a tragic death, and more tragedy followed. It was a professional tragedy that none of his investigations resulted in conviction and that no one was ever held accountable for his murder. It was a personal tragedy that his wife received no pension and that he received no grave marker. Even so, Walker's death was not in vain. "As a result of Walker's murder President Theodore Roosevelt had two laws passed," explains Tom Morton in detailing Joseph Walker's grave maker story. "One provided Federal pensions to families of agents killed in the line of duty, and the other made it a Federal crime to kill an agent while in the discharge of his duty."[65] Still further, Walker' story is now well documented and remembered because of the work of his son and granddaughters.

The one other positive outcome of the Walker case was the eventual establishment of the Federal Bureau of Investigation. "The Secret Service had secured evidence implicating not only rich men and powerful corporations, but far more embarrassing, members of the House and Senate."[66] So Congress saw an opportunity arising out of the Walker case to shut down the land-fraud investigations. As the son of Secret Service chief John E. Wilkie explains, the Walker case is what led to the insertion of a clause into the "sundry civil appropriation bill which was deliberately meant to confine the Secret Service Division to its own bureau."[67] Because the Secret Service had not been created by Congress, its budget came through the sundry bill—a catchall appropriations bill covering things Congress needed in order for the government to do its job but that did not otherwise have Congressional authorization. In order to stop the Roosevelt administration from using the Secret Service Operatives to investigate land fraud and to prevent them from investigating other members of Congress, they inserted a clause in the bill that agents could not be used by other government departments, like the Department of Interior, to conduct their investigations. This ultimately stymied land-fraud investigations, because departments like the Interior did not have their own law-enforcement officials.

In response, the Roosevelt administration created the Federal Bureau of Investigation, but not before fighting a battle that pitted the president against Congress—in particular, the chairman of the House Appropriations Committee, a fellow Republican, Representative James A. Tawney of Minnesota, who led the opposition against Roosevelt. This is the subject of the next chapter.

US Congress Representative James A. Tawney, who served in the House from 1893 to 1911 and was the Chairman of the House Appropriations Committee, formed the greatest opposition to President Roosevelt in the Secret Service controversy, which led to the birth of the FBI.

Photo courtesy of the Office of the Clerk, U.S. House of Representatives, from the Collection of the U.S. House of Representatives.

9

Chairman James A. Tawney

The revelations of the land-fraud investigations of 1907 had culminated in the Colorado case in which Secret Service Operative Joseph Walker was killed in the line of duty. Despite this tragic loss, what had Congress more riled up was that the Department of Justice had used Secret Service operatives to investigate the "private matters" of members of Congress.[1] "The cloakrooms of the Capitol buzzed with excitement" in response to the revelations, writes Secret Service Agent Don Wilkie in his tell-all book about the early years of the agency, and congressmen were left wondering, "Where would this reign of terror end?" Wilkie fully believed that because two sitting members of Congress had been indicted in the Colorado case, word was spreading around Washington that "Treasury operatives were being employed to spy upon the private lives of Congressmen."[2] The legislature was looking to rebuke the president for his administration's actions, which they saw as abusive, but they needed someone to lead the charge. They soon found their man in chairman of the House Appropriations Committee, James A. Tawney.

Representative Tawney saw a way to confine Secret Service operatives to the Treasury Department and limit their activities to investigating counterfeiting and to protecting the president. No longer would departments such as Interior or Justice be able to borrow Secret Service operatives to conduct their investigations. More importantly, no longer would they be able to investigate congressmen involved in private land deals. All Tawney had to do was propose the addition of a short provision to the Secret Service funding bill that would so confine the Secret Service Division of the US Treasury Department.[3] Doing so, however, was guaranteed to create a clash between the executive and legislative branches of government, and it did. "The disturbance over the Secret Service which erupted in 1908 not only prompted a hostile confrontation between Congress and the President," writes Historian Willard B. Gatewood Jr., "it also raised serious questions about the place and role of a secret detective force within a democratic state."[4] More importantly, however, it led directly to the birth of the Federal Bureau of Investigation.

James A. Tawney

James Albertus Tawney was born on January 3, 1855, in Mount Pleasant Township, near Gettysburg, Pennsylvania.[5] Some of his earliest memories were of the Civil War battle being fought near his home when he was only eight years old. At about that same time in his life, he began an apprenticeship under his father as a blacksmith, and he later learned the machinist trade. Tawney left his home state in the summer of 1877, moving west to take advantage of his trade skills in land that was not yet so well settled. It was in Winona, Minnesota, where he found work as both a blacksmith and machinist. He soon joined the Minnesota National Guard and through his contacts there managed to land a job working in the law office of Bentley and Vance. The owners of the firm encouraged Tawney to attend law school and join the bar, so in January of 1881, Tawney enrolled in the law department at the University of Wisconsin in Madison. On July 10, 1882, Tawney was admitted to the bar and was ready to practice law.

Over the next year, Tawney began to make his way up in the world. In late 1882, along with a partner, he opened the Law Office of Tawney & Randall.[6] Then, on March 1, 1883, he was appointed judge advocate in the Minnesota National Guard with the rank of first lieutenant. Soon thereafter, he met a young lady by the name of Emma Beller Newall, and they were married before the close of the year, on December 19.

As his law office prospered, so too did his political connections, and by the end of the 1880s he was being encouraged to run for the Minnesota State Legislature. He did and successfully won election, taking his seat in the twenty-sixth legislative session in 1889. Tawney then used this as a springboard to successfully run for a seat in the fifty-third Congress, representing Minnesota's first congressional district. After his arrival in Washington, D.C., Tawney quickly began climbing the ranks of power where he soon found himself seated on the US House Committee on Appropriations. This was one of the most influential committees in Congress, as it controlled the purse strings: all spending bills must originate in the House, and within the House, all of these bills must start in the appropriations committee.

Tawney, who was elected nine times to Congress (fifty-third to sixty-first Congresses), rose in both seniority and power.[7] When Congress first created the position of House majority whip, it was Tawney who first held the office. Then, in 1905, he was elevated to serve as chairman of the appropriations committee, making him, as historian Wyman writes, "a key figure in the federal government; he was regarded as second only to [Speaker] Cannon in the power wielded in the House."[8]

Despite being from the same party as President Theodore Roosevelt, the two men were from different wings of the party and so did not often agree.[9] Tawney was from the "old guard" of Republicans and "was a steadfast believer in the supremacy of the legislative branch." Roosevelt, however, was from a new, more progressive wing of the Republicans, which believed the president should assert more power to advance American public policies. Tawney's old-guard wing of the Republican Party was opposed to the progressive notions of Roosevelt's wing. And though Roosevelt held the power of the bully pulpit, "the combination of [Tawney's] talent, strong beliefs, and powerful position made him a formidable opponent."[10]

It was Tawney's new role as chairman of appropriations and their difference in politics that soon led to the clash.[11] "As a member of 'the ruling clique' in the House," historian Gatewood explains, "Tawney was generally disturbed by the proliferation of federal investigations and particularly objected to the use of Secret Service personnel in the investigation of 'business arrangements.'" Exercising his power as chairman, Tawney "requested the attorney general to make available complete lists of all inspectors and special agents employed by the Justice Department since 1896."[12] Tawney was now on a collision course with the president, fully intending to keep Congress as the most powerful arm of American government and to shut down the Roosevelt administration's ability to ever investigate another member of Congress again.[13]

The Sundry Appropriation Bill

It all started innocently enough on January 13, 1906. Chairman Tawney called one of the assistant attorney generals, John J. Glover, to testify before the appropriations committee. Glover, chief of the accounts division, had been hired by the Department of Justice on October 2, 1893, as chief bookkeeper and record clerk, and he'd worked his way up 'til on July 1, 1900, he was made chief. When it came to expenditures within the DOJ, Glover was the man to talk to, so when the House appropriations subcommittee needed information on the DOJ budget, Glover was the proper man to call to testify.[14]

The committee had many questions about DOJ expenditures and how they paid their various employees. One question pertained to the use of a special fund of $500,000, which Glover explained was only to fund antitrust cases having to do with "the timber-depredation claims, frauds out in Oregon, Nebraska, and Colorado." Here Tawney saw his opening to get to the bottom of the relationship between the Secret Service operatives from Treasury working for Justice.

"Is there a secret-service bureau maintained in connection with the Department of Justice?" Tawney asked Glover.

"No, sir," he replied.

"Where do you get your secret service?" Tawney then asked.

"Generally from the Treasury Department," Glover replied.

Tawney now saw his opening and smugly asked Glover, "You call on the Treasury Department do you?"

"Yes, sir," was Glover's answer, not realizing the controversy this simple affirmation was about to create—although he had no inclination to lie to the sitting chairman of the House appropriations committee, for this was simply a concurrence with the facts.

Then, hoping to show that the Department of Justice had been violating the law, Tawney asked Glover, "What authority in law has the Department of Justice to call on the Treasury Department for such service?" But Glover continued to address how DOJ funds paid for the agents who'd been reassigned from Treasury.

"Out of your own appropriations?" Tawney asked.

"Yes, sir," Glover replied.

Tawney had him: "You are not authorized by law to do so."

Glover demurred: "We understand that we are authorized to collect evidence in such a way as we may find it necessary to do so." This was not what Tawney wanted to hear, and the conversation turned to laws affecting DOJ investigations.

But Tawney tried another tactic. "The practice of the different Departments in calling upon the Treasury Department for the aid of its secret service force results in effect in giving every Department of the Government a secret service bureau, does it not?"

Glover, again, deflected the question: "I am only here to speak of the Department of Justice."

After another exchange, Tawney decided to make a statement, knowing it would be entered into the Congressional Record. "It is virtually giving to each Department what Congress would never authorize," he said, "the maintenance of a secret-service bureau in every Department, creating thereby a system of espionage in this country which is entirely inconsistent with the theory of our Government."

The congressional boogeyman was now available for all to read about in the Congressional Record. The insinuation that the Secret Service had become an arm of the executive branch to spy on the other branches of government was now part of the official record. But, as he had been asked no question, Glover tried to play it safe and said nothing. Tawney, however, continued to press the issue.

In the end, Glover did eventually say of the practice of borrowing operatives from Treasury, "I am thoroughly satisfied that this is the only way now available, and I don't think it makes any particular difference whether we employ these trained men from the Treasury Department or use the same money in employing outsiders."

Tawney went in for the kill. "It makes this difference," he declared. "The secret service has been created by Congress for a specific purpose." This was incorrect: Congress had not created the Secret Service; the Secretary of the Treasury had in 1865.[15] "It was not contemplated," Tawney continued, "that this service should be employed by the different departments of the Government, for if other departments of the Government have cases in which it is necessary to use secret-service men they should obtain authority from Congress, and then the question of the advisability of maintaining the service throughout our Government would be determined by Congress, which is the only competent authority to determine that question. That is the point."

Placed into the record of the subcommittee was Tawney's political stance on the use of Secret Service agents by the Justice Department and his belief that the agents were being used as spies to practice espionage against Congress. After all, there were congressmen under indictment because of investigations by Secret Service operatives, so the claim had to be true. Although "Tawney's concern could not have been of pressing importance," writes FBI historian John F. Fox Jr. "He did not seriously revisit the issue for two years, though he kept tabs on the use of Secret Service operatives during this time."[16] But politics is often played like a game of chess, which can be a drawn-out game. Tawney had made the first move; now he only needed to wait and see what his opponent would do.

What soon prompted the next move was the publicity and attention derived from the death of Secret Service Operative Joe Walker in Colorado while investigating the land-fraud case.[17] In the wake of that case, according to Don Wilkie, "The operatives who had collected the evidence in the timber and land frauds were withdrawn."[18] This was done under pressure from the legislative branch. Then, a new player in the game was appointed at the end of that year—a new attorney general who, as a member of the executive branch, would soon be making his own moves.

In the fall of 1906, President Roosevelt had the opportunity to appoint a new associate justice to the Supreme Court. Initially, he had tried to convince his secretary of war, William Howard Taft, to accept the nomination, believing he would make an excellent justice, but Taft declined. Roosevelt then turned to his attorney general, William Henry Moody, who accepted the nomination and was confirmed by the Senate on December 12, 1906. Roosevelt now had a vacant cabinet position, so he looked to one of his favorite positions in government—the secretary of the Navy—and nominated Secretary Charles J. Bonaparte for the position.

Bonaparte was born on June 9, 1851, in Baltimore, Maryland, to his parents Jerome "Bo" Napoleon Bonaparte and Susan May Williams.[19] Bo was, in fact, related to the more famous Napoleon, but being an American, the name was more than enough for him; he held no French titles. Charles attended both Harvard University and its law school before returning to Baltimore to practice law. He had a somewhat eccentric personality, eschewing the newfangled technology of electricity and telephone, and traveled solely by way of horse and carriage until his death in 1921. Roosevelt had appointed him secretary of the Navy in 1905 and then as his attorney general after Moody became a Supreme Court Justice. On December 17, 1906, Charles J. Bonaparte was confirmed by the US Senate to serve as head of the Department of Justice.

In no time Bonaparte was having to deal with the issue of borrowed Secret Service operatives from a number of perspectives. For one, his boss wanted the practice to resume so that the investigations into land fraud could continue. However, when Roosevelt nominated and the Senate confirmed James R. Garfield, son of the assassinated President Garfield, to serve as the secretary of the interior, Garfield wanted nothing to do with the Secret Service operatives. So Garfield "dispensed with the services of [Secret service chief John] Wilkie's agents detailed directly to his department," explains historian Gatewood, "because of the friction that had developed between them and investigators in his own department." In the end, Garfield worked out an arrangement with Attorney General Charles J. Bonaparte "whereby agents of the

Interior Department were to have sole charge of land fraud matters until the cases were worked up and ready for prosecution."[20]

It was this particular incident, along with a Department of Justice having to depend on the Secret Service for its investigators, that led Bonaparte to take action. In his first year as attorney general came to a close, he issued the Department of Justice's annual report for 1907, in which he wrote,

> The attention of the Congress should be, I think, called to the anomaly that the Department of Justice has no executive force, and, more particularly, no permanent detective force under its immediate control. This singular condition arises mainly from the fact that before the office of the Attorney-General was transformed into the Department of Justice a highly efficient detective service had been organized to deal with crime against the Treasury laws, which force has been, in effect, lent from time to time to this Department to meet its steadily increasing need for an urgency of this nature, without, however, being removed from the control of the Treasury Department.[21]

Bonaparte's solution to this problem was simple. He argued that if Justice "had a small, carefully selected, and experienced force under its immediate orders," it could better perform its duties, rather than borrowing agents from other agencies and running up against the law. He then drove home this need by frankly stating that "a Department of Justice with no force of permanent police in any form under its control is assuredly not fully equipped for its work."[22]

Congress, especially Representative Tawney, was not pleased.

Soon thereafter, on January 17, 1908, Attorney General Bonaparte was called to testify before the House Appropriation subcommittee. Although he spoke on a number of issues related to Justice's budget, as FBI historian Fox explains, "Bonaparte reminded the House Appropriation subcommittee of his earlier request and complained that the Justice Department had 'to rely on the secret service of the Treasury,' which had just 'gone up in price.'"[23] This last reference had to do with an increase in the cost for other departments to hire Secret Service operatives for their investigations. This was essentially nothing more than the simple issue of supply and demand: the supply of able investigators was low, but the demand was high and rising; as a result, costs went up.

In order to alleviate the issue of supply, Bonaparte offered his proposal to Congress for the creation of a bureau of investigation. He told the subcommittee that "it would tend to more satisfactory administration and also to economy if instead of being obliged to call upon them [the Secret Service] for this service we had a small, a very moderate, service of that kind ourselves." More specifically, he told them, "I think the best plan would be to have a service of that kind under the control of the Department of Justice and let it, if necessary, assist other departments in cases of emergency."[24] What he was calling for was a bureau of investigation run by the Department of Justice: what he envisioned was the FBI.

"In 1907 and again in 1908," historians Althan G. Theoharis and John Stuart Cox explain, "Attorney General Bonaparte formally requested congressional approval to establish an independent investigative division within the Department of Justice, emphasizing the department's inability to meet its increased caseload and the complexity of antitrust and interstate commerce laws."[25] Congress refused both times. Bonaparte was not going to get what he wanted from Congress, while Congress—with Tawney leading the charge—searched for ways to curtail the Secret Service investigations. Throughout February and March of 1908, additional appropriations subcommittee hearings with other departments continued to probe into their use of Secret Service operatives.

By the end of April, Tawney had all of the evidence he needed to make his proposal to amend the Sundry Civil Appropriation Bill. Because Congress had never authorized funding the, Secret Service, the agency's budget had always been generated out of the Sundry bill, which funded a collection of all the extra things government needed to do its business. But the Secret Service had no appropriations bill derived from legislative authority.

On April 21, 1908, the Washington *Evening Star* was one of the first to report on the House appropriations-committee hearings on the Sundry bill. Their article, titled "Loan of Detectives," specifically highlighted the issue of other departments borrowing Secret Service operatives. "Alarmed by the institution here in the National capital of a secret service spy system similar to that of the hated black cabinet of St. Petersburg," the newspaper reported, "the House appropriation committee has included in the sundry civil appropriation bill, which will be reported this week, a drastic and stringent provision prohibiting the detailing, assignment or loan of any member of the government secret service force to any other department of the government for any purpose whatsoever."[26] Tawney had made his move against not only the Secret Service and Justice Department but also against President Roosevelt.

The *Evening Star* wrote of the hearings that day when Secret Service Assistant Chief W. H. Moran testified before the appropriations committee about the agency's operatives. They reported that his testimony "shows that in detailing secret service operators to other departments of the government for detective purposes the law now on the statute books has been repeatedly violated."

In trying to expose the illegality, Tawney asked Moran, "Are these men detailed to the other departments?" to which Moran replied, "No, they are not detailed." If the Secret Service detailed its operatives to other departments, then they would be violating the law. "We do not detail them," Moran countered, then explaining, "What is done, we separate them entirely from our service; in other words, their pay and allowance is stopped the moment they undertake any other work for any other department."

Tawney continued to press. "If a department made request upon the Treasury Department for secret service employees, and you were not able to meet that request with the force you then had in the employ of the secret service of the Treasury Department, how would you supply their demands?"

"Well," replied Moran, "we would tell them we could not supply them."

"Or would you employ other men temporarily?" inquired the chairman.

"Well, we have done that," said Moran; "we have employed men who have performed temporary service for us and found them to be efficient."

"So under the present practice," summarized Tawney, "it would be possible for each department of the government to secure and maintain a secret service force, provided it had the appropriation and the per diem which these people demand and which the Secretary of the Treasury recommends?"

"Yes," admitted Moran, "if we had the proper number of men available. We do not recommend to another department a man for any service, unless we know that man is peculiarly fitted to perform it."

The chairman continued along the same line. "If," he asked, "the demand for this service from another department was such as to require the services of more men than are in your department regularly, and you had applications on file and investigated them to satisfy yourself as to the efficiency and competency of the men, you could, as a matter of fact, supply the entire demand from other departments in this way?"

Moran admitted that this was indeed true. The only problem was, it was also illegal. Moran had admitted that when the Secret Service force was not sufficient to supply all the demands from the other departments, they resorted to using outside private investigators—a practice that had been expressly forbidden by statute ever since the Homestead Strike.[27]

"Now," Tawney questioned Moran, "did you not as a matter of fact know that the restrictions of the law are intended to prevent that very practice?"

"No," replied Moran, "I did not know that. It was never put to us in that way." Now Moran had admitted two things: they were breaking the law, and they hadn't known it.

At that point, other members of the committee wanted to question Moran. In this series of questions, Moran also admitted that when a detective's Secret Service pay was stopped and he was loaned to another department, his chief continued to be his chief, and there was a full record in the central Secret Service bureau of the activities and discoveries.

"So," said Tawney, "to all intents and purposes he remains a member of the secret service department."

"Yes, that is true," admitted Moran.

In order to show how often this was being done, the number of loaned operatives was entered into the record: in 1906, sixty operatives were used, while in 1907 that number increased to sixty-five. Tawney had learned all of this from his questioning of representatives from the various departments in the subcommittee hearings he had held in February and March. "From July 1, 1907, to February 29, 1908," Tawney highlighted, "sixty-six detectives were supplied to the departments by the secret service division, fifty-one going to the Department of Justice, five to the State Department, four to the War Department, five to the Navy Department and one to Porto Rico." As FBI historian Fox explains, "These investigators came from a reserve force of about twenty that the Secret Service kept to help other departments as well as a list maintained by Chief John Wilkie of some three hundred other investigators who had applied for Secret Service positions, were already vetted by the Treasury Department, but for whom no position was available."[28]

Once these numbers were entered into the record, Tawney continued his line of questioning: "Can you tell me, Mr. Moran, from your recollection, about when the practice of using as many detectives as the departments are now using began?"

"Never as many as now," replied Moran. "It has been increasing right along in the last few years particularly."

"Is it not a fact," Tawney then asked, "that prior to about six or eleven years ago men in your secret service were requested by other departments very infrequently?"

"Comparatively, yes," replied the assistant chief.

"Have you kept your force up and do you now aim to keep your force up to supply not only the men that are required in the service for which appropriations are made, but also to meet the requirements of other departments as they are demanded?" Tawney asked.

"Yes; otherwise we would not keep these twenty additional men on the roll," Moran replied.

"You keep in the neighborhood of twenty men in addition to the men necessary to do your work under this appropriation on hand at all times to supply the other departments, and they are employed all of the time?"

"Well," Moran hesitated, "we have had need for them recently in that way."

As the *Evening Star* explained, the committee had discovered that, although the Secret Service division treated loaned detectives as if they were no longer their employees, the operatives

still largely remained their employees and not the other departments'. The other departments, however, treated the agents as if
they were still regularly connected with the Secret Service, not
requiring them to take the oath of office to serve as an investigators in their respective departments. This, it was pointed out by
the committee in no undecided language, was unlawful.

"You say they do not take the oath of other departments?"
asked Tawney.

"Not in all cases," replied Mr. Moran.

"Then how can they be compensated for their service?"
asked Tawney, and without waiting for an answer, said, "The
law expressly prohibits compensation until the oath of office has
been taken."

Moran did not truly answer the question but mumbled that
the Secret Service bureau really did not want this class of work
and would not care if it were stopped tomorrow. The questioning of Moran was finished.

Attorney General Bonaparte was also asked to appear before
the committee to answer questions regarding his department's
appropriations. Much of this testimony centered on the Justice
Department's use of Secret Service operatives for its investigations. But one series of questions from Iowa Representative Walter
I. Smith centered on "spy system." "The growth of the country,"
replied the attorney general, "is such, and the enormous increase
in facilities of communication and the, so to speak, 'cosmopolitiza-
tion' of crime—if I can call it the word for the occasion—is such,
that you are compelled now to have a central agency to deal with."
Bonaparte's testimony continued to come back to the need for a
Justice Department central bureau of investigation in nearly every
one of his responses. "What I recommend on this subject is what I
have recommended all along," he repeated, "that you put into the
hands of the Department of Justice the opportunity to employ a
certain number of men for this purpose. What you have said about
the spy system applies rather to the method of doing the work
than to the work itself. We are obliged to have people who will investigate and report on the facts attendant on crimes or suspected
crimes, and the protection of the community makes it very desirable that you should have as efficient a force as you can."

Bonaparte would not let the central bureau idea go, but neither would Representative Smith let go of his fear that a spy system was operating within American government. His response to Moran was widely reported in the newspapers over the next several days: "Nothing is more opposed to our race, than a belief that a general system of espionage is being conducted by the general government." The allegation was out there: Secret Service operatives were being used by the executive branch to spy on other members of the government.

Historians Theoharis and Cox believe that congressional leaders were "reflecting the strong states' rights and libertarian sentiments of an early day" and that they were trying to "prevent the evolution of 'a Federal secret police.'"[29] Congress was also clearly playing to American fear of anything that undermined the democratic system of government. The newspapers were quick to report on this, and it caused the sensation they knew it would.

Popular reaction was to do whatever it took to shut the system down. So when Tawney proposed the inclusion of a simple paragraph in the Sundry bill that would prevent the temporary transfer of Secret Service operatives to any other department to conduct investigations and that would limit the Secret Service mandate to only investigating counterfeiting and protecting the president, he found was growing support.

"Theodore Roosevelt saw through this ruse," writes Secret Service Agent Don Wilkie, son of Secret Service chief John Wilkie, "and did not hesitate to declare that the real purpose of the amendment was to hamper the Government in its prosecution of the looters of the public domain."[30] Roosevelt was alarmed by what the Tawney amendment if passed by Congress might do to all of the investigations into government corruption, especially in regard to "looters" in the land frauds. So, Roosevelt, being Roosevelt, took action. As historian Gatewood explains, "He immediately lodged his objections to it with Speaker Cannon, who shared Tawney's apprehensions about the use of the Secret Service as an interdepartmental agency."[31]

Writing to Speaker Cannon, Roosevelt wrote, "Of course, the provision about the employment of the Secret Service men will work very great damage to the Government in its endeavor to prevent and punish crime."[32] Roosevelt argued that Tawney's provision would "materially interfere with the administration of justice and will benefit only one class of people—and that is the criminal class." After signing his name to the final letter, but before sending it to the Speaker of the House, in a handwritten postscript, Roosevelt added, "there is no more foolish outcry than this against 'spies'; only criminals need fear our detectives."[33]

Speaker of the House "Uncle Joe" Cannon received the letter, but as historian Gatewood explained, he was "wholly unimpressed by the President's appeal."[34]

Secretary of the Treasury George B. Cortelyou also tried to stop the provision from entering the Sundry bill. He wrote a letter to Chairman Tawney on April 29, 1908, attempting to convince him that the addition of the provision would violate Section 166 of the Revised Statutes, which says that "Each head of a Department may from time to time alter the distribution of the clerks allowed by law as he may find it necessary and proper to do so." However, Cortelyou explained, "the paragraph which it is proposed to incorporate in the Sundry Civil Bill of this year makes it quite doubtful whether, under the terms of this act, I am permitted to detail these employees." Cortelyou finished his letter by telling Tawney, "I wish to convey to you my respectful but none the less emphatic protest against any such abridgement of the rights delegated to the Secretary of the Treasury by existing law."[35]

The opposition had been heard, and now they had to sit and wait to see what Tawney would do. On May 1, 1908, the House resolved itself into a Committee of the Whole to consider amendments to the Sundry bill. All eyes were on the committee, waiting to see what they would do with Tawney's provision.

Once the committee began its deliberations and the Secret Service budget was raised, Tawney approached the issue by first focusing on the agency's mission to protect the president. "The provision in regard to the protection of the President," he said, "was for the first time placed in this paragraph two years ago." "Up to that time," he continued, "no officer or employee in the Secret Service was justified in paying any attention whatever to the protection of the President. If any officer was used, and many were used for that purpose, it was in direct violation of the law, if they were paid out of this appropriation; and they *were* paid out of the appropriation." Tawney explained that the original appropriation had added the clause, "And for no other purpose except for the protection of the person of the President of the United States."[36]

Tawney then brought in Moran's testimony to demonstrate that the Secret Service had violated the law, saying, it "shows that they are maintaining and have for some time maintained on their rolls a force of twenty more men than was necessary for the secret-service work authorized under the appropriation." Tawney also added that this "necessity grows out of the fact, as he informed us, that they are constantly called upon by other Departments of the Government to furnish men for service in their department."[37] For the record, Tawney stated that when the agents were loaned, they remained under the control of the Secret Service and took no oath to the new department under which they were working. In so doing, they had been investigating things unrelated to counterfeiting or having to do with the protection of the president, and were, again, violating the law.

Once Tawney had said his piece, the floor was opened for questions, and the other members of the House took the debate in a number of different directions. New York Representative Herbert Parsons asked him quite bluntly, "Does the gentleman think it desirable to have a general detective service for the Government?" Tawney's reply was short and curt: "No; I do not."

The debate soon focused on the payment of the Secret Service operatives and the retention of the additional men before turning to whether or not the Secret Service should even exist when New York Representative William S. Bennet said, "There is no law whatever on the statute books for a secret-service division. This provision has been carried here for forty-three years and from time to time changed to cover other branches of the Government work in other Departments."[38] Not only did they question the Secret Service's right to exist, the conversation turned nasty when Missouri Representative Clark asked Bennet, "Does the gentleman believe that the secret-service men ever kept anybody from being shot?" Without waiting for an answer he shouted, "They did not prevent the shooting of Mr. McKinley."[39]

Eventually Tawney brought the debate back to the loaning of Secret Service operatives to other departments when he introduced his amendment to the Sundry bill, which read, "No part of any money appropriated by this act shall be used in payment or compensation for expenses of any person detailed or transferred from the Secret Service Division of the Treasury Department, or who may at any time during the fiscal year 1909 have been employed in or under said Secret Service Division."[40] Some of the Representatives, such as John J. Fitzgerald of New York, brought up the Pinkerton law that had passed after the Homestead Strike, which prevented government from hiring private detectives, while others pointed out that the loaning of detectives was already a violation of law, and some asked whether or not there should be one investigative agency in government. The debate continued in circles until many of the representatives were tired of the debate and began shouting for a vote. The debate was closed, the vote taken, and the amendment passed.

The next day, the *Evening Star* commended "Representative Tawney of Minnesota, chairman of the appropriations committee," whom they described as a "bitter enemy of the spy system in the United States" who had "mesmerized the chairman of the committee of the whole, and succeeded in securing the adoption of a paragraph limiting the activities of government detectives to the detecting of counterfeiting and the protection of the president.[41] While soaking up all the accolades, that same day Tawney made an even bolder move—a move made to curtail the Secret Service's ability to ever investigate members of Congress again: "Congress pared the appropriation for the Service to the bone."[42] And to curtail not only Treasury's Secret Service but Bonaparte's and Justice's use of them too, the whole committee also "adopted riders to appropriation bills forbidding the attorney general to use appropriated funds to hire Secret Service agents, temporarily or otherwise."[43] Congress, as led by James A. Tawney, had just sent a strong signal to the president that they, not Roosevelt, ran the government, and they would not tolerate their fellow members being investigated or indicted, ever.

There was still hope that the amendment could be killed, for, after passing the subcommittee vote, the bill still had to go before the entire House for a vote. "Various cabinet members joined the President in seeking to prevent the adoption of the Secret Service restrictions," explains historian Gatewood, many of whom argued that the Tawney amendment was a restriction on them as the head of a department.[44]

Even the *New York Times* came out in opposition of the amendment when it reminded its readers that the Secret Service had restored "more than a million acres of the public domain fraudulently obtained by a powerful 'ring' of land thieves." The bill's inclusion of the Tawney amendment, the *Times* said, showed that the Representatives in the House had "unwittingly become the tool of thieves."[45] A *New York Tribune* editorial added that the restriction was being done by congressmen "whose sympathies have been enlisted by men prosecuted for public land and timber frauds, although it is realized that certain business and transportation interests who could greatly augment their profits by wholesale violations of the law are overjoyed."[46] Politicians, newspapers, and the American people were quickly dividing on this topic, and many began taking action.

After reading the *Times*'s editorial, US Attorney Henry Stimson wrote to Attorney General Bonaparte asking, "Is there no way in which the Bill can be stopped in the Senate?"[47] "I should feel as if the fighting power of my office were almost crippled by such a statute," he added.[48] Roosevelt's administration also began working on the Senate, trying to influence them to remove the amendment from their bill so that when it came to reconciliation between the Senate and the House the amendment might stand the chance of being excised from the final bill. It almost worked. At the administration's request, the Senate removed the provision. However, during a conference committee to reconcile the two bills, "at the House's insistence, the Secret Service amendment was re-added to the final measure."[49]

The bill passed on May 17, 1908.

It then went to the president, who had the ability to veto it, but he quickly signed it, for as FBI historian Fox explains, "his complaints were insufficiently strong to risk significant appropriations for key programs," and besides, "a veto would likely have been overridden anyway giving the margins by which the measure passed."[50] An editorial in the *Chicago Tribune* captured the subsequent mood of the country in the aftermath of the bill when it wrote, "All winter there has been an undercurrent of feeling on the part of the heads of executive departments and those associated with them that Congress has been disposed to embarrass the administration whenever it could do so secretly and without attracting the open hostility of the people." In the end, however, the editorial continued, "Appropriations have been withheld, favorite schemes of the president have been ruthlessly pigeon-holed, and curious little provisos have been inserted in appropriations, all of which tend to embarrass the administration of the government."[51]

There was, however, one more way in which Congress could embarrass the president. Although Roosevelt had already more than doubled the size of the Navy since becoming president, he had asked Congress that winter for four more battleships. "Toward the end of May, 1908, as Congress prepared to adjourn so that its members could hurry to their home districts for the coming campaign," explains Roosevelt biographer Pringle, "the friction between the executive and the legislative branches was obvious. Only two battleships had been authorized," and other requests made by the administration "had been killed."[52] Congress left for the summer having further embarrassed the Roosevelt administration.

Theodore Roosevelt, however, was a man of action and one who was never satisfied with just accepting things as they were. He was forever determined to do things on his own terms. And so "no sooner had Congress placed the restriction upon the Secret Service," writes historian Gatewood, "than Roosevelt began to search for means to continue the work previously done by its agents."[53] Over the month of June, Roosevelt and Bonaparte talked about how to go about doing just that, and they soon found a way.

In July of 1908, with absolutely no fanfare, Attorney General Charles J. Bonaparte quietly signed an executive order creating the Bureau of Investigation, a full-time investigative division within the Department of Justice.[54] If Congress wouldn't allow departments outside of Treasury to borrow Secret Service agents or create a central bureau of investigation inside Justice, then Roosevelt's executive branch would simply resort to method that had been used to create the United States Secret Service in 1865: they just did it.

President Roosevelt pictured with his Attorney General Charles Joseph Bonaparte who was instrumental in the creation of the Bureau of Investigation.
Photo courtesy of the Library of Congress.

10

The Bureau of Investigation

The Constitution of the United States authorizes the president to "take Care that the Laws be faithfully executed."[1] As the head of the executive branch—that branch which is organized to administrate the bureaucracy that ensures the laws are executed—the president wields an enormous amount of power. While Congress is the branch that makes the laws, it is the president who carries them out and ensures they are enforced. And although the Constitution gives Congress the power of oversight, generally exercised through their ability to call forth cabinet-level officials to testify before their committees, the only way they can truly control the executive branch is to modify past laws or create new ones. When it comes to the formal powers of the presidency, then, it is, as Constitutional law expert Arthur S. Miller once explained, "a vessel into which Chief Executives can pour almost anything they wish—or, rather, anything that the operation of the political process permits them to get away with. Nowhere is this better seen than in the area of enforcement of the laws."[2] Thus, when enforcing the laws that Congress passed, in a sense, the president rules supreme.

Theodore Roosevelt, perhaps better than any other president up to that point in time, understood this. He knew that the ability to enforce the law gave the president enormous power, for it was through this enforcement ability that he could influence public policy. Having served as police commissioner of New York City and as a member of the Civil Service Commission, among many other roles, Roosevelt understood the importance of law and law enforcement, which was evidenced by his tough enforcement of the land-fraud laws. By enforcing those laws to the fullest extent, he was also able to control national policy in the area of natural resources, and the public was largely on his side. The only way Congress could take away his ability to control national policy was to modify old laws or pass new ones. By modifying the laws regarding the transfer of the Secret Service operatives to other departments, Congress undercut the president and took away his administration's ability to effectively enforce not only the land fraud laws but many other laws as well. Yet, as Miller said, the system allows the president to do almost anything he can get away with, and Roosevelt understood this too. For "after the restrictive amendment was approved," writes FBI historian Don Whitehead, "word spread through the Department of Justice that President Roosevelt had called Attorney General Bonaparte to the White House."[3] Roosevelt was about to see how much he could get away with.

As Roosevelt saw it, the passage of the Tawney amendment had changed everything. Historian Gatewood explains, "Earlier, when Bonaparte and Roosevelt had broached the subject of such a bureau, both had indicated that its establishment would require congressional approval." However, after the amendment's passage, combined with "the recalcitrant attitude of Congress in general," Roosevelt's perspective changed. This action, Gatewood continues, "apparently helped persuade them"—Roosevelt and Bonaparte—"that some form of detective agency could be created within the Justice Department by executive action alone."[4] For Bonaparte, as criminal-justice historian Friedman explains, "When Congress failed to give him what he wanted, he struck out on his own."[5] As for Roosevelt, Mark Twain once satirically observed, he was always "ready to kick the Constitution into the back yard whenever it gets in the way."[6] Both of these men were ready to take action; they merely needed to find a justification for them.

They first looked at the mission of the attorney general's Department of Justice—and more specifically at its budget. What they found was that under the original 1870 law establishing the DOJ, the attorney general was allowed to disburse funds as he saw fit. Still further, in the current appropriations by Congress, the Department of Justice was authorized funds for "the detection and prosecution of crimes."[7]

Taken together, Roosevelt and Bonaparte had their justification: "Their reasoning was that the department received an annual appropriation for 'the detection and prosecution of crimes,' and that funds from this appropriation previously expended for the services of personnel borrowed from the Secret Service could be used to bear the cost of a small detective force responsible directly to the attorney general."[8] This belief was also shared by many others in the Department of Justice, including Stanley W. Finch, who had joined Justice as a clerk and risen to the position of chief examiner. In a letter to a colleague, Finch explained that, to his mind, Congress had simply left them no choice, having essentially forced them to create a bureau of investigation "for the purpose of doing the work heretofore done by the people borrowed from [Secret Service chief,] Mr. Wilkie."[9] The Department of Justice needed to conduct investigations, and so if they could no longer borrow agents, then within the confines of the laws they were forced to create their own. And that is exactly what Theodore Roosevelt did when he directed Bonaparte "to organize an investigative service."[10]

As President Theodore Roosevelt and Attorney General Bonaparte both realized, the law essentially allowed Bonaparte to take this action on his own. No formal orders were needed, and so none were issued; or, to put it more plainly, there was nothing put into writing. However, word spread throughout the Department of Justice, and everyone knew where the order had come from. "A memorandum in the FBI files written by old-time Agent James G. Findlay" conveys that it was common knowledge in the department how "President Roosevelt directed Bonaparte to create an investigative service within the Department of Justice subject to no other department or bureau, which would report to no one except the Attorney General."[11] Bonaparte, it would seem, had his marching orders.

Bonaparte, of course, did not take action until Congress was back home in their respective states and districts, beginning to campaign for the fall 1908 elections. Once their attention was turned elsewhere, but before the Tawney amendment took effect on July 1, Bonaparte "dipped into the Justice Department's expense fund to hire eight veteran Secret Service agents as permanent full-time investigators."[12] As FBI historian Fox explains, "Within days of this deadline, Attorney General Bonaparte began a small reorganization of [the] Justice Department to address the impending loss of access to the Secret Service operatives. With little fanfare, he began to group together the sundry investigators of the department and nine Secret Service agents permanently hired as Justice special agents."[13]

The actual date is of hire is unconfirmed, as various historians list different dates: Holden says July 26, 1908; Theoharis, June 29; and a letter involving Secret Service chief Wilkie regarding the transfer of the Secret Service operatives suggests it was July 27.[14] Historian Gatewood simply says it was some time "shortly before July 1, 1908."[15] Whatever the actual date was, Secret Service operatives resigned from their positions at Treasury before being given appointments within Justice.

The historical record also is unclear on the actual number of Secret Service men transferred: most say nine, but some say eight, and others, ten.[16] The numbers were further confused by the fact that although Secret Service operatives formed the nucleus of the new agency, many agents already in the employ of the Department of Justice were also transferred over to the new bureau.

For example, FBI historian Henry M. Holden writes that "On July 26, 1908, ten Secret Service operatives of the Treasury Department were transferred and appointed permanent special agents of the Justice Department," and these men, "together, with thirteen investigators who had been employed on peonage cases, and twelve examiners provided for by statute, constituted the founding members of the investigative force."[17] According to another FBI historian, Theoharis, "on June 29, 1908, Bonaparte hired 10 former Secret Service agents as Justice Department employees and funded this through a 'miscellaneous expense fund.'"[18] Yet another FBI historian, Weiner, writes more sensationally that Bonaparte had to "beg, borrow, or steal the money and the men the president wanted."[19] It appears that he neither begged, borrowed, nor stole any money, as the Department of Justice's budget already contained ample funds. All Bonaparte had to do was reorganize both personnel and the accounts from which they would be paid. Neither does it appear he had any trouble securing the men, as the departments involved appeared to be in total agreement and the men transferred willingly.

Evidence of the peaceful transfer comes from a letter chief of Secret Service John Wilkie wrote to his operatives to be transferred. The transfer, he wrote, was "a fortunate solution of what might otherwise be hardship to agents whose services could not be retained in this division beyond the close of the present fiscal year."[20] As Congress had also decided to cut the Secret Service's operating budget, Wilkie knew he was going to have to let some of his men go. Knowing this made it much easier for him to justify letting them leave Justice. As Wilkie explained to them, "You have doubtless observed that the appropriation for Suppressing Counterfeiting was reduced at the last session of Congress, and this in itself would necessitate the curtailment of the field force in the division during the coming fiscal year. The contemplated appointment in the Department of Justice offers a fortunate solution of what might otherwise be a hardship to agents whose services could not be retained in this division beyond the close of the present fiscal year."[21]

So action needed to be taken quickly. Chief Wilkie wrote: "In order to meet certain demands of the Department of Justice for the investigation of crimes, and to conform strictly with the provisions of the Sundry Civil Act for the fiscal year 1909 the Attorney General will appoint as Special Agents in the Department of Justice a number of agents recommended by this division. For the purpose of completing the record of the Treasury Department in all cases in which the Attorney General contemplates an appointment, you will please sign the enclosed resignation and return it promptly to this office."[22] This resignation was in everyone's best interest, but it did run somewhat counter to the spirit of what Congress had intended in the Tawney amendment. When Tawney himself later obtained a copy of this very letter, he was livid.

In the end, as Gatewood explains, some time "shortly before July 1, 1908, the date the Sundry Civil Appropriation Act went into effect, President Roosevelt authorized the transfer of nine men in the Secret Service Division to the Justice Department."[23] Yet this isn't quite accurate. Many have mistakenly claimed President Theodore Roosevelt signed an executive order creating the bureau.[24] However, there exists no presidential executive order creating the new agency. Rather, the executive order was actually issued by the Department of Justice and signed by Attorney General Bonaparte.[25] But this wasn't to happen until later in the month of July, nearly a month after the agents had begun to assemble the new agency.

The first special agent assigned to the newly formed Bureau of Investigation was Harry R. Jentzer. Born on February 11, 1880, in New York City, Jentzer attended public schools there and then worked for a short time as a "resident buyer for several out-of-town department stores." He entered government service in 1904 when he began conducting investigations under US Attorneys Henry L. Wise and Harry L. Stimson. In May of 1906 he was appointed to the Department of Justice to work on naturalization-fraud cases in New York City. In that role, he made a name for himself as a highly successful investigator. So when Justice looked to organize the new bureau in late June of 1908, Jentzer was the first person asked to became a special agent. It was another of the first special agents, Jack Buckley, who recalled how, "On that bright morning of June 29, 1908, when Edward J. Brennan came on duty as an agent he thought he was the first of the crop but when he walked in there was Harry J. Jentzer acting like a veteran because he had been around since 1906. It seems beyond dispute that Harry was the first as far as members of . . . [the Society of Former Special Agents of the FBI] are concerned."[26]

Special Agent Jentzer went on to make a name for himself, including the capture of several German spies during World

War I and tracking down con man David Lamar in Mexico, the original "Wolf of Wall Street." Jentzer retired from the FBI in 1926 and died on December 26, 1958.

The special agent who'd been surprised to learn he wasn't first in the bureau, Edward J. Brennan, did, however, hold the distinction of being the first of the nine Secret Service operatives to be transferred from the Treasury Department to the Justice Department to serve in the new Bureau of Investigation. Born in Saint Louis, Missouri, Brennan had begun his law-enforcement career in 1894 when he was appointed deputy marshal. He later transferred to the Saint Louis Police Department, where he worked as detective. Then in 1907 he accepted a position with the Secret Service, where his extensive background in investigations quickly mad him a prized operative. So in June of 1908 he was the first of the Secret Service operatives asked by Chief Wilkie to transfer to the new bureau.

Brennan went on to conduct successful investigations in the "sugar fraud" cases of that time period—cases in which the sugar industry was attempting to cheat the government of tariffs from the importation of sugar—and he was involved in the investigation into the 1910 bombing of the *Los Angeles Times* Building.[27] He eventually transferred to the Chicago office, where he rose to the rank of special agent in charge. He retired from the bureau in 1924, but by then, his son, John Brennan, had been appointed special agent, working the famous John Dillinger gangster case and helping track down Martin Durkin, murderer of Special Agent Edwin C. Shanahan, the first bureau agent killed in the line of duty.

The nine men who transferred from the Secret Service, along with an estimated thirteen personnel "already employed in the department in connection with land fraud and peonage cases, were designated special agents," and they were "directly responsible to Chief Examiner Stanley W. Finch, who received from them daily reports, which he summarized for review by the attorney general." Finch had been in on the creation of the new agency, and Bonaparte had asked him to take over leadership of the men. Then, in a series of letters, Bonaparte and Finch, along with the assistance of federal attorneys Stimson from New

York and Edwin W. Sims from Illinois, worked out the legal details and mission of the new bureau.[28]

Bonaparte and Finch focused on the investigations the new agents would undertake, while Stimson and Sims worked out the legalities of how to operate within the existing laws and the Constitution. As Bonaparte and Finch worked over those weeks, they avoided bringing any attention to the new organization. Their plan was to work out all of the details in advance of Congress's return for the fall session, making sure the agency was up and running, conducting investigations, and that all the legalities were settled before objections could be made.

Not of least importance was what to call the new agency. Although the Bureau of Investigation was favored, they felt it would draw too much attention, especially after Bonaparte had used that very name for the proposed agency when he had testified before Congress. So they took to calling their new organization "the new Special Agent Force."[29] That was considered sufficiently vague.

Then, on July 26, 1908, the day typically given as the birthdate of the Federal Bureau of Investigation, Attorney General Bonaparte issued the Department of Justice executive order formally establishing "a new investigative division with a thirty-man force of 'special agents.'"[30] "All matters relating to investigations under the Department," Bonaparte wrote,

> except those to be made by bank examiners, and in connection with the naturalization service, will be referred to the Chief Examiner for a memorandum as to whether any member of the force of Special Agents under his direction is available for the work to be performed. No authorization of expenditure for special examination shall be made by any officer of the Department, without first ascertaining whether one of the regular force is available for the service desired, and in case the service cannot be performed by the regular force of Special Agents in the Department, the matter will be called to the attention of the Attorney General, or Acting Attorney General, together with a statement from the Chief Examiner as to the reason why a regular employee cannot be assigned to the work, before authorization shall be made for the expenditure of any money for this purpose. Charles J. Bonaparte, Attorney General.[31]

Bonaparte had simply ordered all attorneys at Justice to refer any investigative requests to Stanley W. Finch, the chief examiner, and he would determine if there were enough special agents available to conduct the investigation.[32] The organization was, for all intents and purposes, up and running.

And while the new Special Agent Force was busy organizing and conducting the first of its investigations, the two men who would clash head-on were busy with summer vacations and preparations for fall elections. Roosevelt spent his final summer as president in Oyster Bay at his home on Sagamore Hill, known widely as the "Summer White House." The US Olympic team and their managers, having earned forty-seven medals, including twenty-three gold, at the London games, went to visit him at his home toward the end of that summer.[33] Despite the appearance that he was having a relaxing time at home, entertaining various guests, behind the scenes Roosevelt was doing what he could to help elect his chosen successor, William Howard Taft.

At first it seemed Roosevelt was going to play a major role in Taft's campaign, but that was not to be. When Grover Cleveland had died, Taft had visited Roosevelt at Oyster Bay to—as he openly told the press—confer about his speech, which he'd then delivered at the funeral in Cincinnati.[34] This had proven, however, to be the beginning of the end of Taft's dependency on Roosevelt; for upon announcing a visit, Taft had declared himself in need of "the President's judgement and criticism,"[35] which was taken as a sign of weakness, leaving his detractors to say that Taft was unable to act independently. His opponents took full advantage in exploiting this perception, which damaged Taft early in his campaign. And so he quickly began to distance himself from Roosevelt.

As the summer came to a close with the Labor Day weekend, the importance of the Secret Service was underscored for Roosevelt when a mentally unstable man came calling to Oyster Bay, possibly to assassinate the president. According to the Washington *Evening Star*, "A crank armed with an antiquated 'bull-dog' revolver was caught near the President's house at Sagamore Hill by the secret service guards."[36]

The man had reached Oyster Bay station on the 12:18 train and then walked the three miles to Sagamore Hill. He arrived on the grounds shortly after two o'clock in the afternoon, approaching on the road that led to the president's house, forking at the tennis courts some two hundred yards from the house, where it forms a loop in front of the home. The two Secret Service operatives on duty that day had been stationed at either end of the house. Because the house sits atop a hill, their position commanded views of both roads after the fork at the tennis courts.

One of the rules for visitors at Sagamore Hill during Roosevelt's presidency was that "no one shall come on foot." So when Secret Service Operative John Adams caught sight of a man "toiling up the hill road, he guessed that something was wrong and motioned for the man to go back." The man did not stop and continued walking toward Adams, who then moved toward the suspect. As Adams approached him, he demanded to know what he was doing there, prompting the man to present his "card," which bore the name John Coughlin and identified him as a detective and an "officer." He claimed he had come "to confer with President Roosevelt concerning the recent outrages by yeggmen [burglars] in Boston and to lead back such troops as the President thought it fit to order out."[37]

Operative Adams informed Coughlin that the president was not seeing visitors at the moment and that Coughlin needed to leave the grounds immediately or face arrest. That was when Coughlin reached behind his back, into a back pocket of his pants. Adams reacted, grabbing Coughlin and placing him in his custody. The struggle did not last long, for Coughlin was described as a "slightly built man." At this point, Operative James Sloan Jr. arrived to assist and, after searching him, they pulled a ".32-caliber revolver of the 'bulldog' type" out of Coughlin's pocket.[38] The gun, which had been wrapped in a small wool bag, was not loaded.

They soon identified the man as John Coughlin of Walpole, Massachusetts. He had been in and out of mental institutions and had been missing from his home for the past ten days. He was taken into custody and evaluated by physicians, who declared him insane and ordered him to be sent to the asylum at Kings Park.[39]

The *New York Times*'s story was a bit more sensational, reporting that Roosevelt had been out horseback riding with a friend when a gun was fired. It was said that the "bullet went over the President's head." The *Times* also noted that the "whizz was so distinct that the President reined in his horse, looked sharply about, and not seeing anyone or hearing any further noise, galloped home." The Secret Service searched for the shooter, but they were unable to find anyone; later, Coughlin showed up. The paper did add that Coughlin claimed he was a detective for the "Unelected Congress of Massachusetts."[40]

The following day, the *Times* clarified the shooting story, saying the president and his friend had heard gunshots in the distance, once while riding and once while swimming in Cold Spring Harbor. They later learned it had been Jack Roosevelt who had been target shooting out back. This report added that Secret Service chief John Wilkie had visited Coughlin's home in Walpole and, after speaking with many people there, had learned that Coughlin was known to have a long history of mental illness.[41]

After this little incident at Sagamore Hill was resolved, all eyes turned toward politics, for the campaign season "began in earnest after Labor Day." Roosevelt was ready to throw himself into the campaign after his summer rest, still hoping to play a major role in Taft's election. Yet the further the campaign moved along, the less Taft sought out the president's advice. Taft now had his own handlers advising him, and avoiding Roosevelt was one of their foremost suggestions. So, after returning to Washington in mid-September, Roosevelt "plunged into the only kind of campaign work he could do, barring a request (which never came) to tour on behalf of Taft. He fired off a series of press statements and public letters attacking every candidate in the Democratic ranks who seemed vulnerable to charges of corruption, or any other sins on the calendar of human frailty."[42] The president's October proved to be very busy.

The election was held on November 3, 1908. President Roosevelt had kept his promise to not seek a third term of office and had been explicit in his support of William Howard Taft, his close friend and Secretary of War, to become his successor in office. Taft's Democratic opponent was William Jennings Bryan, the three-time Democratic nominee who had run previously in the 1896 and 1900 campaigns, losing both times to William McKinley. After sitting out the 1904 election, Bryan had been brought back to run against Taft. Although he had handily captured the Southern vote, it was not enough to overcome either the popular vote or, more importantly, the electoral vote, which he lost, 321 to 162. Upon hearing the election results, Roosevelt was heard to say, "We have beaten them to a frazzle!"[43]

Now entering a transition period—one to power and one to retirement—both men were somewhat apprehensive over what was to come. Taft was described as being "in reality depressed and wishing that he was headed for the Supreme Court," while Roosevelt lamented, "If I had conscientiously felt at liberty to run again, and try once more to hold this great office, I should greatly have liked to do so and to continue to keep my hands on the levers of the mighty machine."[44] Alas, it was not meant to be. Taft was to become the twenty-seventh president of the United States when he took office on March 4, 1909, and Theodore Roosevelt was now a lame-duck president. However, in typical Rooseveltian fashion, he chose not to act like one.

Meanwhile, in Minnesota, James A. Tawney had been re-elected to Congress to serve his states' first congressional district in the House of Representatives. He had run against Democratic candidate Andrew French, handily beating him, and thus was headed back to Washington to resume his position as chairman of the House Committee on Appropriations. Upon his return to the capital, Tawney found a House of Representatives that was very little changed for the coming term: the Democrats had managed to gain a small number of seats, but the Republicans had retained their power, which was good for Tawney. While it is unknown exactly when Tawney learned of the creation of the new bureau, it was most likely some time during the late summer or before the election. The election assuredly overshadowed anything in that regard, and although the fight was by no means forgotten, the election of Taft had changed the dynamic.

Everyone felt the new president-elect was more malleable than Roosevelt, and certainly less polarizing. So, though Tawney continued to gather information on the new bureau—such as obtaining a copy of the letter from Chief Wilkie to the transferring operatives—he took no immediate action and remained silent on the issue for the time being upon his return to Washington.

Tawney would likely have received information on the new agency, and the justification for its existence, through the attorney general's annual report. The release of the report had been, in truth, the first formal announcement of the new agency's existence. As FBI historian Fox surmises, "When Bonaparte announced the creation of a special agent force to Congress that fall in his Annual Report, he must have considered the action a *fait accompli*."[45] The agency had already been created, Bonaparte surely thought, and the new agents were hard at work, meaning, therefore, that any discussion of their work must consider them to be just another part of the existing Department of Justice.

The AG's report was issued publically on December 18, 1908, but no doubt Congress had already received their copies earlier. "It has been the duty of this department," Bonaparte opened the report, "to continue the enforcement of the several statutes intended to protect the interstate and foreign commerce of the country."[46] While he spoke of enforcing the laws, he did not initially mention the new bureau of investigation. Several pages later he did mention the "peonage and land-fraud prosecutions" but still made no mention of the bureau. When he did finally get to it, it was given its own section, titled "The New Special Agent Force," at which point he introduced to Congress what he and Roosevelt had been up to during the summer.[47] Bonaparte wrote:

> In my last annual report I called attention to the fact that this department was obliged to call upon the Treasury Department for detective service and had, in fact, no permanent executive force directly under its orders. Through the prohibition of its further use of the secret service force, contained in the sundry civil appropriation act, approved May 27, 1908, it became necessary for the department to organize a small force of special agents of its own. Although such action was involuntary on

the part of the department, the consequences of the innovation have been, on the whole, moderately satisfactory. The special agents, placed as they are under the direct orders of the chief examiner, who receives from them daily reports and summarized these for submission each day to the Attorney-General, are directly controlled by this department, and the Attorney-General knows, or ought to know, at all times what they are doing and at what cost. Under these circumstances he may be justly held responsible for the efficiency and economy of the service rendered. The experience of the past six months has shown clearly that such a force is, under modern conditions, absolutely indispensable to the proper discharge of the duties of this department, and it is hoped that its merits will be augmented and its attendant expense reduced by further experience.[48]

For Bonaparte, it was indeed a fait accompli: he'd had had no choice but to create the new bureau. And "after the return of Congress, Mr. Bonaparte defended his actions on the grounds that his police force was very small, that it was an 'innovation,' and that in any events its creation was 'involuntary' as far as he was concerned. He took the position that the responsibility for the birth of the new police organization could not be laid at his door; Congress, by preventing him from hiring Treasury detectives, had forced his hand."[49] And now that the bureau was up and running, Bonaparte added that it was doing an excellent job and should be funded by Congress.

From the perspective of the legislature, however, this was an affront—both to them and to the intent of the Tawney amendment. Roosevelt and Bonaparte's brash move could have proven to disastrous, for "the establishment of the Bureau of Investigation contravened the spirit of Congress's actions of 1907 and 1908, and Bonaparte's decision alone did not ensure the Bureau's status—Congress could have countered his move by restricting the use of contingency funds or by rescinding the 'detection' section of the 1870 statute defining the Justice Department's power."[50] However, they chose not to do so. Why is largely unknown, but perhaps they intended to address the problem after the New Year or after the new Congress and president were seated. In any case, they never got the chance, because Roosevelt, despite being a lame duck, went on the attack, entirely changing the game.

Perhaps knowing that Congress could have attacked first upon their return is why Roosevelt stole the initiative. Or, perhaps it was because he wanted to expose what Congress had been trying to cover up with the passage of the Secret Service amendment. Or perhaps Roosevelt's pugnacious nature learned from his days of boxing insisted that he keep fighting until the bell rings. Whatever the case may be, on December 8, 1908, when Roosevelt released his Special Message to Congress, the he went on the attack, sending Congress—and especially James A. Tawney —into a tailspin.

Official portrait of Stanley Willington Finch, the first director of the [Federal] Bureau of Investigation.
Photo courtesy of the Library of Congress.

11

Born in Controversy

With the results of the fall elections of 1908 tallied, Congress began its return to Washington for the remainder of their session before the Christmas break. There was little discussion among them about the Tawney amendment to the Secret Service appropriations bill, and neither was there apparently much discussion regarding the creation of the Bureau of Investigation. The bureau was up and running, and everything was proceeding as if the agency had always. It truly was a fait accompli—that is, at least until December 8, 1908, the Tuesday on which Roosevelt delivered his eighth, and final, annual message to Congress.

The message was delivered simultaneously to Congress and the press.

In past administrations the messages had been issued to Congress in advance of its public release, which made this release a break in protocol. Speaker of the House Joe Cannon noted this in his memoir: "I was not consulted about President Roosevelt's last annual Message, nor was it submitted to me in advance of publication, as had been all of the former Messages of Mr. Roosevelt."[1] It mattered little, for it was the last message of a lame-duck president who would no longer be in office come March 4, 1909, only three months away.

It is said that the members of both chambers were gathered together to hear the president's message "read from the desk."[2]

Several clerks had been assigned to read the entire message to those in attendance, which were, in actuality, very few. "In part because the president was now a lame duck, and therefore his words no longer mattered much to Congress, and in part because he had written so confoundingly of them," writes historian Jim Rasenberger, not much attention was paid to Roosevelt's message. In fact, "both chambers were nearly empty as the reading clerks droned through it," and "those few in attendance chatted among themselves, wrote letters, and scanned newspapers." It was a monotonous affair, for "Page after page, the message promised little in the way of news." It was nothing more than "boilerplate Roosevelt."[3]

As the clerks took turns reading, the message at first mentioned the government's finances, which Roosevelt believed to be "excellent."[4] He then addressed the issue of corporations, the Interstate Commerce Commission, and antitrust laws. He addressed the work of labor and the courts before turning to his esteemed conservation policies, including the forests, inland waterways, and national parks. He gave a quick mention to denatured alcohol, pure food, and Indian service, among other topics, before finally turning attention to the Secret Service, which, Rasenberger noted, "was buried about fourteen thousand words into the message."[5]

"Last year," Roosevelt opened this section,

> an amendment was incorporated in the measure providing for the Secret Service, which provided that there should be no detail from the Secret Service and no transfer therefrom. It is not too much to say that this amendment has been of benefit only, and could be of benefit only, to the criminal classes. If deliberately introduced for the purpose of diminishing the effectiveness of war against crime it could not have been better devised to this end. It forbade the practices that had been followed to a greater or less extent by the executive heads of various departments for twenty years. To these practices we owe the securing of the evidence which enabled us to drive great lotteries out of business and secure a quarter of a million of dollars in fines from their promoters. These practices have enabled us to get some of the evidence indispensable in order in connection with

the theft of government land and government timber by great corporations and by individuals. These practices have enabled us to get some of the evidence indispensable in order to secure the conviction of the wealthiest and most formidable criminals with whom the Government has to deal, both those operating in violation of the anti-trust law and others. The amendment in question was of benefit to no one excepting to these criminals, and it seriously hampers the Government in the detection of crime and the securing of justice. Moreover, it not only affects departments outside of the Treasury, but it tends to hamper the Secretary of the Treasury himself in the effort to utilize the employees of his department so as to best meet the require-ments of the public service. It forbids him from preventing frauds upon the customs service, from investigating irregu-larities in branch mints and assay offices, and has seriously crippled him. It prevents the promotion of employees in the Secret Service, and this further discourages good effort. In its present form the restriction operates only to the advantage of the criminal, of the wrongdoer.[6]

The first paragraph was really nothing more than a review of the problems the president saw coming out of the inclusion of the Tawney amendment and the problems it posed for the executive branch. While Congress probably did not want to have the issue put before the American people in this manner, had Roosevelt left it at that, it probably would have angered Congress but likely would not have evoked an official response. But in the second paragraph, Roosevelt's disgust with Congress came into full display, and he had to have known it would un-leash the full wrath of Congress. "The chief argument in favor of the provision," the president continued,

was that the Congressmen did not themselves wish to be in-vestigated by Secret Service men. Very little of such investiga-tion has been done in the past; but it is true that the work of the Secret Service agents was partly responsible for the indict-ment and conviction of a Senator and a Congressman for land frauds in Oregon. I do not believe that it is in the public inter-est to protect criminally in any branch of the public service, and exactly as we have again and again during the past seven years prosecuted and convicted such criminals who were in the executive branch of the Government, so in my belief we should be given ample means to prosecute them if found in the legislative branch. But if this is not considered desirable a special exception could be made in the law prohibiting the use of the Secret Service force in investigating members of the Congress. It would be far better to do this than to do what actually was done, and strive to prevent or at least to hamper effective action against criminals by the executive branch of the Government.[7]

Those few in attendance were astounded by the president's allegations and likely did not hear the rest of the message. Many approached the clerks for a copy of the message to verify what they had heard—that the Tawney amendment had been created and passed to prevent members of Congress from being investigated. Word began to spread to those who either had not been paying attention or had not been in attendance. "By the next morning, members of Congress had been alerted to the offending section of Roosevelt's message and had worked themselves up into a lather of indignation. The president had essentially accused them of criminal conduct, it was an outrage, a calumny that demanded a strong rebuke."[8] As the *New York Times* so plainly stated it, "Nothing that Mr. Roosevelt has done in his seven years in the White House has so stirred up members of Congress."[9]

Why kick the hornet's nest? Roosevelt was a lame-duck president, unlikely to change Congress's mind on the matter, and his Bureau of Investigation was already operational. So why would the president decide to make a statement knowing full well it would raise the ire of Congress? "In view of the circumstances," Gatewood points out, it makes sense to "ask why Roosevelt renewed the controversy by a pointed reference to it in his last annual message in December 1908."[10]

Perhaps the most obvious answer to the question is the president's nature. Roosevelt was always known for having "a reputation for impetuosity and pugnacity." As his biographer Miller explains, "Roosevelt's aggressiveness is often linked to his boyhood struggle against illness, to his father's failure to fight in the Civil War, and the tales of derring-do related by his Confederate uncles."[11] Yet, as his biographer Edmund Morris explains, "In youth, the aggressive impulse had predominated, but in maturity he had strengthened himself to a state of containment."[12] And yet he still decided to insult Congress. As Gatewood asserts in his book on *Theodore Roosevelt and the Art of Controversy*, "Despite what has been called the 'impolitic' nature of the message generally, his 'affinity for controversy' scarcely seems to offer a satisfactory explanation." Having explored Roosevelt's political astuteness when it came to engaging in controversy, Gatewood believes Roosevelt's impulse originated from "something more than merely a desire to strike back at a Congress which had stubbornly rejected his proposals was involved."[13]

Considering Theodore Roosevelt's beliefs, much of the controversy would have centered on his life's work in public service—exposing and stopping corruption. The fact that his administration had exposed corruption within Congress, which had led to indictments and, in at least one case, imprisonment, may very well have been his motivation. "He was convinced," Gatewood explains, "that his role in sending certain members of Congress to the penitentiary for violations of the land laws was the primary reason for the passage of the restrictive amendment."[14]

One of the president's closest friends, military officer Archibald Butt, once conveyed that Roosevelt believed corruption had "made its last stand just where it was least expected, namely Congress."[15] Roosevelt discussed his frustration on this very topic with his friend, writing, "How can I hunt out corruption, or even know that it exists unless I have the use of men who know where it is and how to get at the facts? I have pledged myself to wage war on corruption and graft wherever they can be found, and the higher up the criminal may be, the more necessary it is to strike him down. I want the people to know what I know and then it makes no matter how lenient a President may want to be, he will have to account to the people if corruption goes unchastised."[16] The Secret Service amendment embodied this most important issue, central to Roosevelt's life's work, which goes a long way in explaining his willingness to fight Congress to the end on the subject.

But this letter to Butt suggests something interesting: In addition to the issue of corruption, Roosevelt mentions the importance of letting the people know what was going on. When the Tawney amendment had been debated, the press mostly covered the Congressional viewpoint, leaving Roosevelt to feel that his administration's reasons for killing the amendment had not been adequately explained to the American people. "It is also conceivable," explains Gatewood, "that Roosevelt, always concerned about his historical reputation, may have addressed his remarks on the Secret Service as much to posterity as to the public of his own day."[17]

But there is yet another possible explanation for Roosevelt's shot: There may have been little hope that the Tawney amendment would ever be repealed or the Secret Service budget increased in the coming years, thus hamstringing that agency. Furthermore, there was nothing to say that Congress couldn't do the same thing with the newly created Bureau of Investigation—restricting its budget and ability to use its own detectives. And were other means by which Congress could hamper the newly formed bureau; as FBI historian Theoharis explains it, "Congress could have countered his move by restricting the use of contingency funds or by rescinding the 'detection' section of the 1870 statute defining the Justice Department's power."[18] This makes it all the more likely that Roosevelt went on the attack to expose the issue to the public in order to check the possibility that Congress would try to alter his creation of the new bureau.

Regardless of the reason for his decision to reprimand Congress for its Secret Service amendment, "the reaction in Congress was immediate and vehement."[19] As Congress absorbed what the president had said and began reacting to it, the newspapers were there to record it all.

On the following day, the *Washington Post* reported, "About the only thing in the last annual message of President Roosevelt talked about by members of the two houses of Congress yesterday was that portion relating to the secret-service branch of the Treasury and the alleged plain intimation that Congress placed limitations upon the appropriations for that bureau, so that these detectives could not be utilized to investigate the affairs of congressmen themselves." The editors of that newspaper also added, "It is idle to attempt to conceal the fact that both senators and members of the House are indignant over the language used by the President, and while none would discuss the matter for publication, many privately asserted that the President went out of his way to arraign Congress."[20]

Even members of Roosevelt's own party and those who were sympathetic to him were taken aback by the message. Speaker of the House "Uncle Joe" Cannon certainly had an insightful view to his chamber's reactions. In his memoir, relayed to his private secretary, L. White Busbey, Cannon later recalled, "I was a much surprised as any one when it was found that this Message contained an assault upon Congress, and especially upon the House of Representatives, because of the amendment limiting the activities of the Secret Service." Because of his position as the speaker, Cannon was well aware of how Roosevelt's move was perceived by both chambers of Congress. "It caused a storm on both sides of the Chamber, and members were ready and eager at once to pass a vote of censure and return the Message to the President with the announcement that the House of Representatives would not receive a message of that character from the President."[21]

And Cannon had taken action as soon as the clerks had finished reading the annual message—including the parts read after the Secret Service section, about education, public health, and foreign affairs, which no one heard. Cannon "called to the desk leaders on both sides of the Chamber, counselled moderation and suggested that the House could not afford to be precipitate or do an offensive thing because it believed that the President had been offensive and advised adjournment without taking any action." He then asked key leaders to move the discussion to the privacy of his own office. Once there, "In further conference in the Speaker's Room it was decided a special committee should be appointed to consider the action to be taken. It was also agreed that no member of the Committee on Appropriations to whom the President had made personal reference, or any other member who had cause for personal feelings, should have anything to do with the decision."[22] Cannon had, wisely, called for a cooling-off period.

On December 11, 1908, when the House was once again in session, the issue was first visited. Representative James Breck Perkins of New York "rose to a question of privilege and offered a resolution calling attention to the offensive language used by the President and providing for a special committee to report to the House."[23] Perkins put forth House resolution 451, resolved "whereas there was contained in the sundry civil appropriation bill which passed Congress at its last session and became a law a provision in reference to the employment of the Secret Service in the Treasury Department." The recital portion of the resolution referenced the President's address, repeating almost the entire second paragraph. It then concluded, "Now, therefore be it *Resolved*. That a committee of five Members of this House be appointed by the Speaker, to consider the statements contained in the message of the President and report to the House what action, if any, should be taken in reference thereto."[24] The counterassault had begun.

After the resolution had been read to the House by the clerk, Perkins, as most congressmen are wont to do, felt obliged to make a short speech. "It is of importance to the Republic," he told the chamber, "that all of the coordinate branches of the Government should possess, in a high degree, the confidence and respect of the people. I yield to no one in my respect for the Chief Executive of the United States; and I yield to no one in my respect for the Congress of the United States."[25]

This was met by loud applause.

Perkins, after a short pause, continued: "To the Congress is granted great power, and upon it are imposed great responsibilities. We can not neglect our duties nor shirk our responsibilities. . . . The dignity of that body should not be punctiliously insisted upon, but it should be properly maintained. The statements made by the President of the United States can not be lightly disregarded. They may be so construed by the public as to lessen the dignity and thereby impair the usefulness of the Congress of the United States."[26]

The speech was short, and when he had concluded he asked that the resolution be adopted "without debate and without dissent."[27] This too was met with loud applause.

The question was then taken, and the resolution was agreed to. Speaker Cannon then made his appointment of five members—"Mr. Perkins, Mr. Denby, Mr. Weeks, Mr. Williams, and Mr. Lloyd"[28]—chosen for their perceived impartiality. The committee chair, Congressman Perkins, a fellow Republican, "was one of the President's warm personal friends," Cannon later recalled in his memoirs, "from his own state, and had always been identified with his supporters in New York. He was Chairman of the Committee on Foreign Affairs, a scholar and an author, and one of the most even-tempered men in the House. No better man could have been selected for such a delicate duty." As for "Mr. Denby, of Michigan, Mr. Weeks, of Massachusetts, Republicans; and Mr. Williams, of Mississippi, and Mr. Lloyd, of Missouri, Democrats," he recalled, "the three Republicans were all warm personal friends of President Roosevelt and none of them had ever had any differences with him over legislation or patronage. Mr. Williams was the minority leader of the House and Mr. Lloyd was the Chairman of the Democratic caucus."[29]

The Senate waited a few days after the House had formed its committee to take action. On December 16, resolutions were introduced in the Senate to place the matter in the hands of the committee on appropriations to determine what action, if any, should be taken. The resolution was introduced by Senator Aldrich from New Jersey and was read aloud to the Senate. The resolution asked the committee to determine whether the Sundry bill had "impaired the efficiency or sufficiency of the force employed in the secret service." It also directed the committee to ascertain "what persons other than those included in the Secret Service were paid from the Public Treasury during the fiscal year [1908] for service in connection with the enforcement of the laws or for work in the detection or investigation of possible crimes." And, finally, the committee was ordered to "report as soon as practicable, from time to time," the progress of their inquiries.[30]

Shortly thereafter, Senator Joseph Bailey of Texas took the floor. "Mr. President," he began, "the President of the United States was not careful of the feelings of Congress, and I can not comprehend the delicacy that moves Senators and Representatives to be very careful about what they say in respect of him. He charges, in effect, that the Congress of the United States withheld an appropriation which the Government needed to enforce its laws, and then says the argument which was used to induce Congress to withhold that appropriation was that if the appropriation was granted and used it would be employed against some dishonest members of the Congress." He then added in exasperation, "I am totally at a loss to understand how this body or the other body can receive a message of that kind and make no protest." Then, as an aside, "I doubt, if in the history of this Republic, any mayor ever sent such a message to a corrupt city council."[31]

Senator Eugene Hale of Maine then took the floor, trying to argue that the Senate had taken action by referring the issue to the committee on appropriations. But Bailey would hear none of it. "The question which addresses itself to the self-respect of Congress," he said upon once again taking the floor, "is the imputation of the President that it was governed in limiting this appropriation by a desire to shield its guilty members."[32]

The next senator to take the floor was the rather colorful Benjamin "Pitchfork Ben" Tillman of South Carolina. He was notorious for his previous run-ins with the president, so when he took the floor, everyone quieted to hear what he had to say.[33] Addressing Senator Hale, Tillman said, "If we are accused of dishonesty, of shirking the appropriation . . . because we are afraid our own shortcomings will be found out by this very same instrumentality, it looks to me as though we shall rest under the accusation of being a lot of rascals and scoundrels who belong in the penitentiary, unless we assert our manhood and self-respect and say it is not true."[34]

Tillman's statement began to garner a response, but Senator Hale was quick to reply, "I would not go, Mr. President, quite so far as the Senator does. I think there has been a great deal of restive and indignant feelings in the Senate about this matter."[35]

Tillman, who was always good for a laugh, responded wryly, "There is no restlessness at the White House. They are calm and serene up there."[36]

Laughter immediately broke out among the senators.

Senator "Pitchfork Ben" Tillman had received his famous moniker in 1896 when he ended up in a dispute with presidential candidate Grover Cleveland and declared him to be "an old bag of beef" and that he was "going to Washington with a pitchfork and prod him in his old fat ribs." The imagery was colorful enough to please the editorial cartoonists, and the appellation stuck. Tillman, with a seeming penchant for agitating presidents, also had a run-in with Roosevelt early in the president's tenure. Tillman had been invited to dine at the White House, but after he'd assaulted his fellow South Carolina Senator, John L. McLaurin, on the floor of the senate chamber, Roosevelt had rescinded the invitation to dine. Tillman never forgave the slight, and it was exacerbated when Roosevelt later invited Tuskegee Institute educator Booker T. Washington to dine at the White House. Tillman, a racist by every definition of the word, was incensed that a black man had been invited to dine at the White House when he hadn't, and he stated rather crudely, even by the standards of the time, "the action of President Roosevelt in entertaining that n----- will necessitate our killing a thousand n-----s in the South before they learn their place again."[37]

But back in the Senate that December day, as Tillman ridiculed and joked, other senators voiced their own concerns about the president's annual message, with many focusing on the Secret Service, while others concentrated on the land-fraud investigations. Picking up on the land-fraud discussion, Tillman weighed in once more. "I call attention to the fact that the President alleges, or at least indicates, that the land frauds in the West perpetuated by a certain Senator, who was convicted, were of a part with the investigation which he had been following; not that we have been breaking the revenue laws and thereby laying ourselves open to the charge of disobeying our own laws, but that he is investigating us generally—that we are a lot of rascals who need investigation." Tillman paused before adding, "Now, there may be men here who feel that way, but God knows I do not."[38] In light of Tillman's past, he brought down the Senate with laughter.

Oddly enough, the only real defense of the president came from a Democrat, Senator Francis G. Newlands of Nevada. "I do not intend to establish myself, or to attempt to establish myself, as the defender of the President of the United States," he hedged. Yet he proceeded to argue that the Secret Service was a necessary agency of the national government "for the purpose of inquiring into violations and evasions of law." He further believed that "members of Congress, equally with all other citizens of the United States, shall be subject to inquiry regarding violations and evasions of the laws which have passed Congress and been approved by the President of the United States."[39] His claim was simply that Congress was not above the law and could be investigated like any other American.

For Senator Newland, the only real issue was whether Roosevelt had the right to say what he had said to Congress, and on this point he instructed his fellow senators. "Under the Constitution," he reminded the assembly, "the President of the United States is a part of legislative action. He has the power of recommendation." Nelson believed, therefore, that "it was the duty and the right of the President to make his recommendation to Congress" and that only "his language may deserve the condemnation of the body."[40] His fellow Senators, however, believed that not only did the president insult Congress, he had also accused them of malfeasance. They insisted the president be forced to provide evidence for the charge. Senator Newland's suggestion was, at first, countered and then simply dismissed.

The Senate closed out discussion on this topic and moved on, but the following day, December 17, the issue was once again at the forefront of the Representatives in the House. At noon that day, after the invocation by the chaplain, Reverend Henry N. Couden, Representative James Breck Perkins of New York asked the clerk to read the special committee's resolution, which they had finalized. Speaker Cannon asked the clerk to comply, and the resolution was read. The resolution reiterated the issue of the Sundry Civil Appropriation Bill, the president's annual message, and the particular line about congressmen constraining the Secret Service so as to avoid being investigated. The resolution resolved

that the President be requested to transmit to the House any evidence upon which he based his statements that the "chief argument in favor of the provision was that the Congressmen did not themselves wish to be investigated by secret-service men," and also to transmit to the House any evidence connecting any Member of the House of Representatives of the Sixtieth Congress with corrupt action in his official capacity, and to inform the House whether he has instituted proceedings for the punishment of any such individual by the courts or has reported any such alleged delinquencies to the House of Representatives.[41]

The House was demanding that the president prove his allegations.

Once the resolution was entered into the Congressional Record, debate ensued, and Representative John Sharp Williams from Mississippi asked to take the floor. "The object of the resolution," he said, "is to give the President of the United States an opportunity to show upon what grounds he made his late seemingly unprovoked and unjustified attack upon the honor, the honesty, and the reputation of the legislative branch of the Government. So far as this committee has been able to discover, there is not a scintilla of evidence to support these statements." He also added that if the President "does not furnish any evidence, or furnishes insufficient evidence, to support his statement, then the country, which is the master of both of us, will come to its own judgment of his conduct."[42] Williams was hoping to not only put more pressure on the president to show some evidence but also to sway public opinion over to Congress's side. After some discussion regarding the details and final wording, the resolution passed the House with only one dissenting vote.[43]

According to Speaker Cannon, it was only after the session that he learned a phone call had been placed to his office by the president's secretary. The president had called to discuss the resolution. Speaker Cannon, however, explained in his memoir that he'd "had no knowledge that the President desired to confer with me until after the opening of the House on December 17." The message was, as he saw it, a "preemptory command for the Speaker to come to the White House for a consultation with the President. It was to be at once." Cannon's secretary, L. White

Busbey, had relayed the message to Cannon, even though he had already taken the chair in the House chamber and the session was underway. In fact, Busbey brought it to Cannon just as Perkins was beginning to speak, and Cannon believed that the message "was probably the only one of its kind ever sent by a President to a Speaker of the House." Cannon, who claimed he was "indignant," continued on with the session, believing that Roosevelt's timing "looked like a test between respect for the President and duty."[44] Cannon chose duty over the president.

The Speaker of the House did, however, go straight to the White House when the session was finished. According to the *Washington Post*, Cannon arrived "shortly before 1 o'clock" at the White House.[45] Everyone presumed, rightly, that the conversation was about the House resolution, but neither man openly discussed it at the time. Later Cannon presented his side of the story. "The President was in an ugly mood," Cannon recollected, "and we came nearer a personal quarrel than at any other time of our acquaintance." Cannon was indignant and believed the president threatened coercion against him. There was no history of goodwill between the two men, and nothing was resolved by the meeting other than for each to become more entrenched in his personal position: the president determined to respond to the request for evidence, and the speaker to remain "indignant" over the president's words in the annual message.[46]

President Roosevelt, of course, had his own opportunity to divulge his side of the conversation in his autobiography, but he chose to be less specific than Cannon had been. "There were many points on which I agreed with Mr. Cannon," Roosevelt claimed, but "with increasing friction." Roosevelt then explained that "for some years" he had kept "pushing forward," while Cannon had kept "hanging back." However, as his tenure as president was coming to a close, Roosevelt wrote, "I was forced to abandon the effort to persuade them to come my way, and then I achieved results only by appealing over the heads of the Senate and House leaders to the people, who were the masters of both of us." It was clear he was referring specifically to the Secret Service issue, especially when he added, "I continued in this way to get results until almost the close of my term."[47]

Almost being the key word in that sentence. For by that December of 1908, "the leaders of the House and Senate, or most of them, felt that it was safe to come to a break with me, and the last or short session of Congress, held between the election of my successor and his inauguration four months later, saw a series of contests between the majorities in the two houses of Congress and the President—myself,—quite as bitter as if they and I had belonged to opposite political parties." As doggedly as ever, Roosevelt believed he had "held his own," and that was pretty much all he had to say in regard to the final dispute in his own memoirs.[48]

In light of the senate's actions of December 16 and the House's actions of December 17, according to Gatewood, "public interest in the Secret Service controversy assumed a new dimension."[49] Any comment on or off the record by any member of Congress regarding anything revolving around the issue was suddenly reported by the press. At first there was talk of the Senate ordering a full investigation of the Secret Service and its practices.[50] Next came the headline that "ABOLITION OF THE SECRET SERVICE MAY BE PROPOSED," based on a congressman's belief that this was a forthcoming proposal from the president.[51] Then, in another headline, the *Washington Post* declared, "PLANS SLEUTH MERGE," which declared, "President Roosevelt is considering incorporating in his message to Congress, in regard to the secret service, a recommendation that a bureau of criminal investigation be added to the Department of Justice, which shall include Chief Wilkie's secret service, the post office inspectors, the customs inspection service, the internal-revenue special agents, pension examiners, and land office agents."[52] Another rumor said the Senate appropriations committee was planning to call President Roosevelt to testify in regard to the evidence he held; but this was dispelled by Senator Hale, acting chair, who called it an "imaginative statement in this morning's *Washington Post*."[53]

Unlike so many of the papers reacting to every rumor picked up by the press, the *New York Observer* took a more historical view of the situation. "President Roosevelt and Congress are now at odds, one with the other," wrote the editor, "and the situation presented to-day recalls to the historian of American affairs the tense conditions that prevailed when Congress expressed strong disapproval of the actions of President Tyler, and again took sharp issue with President Jackson."[54] Tyler had become president after William Henry Harrison died in office thirty days into his tenure in the White House. Tyler had run afoul of his own party, the Whigs, in Congress, and the backlash was severe—so much so that he was the first president for which an impeachment resolution was ever considered.[55] As for President Jackson, always a controversial president, Congress, under Whig Control, voted to censure him for withholding documents when he decentralized the Bank of the United States. In 1834, Jackson earned the dubious distinction of being the first president to ever have been censured by Congress. The censure did not sit well with the American people, however, and three years later, in 1837, the censure was expunged from the record.[56] But this *New-York Observer* editorial did, however, call out Roosevelt for being too sarcastic in his message, as well as Congress for pretending their ranks were filled with angels. The editorial did add, wrongly, that "the people at large have no interest in personal squabbles between men in public life," but it went on to call for both parties to cease recriminations.[57] It was a nice sentiment, but that did not happen.

As the American people prepared to celebrate Christmas that year, the activities on the part of the administration were coming into greater focus, clearly suggesting that the recriminations would continue. The *Washington Post* ran the headline, "THE PRESIDENT WILL REPLY," explaining in its article that, "President Roosevelt is preparing a message to Congress on the subject of the secret service, which is likely to cause commotion at the Capitol and throughout the country when it is made public shortly after the conclusion of the holiday recess."[58] The *New York Times* further explained that "President Roosevelt has begun preparing for submission to Congress a mass of evidence upon which he based the statements in his annual message regarding the Secret Service."[59] The Washington *Evening Star* also added that, "Cabinet officers have been submitting to President Roosevelt their reports in reply to the Aldrich resolution on the secret service, and it is considered likely that the President will have all these reports ready to send to the appropriations committee of the Senate soon after the reassembling of Congress."[60] So the rhetoric began to die down, allowing everyone to enjoy the holidays. Everyone, that is, except Theodore Roosevelt and his administration. They had a response to put together for Congress.

President Roosevelt, pictured at his desk, in his final annual message to Congress, addressed the restrictions placed on the use of Secret Service operatives that sparked the controversy over the Secret Service, but drew attention away from his newly created Bureau of Investigation.

Photo courtesy of the Library of Congress.

12

The Battle over the Bureau

Before Christmas of 1908, President Roosevelt had promised to respond to the Congressional resolution. Rather than backing down or simply delaying until the end of his term, which was a few mere months away, Roosevelt did what Roosevelt had always done: he threw himself into action. He ordered his departmental secretaries to begin drafting their responses to the resolution, which would also serve to provide him with additional documentation to draw from as he wrote his response. Because his annual message had been so widely read by not only politicians but the American public generally, he knew his response would also be so scrutinized. He knew he had to weigh his every word carefully. In a letter he wrote to his friend William Sewall just before Christmas, he detailed his delicacy in choosing wording. "I was careful never to condemn all Congressmen, but my business is to war against all crookedness wherever I find it, and I am not going to let up as long as I am President."[1] Roosevelt's intent was to be just as precise when it came to his response to the resolution.

Roosevelt also paid special attention to the timing of his response message's release. Rather than publishing it as soon as possible, he planned to wait until Congress had returned to Washington after the holidays, in order to gain the greatest political advantage. "He was not only careful in framing his response to the House request," explains historian Willard B. Gatewood Jr., but he also "delayed its release so as to reap maximum advantage."[2] More specifically, Roosevelt let the press know that his response would be worth the wait, and that was enough to cause them to help build excitement for its eventual release. As one veteran journalist, Arthur Wallace Dunn, explained, "Roosevelt let the idea circulate through his well organized press service that reports of secret service men on Congressmen would provide interesting reading if sent in a special message."[3] The press did its job—and did it well—for the excitement began to build, and it was talked about extensively by nearly everyone over the holidays. This had its intended effect, for as Gatewood acknowledges, "By the time it was presented to the House on January 4, 1909, popular opinion appeared to be solidly behind the President in the Secret Service matter."[4] Roosevelt, it appears, was winning the battle on the field of public opinion.

Yet there was one additional reason Roosevelt had decided to delay his response. The president realized that the longer he waited, the greater the doubts would grow among congressmen who had all but forced his response. The delay had the effect of creating an agonizing sense of foreboding among them. This fear turned into doubts that they may have been too impetuous in trying to call the president's bluff, for perhaps—just perhaps—he might indeed have compelling evidence against them. By the time Congress was prepared to go back into session, on January 4, 1909, the confidence on the part of many members of Congress had eroded, giving way to fear and trepidation.

On that day, "promptly at noon," wrote the Washington *Evening Star*, "Mr. Latta, one of the President's secretaries, was at the main door of the chamber bearing the message which was read as soon as the Italian relief measure was put through."[5] The House had decided to first vote on a relief package for southern Italy, which had just been hit by a devastating earthquake. Congress had voted to provide eight hundred thousand dollars in Italian relief before all eyes turned to the bearer of the special message: Mr. Latta walked the special message to Speaker Cannon, who, after opening and scanning it, handed it to the clerks to be read aloud.

The president's special message to congress opened with the acknowledgment of their resolution by stating, "I have received the resolution of the House of Representatives of December 17, 1908."[6] He then reprinted every word of the resolution in order to be entirely clear about what he was referring to in his own message. And then he launched into an attack on the resolution itself.[7]

"I am wholly at a loss to understand the concluding portion of the resolution," Roosevelt began. "I have made no charges of corruption against Congress nor against any Member of the present House. If I had proof of such corruption affecting any Member of the House in any matter as to which the Federal Government has jurisdiction, action would at once be brought, as was done in the cases of Senators Mitchell and Burton and Representatives Williamson, Hermann, and Driggs at different times since I have been President. This would simply be doing my duties in the execution and enforcement of the laws without respect to persons."[8] Roosevelt was careful to point out that he had accused no one of any crime, but he also craftily inserted the fact that the Senate and the House were not beyond reproach, specifying those among them who had either been indicted or convicted.

To clarify, Roosevelt explained how he believed the House had misconstrued "the meaning of my words." In order to be very clear, with an eye toward the record, he then reprinted the two paragraphs referring to the issue of the Secret Service from his annual message of the month before. From there, Roosevelt launched into his own defense:

> A careful reading of this message will show I said nothing to warrant the statement that "the majority of the Congressmen were in fear of being investigated by the Secret Service men" or "that Congress as a whole was actuated by that motive." I did not make any such statement about Congress as a whole, nor, with a few inevitable exceptions, about the Members of Congress, in any message or article or speech.

From there he explained that he would not launch an attack on Congress as a whole because to do so would threaten the "safety of free government."[9]

Having dismissed any notion that he had or intended to make a blanket attack on Congress, he concluded that "this allegation in the resolution, therefore, must certainly be due to an entire failure to understand my message."[10] The president restated the claims he'd made in his annual message to ensure everyone understood exactly, after which he began introducing the evidence for these claims.

Roosevelt immediately zeroed in on the line in his message that had most offended congressional sensibilities. He again drew attention to the part of the resolution asking for the president to show evidence that Congress had passed the amendment because they did not wish to be investigated themselves by the Secret Service. In reply, Roosevelt asked them to simply turn to their own Congressional Record of May 1, 1908, for the requested evidence. "Mr. Tawney of Minnesota, Mr. Smith of Iowa, Mr. Sherley of Kentucky, and Mr. Fitzgerald of New York," wrote the president, "appear in this debate as the special champions of the provision referred to."[11]

As an aside, he said it would have been most helpful to identify how members of the House had actually voted in regard to the amendment, but as there had been no roll-call vote, this was not possible. This, of course, suggested that perhaps members of the House were trying to hide something by not revealing how they voted. Roosevelt also craftily noted here that ordinarily he would not call out specific members of the House, but because of his need to answer the resolution as demanded, he had no choice. Then he went in for the kill, using their own words against them.

The president argued that the House debate on May 1 fully supported his statement that members of Congress did not want to be investigated: "Two distinct lines of argument were followed in the debate," he wrote. "One concerned the question whether the law warranted the employment of the Secret Service in departments other than the Treasury, and this did not touch the merits of the service in the least." It was the second line of argument, however, which did."[12]

"The other line of argument," Roosevelt continued, "went to the merits of the service, whether lawfully or unlawfully employed, and here the chief if not the only argument used was that the service should be cut down and restricted because its members had 'shadowed' or investigated Members of Congress and other officers of the Government."[13] It was this line of debate, Roosevelt believed, that caused the House to vote to prevent the Secret Service from transferring its operatives to other departments and reduced its budget.

Then Roosevelt specifically went after Tawney, whom he believed to be at the forefront of the opposition. "Mr. Tawney, for instance, says: 'It was for the purpose of stopping the use of this service in every possible way by the departments of the Government that this provision was inserted.'" Roosevelt was setting up his argument here that Tawney and other members of the House believed, "both by implication and direct statement," that it "ought to be the law" that "the Secret Service should be used to suppress counterfeiting." If that were the case, then the Secret Service would not be able to investigate Congress, unless its members were engaged in the crime of counterfeiting. Roosevelt then argued that, regardless of the specifics, there was plenty of evidence that the Secret Service had long had "ample legal authority," given by both Congress and the chief executive, to investigate violations of the federal laws outside of that solitary crime.[14]

He then added another layer to his argument, pointing out that "A careful reading of the Congressional Record will also show that practically the only arguments advanced in favor of the limitation proposed by Mr. Tawney's committee, beyond what may be supposed to be contained by implication in certain sentences as to 'abuses' which were not specified, were those contained in the repeated statements of Mr. Sherley." Representative J. Swagar Sherley had stated that the Secret Service had investigated members of Congress and that they should not have done so. Roosevelt then highlighted every instance in which Sherley made this statement, including "in column 1 on page 5556," where Sherley mentioned that military officers and members of Congress should not be investigated, and again "in column 1, page 5557," where "he refers only to Members of Congress." "His speech," Roosevelt summarized, "puts most weight on the investigation of Members of Congress."[15]

Roosevelt then took some time discussing and refuting a 1904 article written by L. White Busbey, Speaker Cannon's private secretary, in which Busbey had railed against the use of the Secret Service to investigate members of Congress. Here Roosevelt hoped to show where some of the congressional animus had originated and that more than likely—via guilt by association—it had originated with the speaker himself.

After this somewhat-awkward aside, Roosevelt then stated what he believed to be the real issue at the core of the entire flap over the resolution, the annual message, and the Tawney amendment: "Does Congress desire that the Government shall have at its disposal the most efficient instrument for the detection of criminals and the prevention and punished crime, or does it not?"[16] Stated so baldly, Roosevelt was hoping to maintain the high ground: If the answer was yes, then the Tawney amendment was problematic. If the answer was no, then members of the House were trying to protect themselves from investigations as he had claimed in his annual message. Roosevelt had given Congress Hobson's choice.

Having made his most crucial challenge to the members of the House, Roosevelt began to return his special message to a defensive posture. He claimed that he had attempted to wage a protest over the amendment but concluded that "Messrs. Tawney and Smith and their fellow members of the Appropriations Committee paid no heed to the protest." Roosevelt then claimed that as the House had left him no other means available to protest the amendment, he had been left with no other choice but "discussing it in my message to Congress."[17]

The rest of the president's message covered all of the land-fraud investigations, noting the "far-reaching and widespread system of fraudulent transactions," how in "Colorado one of the Secret Service men was assassinated," and that Senator Mitchell and Representative Williamson "were convicted on evidence obtained by men transferred from the Secret Service." Their work, he conceded, was both necessary and dangerous and therefore, "In conclusion, in the name of good government and decent administration, in the name of honesty and for the purpose of bringing to justice violators of the federal laws where they may be found, whether in public or private life," Roosevelt demanded "that the action taken by the House last year be reversed."[18]

Having anticipated the reading of this special message since mid-December, the press was present in abundance to record every word and reaction on the part of the House. The *New York Times*, in their coverage of the reading, reported what had occurred while the message was still being read by the clerks. "The message itself went along so smoothly," the paper wrote, "that many of the paragraphs that are now forming the theme of heated discussion and condemnation were greeted with ripples of laughter that swept over Democrats and Republicans alike." In fact, it noted that, "Once the reading of the clerk was interrupted by loud applause." However, "when the end came there was dead silence." The newspaper concluded, "The House saw it had been laughing at itself." Representative J. Warren Keifer of Ohio was the first to realize this: "He called us rascals before, and now he says we are fools."[19]

The *Washington Post* noticed something the *New York Times* had overlooked. "While the reading was going on," the *Post* wrote, "Representative Perkins consulted with the Speaker, the Republican floor leader, Mr. Payne, and John Sharp Williams, who is a member of his special committee, with the result that as soon as the message had been finished, he moved that it be referred to his committee."[20] Yet when the speech had ended, Perkins too had sat in stunned silence, his plan of action momentarily forgotten. However, "After a moment's delay Mr. Perkins of the so-called 'Spanking Committee'"—as it had come to be called, as its primary mission was to "spank the president"—"moved that the whole message be referred to his committee." Representative Griggs of Georgia, however, voiced his objection, believing the message should be sent back to the president "without delay." But calmer heads prevailed, and Perkin's committee received the task of determining how best to respond.[21]

The first paper to actually get the story to press was the Washington *Evening Star*, which included the story in that evening's paper with the headline that the House of Representatives was "RILED UP BY MESSAGE." They reported on the many statement overheard in the House that afternoon, including such gems as, "The President has much nerve and little logic—a poor combination in the long run," "The President has side-stepped the issue; he is audacious but ridiculous," and "The President is a four flusher; It is time the people of the United States were waking up to the fact."[22] The term *four-flusher* derived from the game of poker, meaning one card short of a full flush, and had come to mean someone who was a welcher, a piker, or a braggart.[23] The *Evening Star* had its own way of describing the special message: it was, the said, as "a beehive just after a naughty but active small boy has stirred up the occupants with a stick."[24]

As could be expected, much of the press attention was placed on James Tawney because of how he had been named, often, in the message. "Chairman Tawney of the appropriations committee, whom the President picked out as head devil in the congressional movement against the secret service," noted the Washington *Evening Star*, "is red-faced, but non-committal." "Now, however," the paper continued, "it is generally conceded that Mr. Tawney has been smoked out and that he must reply."[25] But before that could happen, Representative Perkin's special committee had to decide how to respond. Tawney would have to wait his turn to take the House floor.

But Tawney was under no obligation to wait to talk with the press, and it was there he raised his first outcry over what he believed had been direct attacks made upon him by the president. "I have been elevated from the ranks of the criminal class to the Ananias club," began Tawney,[26] referring to a story in the Acts of the Apostles in which Ananias, after telling a lie to Peter, falls dead. As Tawney's lie had originally been about a financial transaction, and combined with the yellow journalism and the conservation frauds at the time, the reference was, Roosevelt believed, fitting, and he had used it several times before to describe these individuals.

"I have nothing to say to the President's message at this time," Tawney told the pressmen, before continuing, "except that he has misinterpreted my speeches to the House. This controversy lies between the chief executive and the legislative department of the government, and there it should rest until settled. The President is wrong in trying to make it an issue between himself and the appropriations committee."[27] Tawney would have much more to say in the coming days.

Even Speaker of the House Joseph Gurney Cannon could not help but comment on the president's special message— even before Perkin's committee had determined their response to the president. He had his own suspicions about who had actually orchestrated the president's message, if not written it entirely. "Speaker Cannon interpreted the message as primarily the work of Secret Service Chief Wilkie," explains Gatewood.[28] In his memoirs Cannon later wrote that Chief Wilkie "constructed for the President a fantastic story" and that the special message had been "more offensive than the one to which the House had taken exception."[29]

Cannon also believed that the blame for this "whole mess"[30] could be placed on Busbey's 1904 article in which he'd railed against using Secret Service to investigate Congress. "The use of that old newspaper article by President Roosevelt," Cannon told the papers, "was the weakest political move I ever knew him to make."[31] It was believed that Roosevelt had been attacking Busbey because of his disagreements with Cannon, but Busbey had, in fact, written the article a year before Cannon had even become speaker and Busbey his private secretary. In fact, Busbey told Cannon that he had based the article on certain things Roosevelt had said early in his presidency. Nevertheless, Gatewood also points out something that few actually knew at the time: "the old enmity which had existed between Busbey and Wilkie ever since their days as rival newspapermen in Chicago."[32] It seemed that there were many layers of discord in regard to this issue.

As members of the House criticized the president for his special message, members of the Senate were digesting the letter President Roosevelt had sent to Senator Eugene Hale the following day, January 5.[33] The Senate had handled things differently, requesting specific reports from the various departments within the executive branch pertaining to the issue of the Secret Service. Over the Christmas break, in addition to providing Roosevelt what he had needed in order to respond to the House, reports for the Senate were being prepared by various departments and agencies, including the secretaries of both the State Department and the Treasury, as well as the attorney general in the Justice Department.

Roosevelt explained in his letter to Senator Hale that he agreed with the request for evidence and documentation regarding the Secret Service by the Senate. "Let me at the outset," Roosevelt wrote Hale, "most earnestly express my cordial agreement with the view that it is not only the right but the duty of Congress to investigate the workings of the Secret Service or detective agents by which alone the Government can effectually safeguard itself against wrongdoing, punish crime, and bring to justice criminals."[34] He said he understood that in any detective system there is the possibility of abuse but that the system is nonetheless needed.

He continued, "In my communication of the 4th instant to the Lower House I have set forth at length the reasons why, in my judgment, it is eminently desirable that, in addition to the special detectives or inspection service of each department, there should be in some one department, preferably the Department of Justice, a service which can be used at need in any department in order to achieve the ends I have described."[35] It is interesting to note that Roosevelt had already created an agency for that express purpose—the Bureau of Investigation—but despite its existence, it was not receiving much attention, and neither was it doing anything that would invite attention. It was almost as if Roosevelt were trying to draw attention away from its existence, by writing of his hopes for such an agency and spending more time addressing the Secret Service.

At this point in the letter, however, Roosevelt starts to turn the tables on Senator Hale. The president had been called upon to furnish reports of the activities of the Secret Service and possible wrongdoing in Congress. Yet Roosevelt asked Senator Hale to return the favor. As he explained, "very frequently accusations have been made to me privately by Members of the two Houses to the effect that the Secret Service has been used as a 'police of morals' or to shadow Senators, Congressmen, and other public officials." He continued, "I should be greatly obliged if any information could be furnished me tending to show any instance where this has been done in times past."[36] Roosevelt was responding in kind to Congress: he was calling their bluff.

Then, just as he had done in the special message to the House in singling out Tawney for special attention, Roosevelt now singled out Senator Tillman. He focused on Tillman's possible land fraud, presenting evidence that caught the senator in a lie. On February 8, 1908, Tillman had said, "I have not bought any land anywhere in the West nor undertaken to buy any." Roosevelt then reprinted a letter by Tillman that read, in part, "I wired you from Wausau, Wis., as follows, and write to confirm it. 'Wm. E. Lee, my agent, will see you about land. I want nine quarters reserved. Will forward signed application and money at once.'"[37] This suggested merely that Tillman had been caught in a lie while speaking on the floor of the Senate, not that he had committed a crime.

But Roosevelt then presented a copy of this William E. Lee's letter, in which he wrote to those setting up the land deal, "In case Senator Tillman gets in on this deal with some good land in the eight quarters we want, I am satisfied that he can be of great help in getting matters started from Washington and cause the Government to get busy and do something along the line you desire." Several days after this letter had been written, Tillman, on the floor of the Senate, had raised the issue of land grants going to railroads, attempted to block it, and moved that land grants instead go to the people. Tillman had then written Lee, his agent, "If I can succeed in causing the Government to institute suit for the recovery of the land and make it easier for others *as well as myself* to obtain some of it, I shall do it without any regard to the dealings of your firm."[38] Roosevelt emphasized the words *as well as myself* in the letter to Senator Hale, noting that Tillman had fully intended to benefit from his actions in regard to the land deals.

Upon hearing the president's letter to Hale read before the Senate, Tillman, usually good for a sensational quotation or a joke, grew rather sober. "It is a serious matter for the President of the United States to attempt to hurt the honor of a Senator of the United States, and therefore, I suppose he must have some evidence which, in his own mind, convicts me," was all he offered as a response. He then made his intentions clear: "I am going to proceed slowly and carefully, so that the whole matter may be handled in as grave a manner as it deserves. Of course, I know that I have not done anything unlawful, and therefore I have no fear of the outcome. But I cannot afford to be hasty."[39] When pressed as to when he would answer the president's allegations, Tillman responded, "When I make answer it will be on the floor of the Senate Chamber."[40]

America was now waiting to see how the House and Senate would respond to the president's message and letter. In particular, they were waiting to see how Representative James A. Tawney and Senator Benjamin "Pitchfork Ben" Tillman were going to respond. The president had the public's support, but within Congress, most members were apparently siding with Tawney and Tillman. At least it could be said that the incident managed to unite Democrats and the Republicans.

Senator Tillman had the most to lose, as he was potentially walking into a legal issue over his involvement in the possible land deal. He knew he had to tread carefully. He had thought he'd called the president's bluff but had come up wanting. Tillman had suffered a stroke in 1908, which prevented his chairing the Senate's appropriations committee, so politically he had not much to lose but everything to gain. Yet if he pressed too hard he might be exposed to legal troubles and then, like Senators Mitchell and Burton, find himself under indictment. Tillman was in a precarious position.

Representative James Tawney, on the other hand, chaired the House's appropriations committee, and he had the most to lose politically speaking. Tawney knew he had to go on the offensive to get his position on matters out before the people, by going to both the press and the people directly. Tawney thus sat down to prepare a letter he could mail to the right people, use as a letter to the editor, and draw on in making speeches, all with the intent of framing his side of the debate in advance of the House's hearings on the president's special message.

Tawney began drafting a boilerplate letter, to be changed as needed, as follows: "I am sending you under separate cover a copy of my speech on this subject which contains the facts which led to its adoption. After you have read the speech I would like to know whether in your opinion the President was justified in assailing a coordinate branch of Government up on the grounds stated by him in his message, and whether or not he was justified in misquoting what I said concerning the letter of the Secretary of the Treasury."[41] He then summarized his attached speech in ten bullet points, in which he argued his position. He put forth his belief that the limitations placed on the Secret Service by his amendment the previous year had not affected that agency's ability to investigate counterfeiting, that other agencies had the ability to conduct their own investigations, and that the limitation had hampered no agency whatsoever.

Tawney more pointedly argued that the president had been dishonest in using only a portion of his words from previous congressional testimony in his special message. The president had said that Tawney claimed to have a letter from the secretary of the Treasury saying that he "himself admits that the provisions under which the appropriation has been made have been violated year after year for a number of years in his own Department." This pertained to the loaning of Secret Service agents that had become common place but for which there was no authorization. Tawney argued that Roosevelt had left off the word *whereby* from the secretary's statements. The inclusion of this word, Tawney argued, made this his own conclusion rather than a "statement of fact or an express admission upon the part of the Secretary."[42]

Tawney, it seems, was mincing words. Or perhaps Roosevelt was. In either case, it seemed rather pathetic for a senior member of the House to be whining about such minor details in order to show who was right or who was wrong. "It is unfortunate that the President did not deem it necessary to quote me correctly," Tawney sniffed, "but inasmuch as he has misrepresented me in this way, and has based his criticism of me largely upon what he thus made to appear a misrepresentation upon my part, it is only right that attention should be called to this misquotation."[43] Tawney had been hoping to win over the press and the American people, but the letter and his subsequent speeches failed to do it. In fact, in time, they would actually work against him.

Still, despite the letter's devolving into minutiae, Tawney felt he was even more justified in raising his compliant and that it gave him an even stronger case. He concluded his letter with an affirmation of all he saw in his own narrative: "In closing I wish to say that I am convinced now more than ever that my position in respect to the restriction placed upon the activities of the Secret Service Division of the Treasury Department was justified by the facts, and I shall continue to hold that position regardless of any attacks upon me from whatever source, as I believe that the position I have taken, when the facts are known to the people, will be found by them to be proper."[44]

Tawney then sat back and waited for the people to tell him how right he had been and how wicked President Roosevelt's special message was, especially where it had attacked Tawney's honor. Only it didn't work out that way. A few people said they agreed with him, but many told Tawney they were not willing to commit just yet, especially in writing. Most of the letters, however, condemned Tawney for his pettiness.

One such letter, received almost immediately, came from A. B. Blair, president of the Winona Seed Company. He wrote to Tawney "with re to the secret service appropriations controversy, which is apparently on between the President and Congress and which involves yourself," specifying what he could expect from him. "Of course you are aware I have always stood you, thro thick and thin—and will perhaps continue to do so, but not as against President Roosevelt, and anything he may ask in connection with the land frauds." Blair then tried to explain to Tawney that his arguments were falling on deaf ears, as this situation was different from politics as usual: "Explanations do not count, as against his message, published in last nights Republican. People who, rarely if ever, read a President's message, read this, every word." Then, landing what had to be a crushing blow, Blair concluded, "I very much doubt if you could be re-elected to day."[45]

Tawney wrote back, attempting to bring Blair around, expounding on Roosevelt's unpresidential behavior and his misuse of the Secret Service. But Blair would hear none of it and countered with his own letter, once again refuting Tawney's arguments. Tawney tried yet again, but in the end, Blair put it to him as plainly as he could: "Those of us, and there are many, who have lived in Minnesota and Wisconsin for a generation are familiar with the gossip of the land and timber steals and have no doubt it is being repeated in the West on an even larger scale, and we care little about the method of the man who pushes it thru and will stop it."[46] Blair sided with Roosevelt in this dispute between the legislative and executive branches of government, and it seemed nothing was going to convince him otherwise.

Blair wasn't the only one to voice disagreement with Tawney. In fact, the majority of the letters Tawney retained were actually against him, and it is clear he tried to counter each individually. E. A. Agard, a lawyer from Illinois, wrote Tawney on January 9, telling him that in his public fight against the president, "politically you have committed hari kari, and from this on are a 'dead one.'"[47] It seems Tawney was alienating not only the average American but also his sometime supporters.

Tawney sent his letter to many newspapers, most of which published it, but the response against him was much the same, made all the worse because it was now in the public forum. In an editorial published in the weekly *Musical Courier*, Oscar H. Halwey wrote Tawney, "We are under the impression that he is right and that you and the others who would hamper him are wrong . . . the graceful thing for you to do would be to accept the suggestion of the president and get in line with him."[48] In fact, all of the newspaper editorials ere against Tawney, some to a lesser degree than others, but the one editorial response that incensed Tawney had come from the *Albert Lea Tribune*.

"WHO ARE THESE MEN?" actually opened with a reprint of what one of the Eastern papers, the *Philadelphia North American*, had been saying about the dispute: "Who are the spokesmen now set up to thunder against Roosevelt on behalf of this Congress, whose dignity is injured. Tillman, who in his recent shame seems to have the sympathy and not the censure of his colleagues . . . Tawney, proved a falsifier of public documents by his misquotation upon the floor of Congress of a letter from the Secretary of the Treasury and his misstatement of facts with respect to an investigation and exposure in the Bureau of Engraving and Printing."[49] Tawney, the paper felt, had twisted the secretary's words by omitting from the debate some of what had been testified. Further, in his arguments about the Secret Service, Tawney had claimed that Moran was nothing more than a clerk for that agency and not a Secret Service operative despite the fact he was.

The notion that a newspaper from the state he represented would have the audacity to reprint this editorial, claiming he had lied in official congressional testimony, pushed Tawney over the edge. His fight was no longer with just Roosevelt: Tawney was now fighting the world.

He immediately fired off a letter to the *Albert Lea Evening Tribune*, demanding a retraction. And in his fury at having been condemned by a Minnesota newspaper, Tawney filed a civil suit for libel against the newspaper the following day. He was determined that the world see things his way, even if it meant destroying his political career to do so. He steadfastly believed that in the end he would be vindicated.

Set on a path to destroy the president, Tawney was about to destroy himself.

Senator Benjamin "Pitchfork" Tillman, was one of the most visible antagonists against the president in the Secret Service controversy.

Photo courtesy of the Library of Congress.

13

Sore Losers and Petty Politics

After the president had his say, America, its media, and especially those in Washington all waited to see how Representative James A. Tawney would respond in the House and how
Senator Benjamin Tillman would respond in the Senate. The
so-called "spanking committee," formed first in the wake of the
president's special message to the House, met throughout the
week of January 3, 1909, to determine how best to respond to
the president. Tawney was left off the committee, as was anyone
named in the president's special message, so the House could be
seen as remaining above the fray. Tawney, however, was kept
well apprised of the committee's activities. He learned the committee was going to put forth a resolution regarding the annual
message that was specifically focused on the two paragraphs
that dealt with the Secret Service. The resolution would call for
the House to table those two paragraphs, which would effectively mean they would be deleted: when the annual message
was printed in the Congressional Record, the two paragraphs
pertaining to the Secret Service would be excised, as if they had
never been written. While that sounds both petty and insignificant, it was, in fact, a major rebuke of the president, something
Congress had not done since the House had censured President
James K. Polk for starting what they called an unconstitutional
war against Mexico in 1848. Tawney made ready his speech that

week in preparation for the House debate that had been set for that Friday.

And so it was that on January 8, 1909, at noon, the House of Representatives opened its session. The invocation was given by the House chaplain, Reverend Henry Noble Couden, a Universalist minister who had lost his vision from a wound received in battle during the Civil War. The prior day's proceedings were read and approved before House business was heard, including the status on many of the concurrent House-Senate resolutions.

That Friday, "the galleries of the House of Representatives were jammed to capacity." In fact, "the throng was so great that the wives of several congressmen had to sit on the steps."[1] The wife of one Texas congressman had come to see President Roosevelt "metaphorically 'thrown to the lions.'"[2] And so she crowded into the House gallery with so many others to watch the spectacle unfold.

Noticeably missing from the floor of the House or among the galleries, however, was anyone from the president's administration, including the conspicuous absence of Representative Nicholas Longworth, the president's son-in-law. Roosevelt understood full well what was about to happen and so chose to not to have anyone from his administration present. In part this was to send a signal that he was so powerful he did not care to concern himself with any negative comments the House might voice against him. He remained at the White House, no doubt amused by the thought of what members of the House might be saying.

After all of the preliminaries were out of the way, the show—as many of the spectators, including the media, saw it—began. Representative James Breck Perkins from New York, chair of the "spanking committee," stood up and addressed Joseph Cannon. "Mr. Speaker," he said, "I offer a privileged resolution, and ask that it be reported by the Clerk."[3] Speaker Cannon then had one of the clerks read the resolution. The preamble of the resolution summarized the president's annual message, the House's subsequent request for evidence of the president's charges, and the president's special message by way of response. Then three resolutions were then set forth: The first "Resolved, That the House, in the exercise of its constitutional prerogatives, declines to consider any communication from any source which is not in its own judgment respectful"—this to make clear the House's distaste for Roosevelt's charge that the Tawney amendment had only been written because congressmen did not want to be investigated by the Secret Service.

The second "Resolved, That the special committee and the Committee of the Whole House on the state of the Union be discharged from any consideration of so much of the President's annual message as relates to the Secret Service, and is above set forth, and that the said portion of the message be laid on the table," indicating the House's refusal to accept those two paragraphs of censure. And, finally, the third "Resolved, That the message of the President sent to the House on January 4, 1909, being unresponsive to the inquiry of the House and constituting an invasion of the privileges of the House by questioning the motives and intelligence of Members in the exercise of their constitutional rights and functions, be laid on the table." So, not only would the House strike the Secret Service paragraphs of the annual message from official record, they would also strike the entirety of the president's response to it—a response the House had specifically requested. This resolution was primarily made because of the attention the president's response had focused on four specific members: "Mr. Tawney of Minnesota, Mr. Smith of Iowa, Mr. Sherley of Kentucky, and Mr. Fitzgerald of New York."[4]

Once the clerk had finished reading the resolution, Representative Perkins then delivered a speech that mostly recapped all of the House grievances with the president, using them to justify the resolution. He informed Speaker Cannon that his committee had looked at the issue at hand "with due regard for the rights of the Chief Executive, with due regard for the rights of the Congress," and concluded, "we are unanimously of the opinion that the portions of the message objected to do constitute a breach of the privilege of this House." This was met by the first of many rounds of applause that day in the chamber. Perkins said the House had the "utmost confidence" in the appropriations committee, which was met with applause. He said that no congressman was in fear of being investigated, which was met with applause. And at the close of his speech, when he beseeched "every man who is a member of it this day [to] vote on the question that is presented in the manner that seems to him worthy of the traditions of which we are the heirs, of the institutions of which we are the protectors, and of the people of whom we are the representatives," his sentiments were met with a long, sustained applause. Now that the resolution had been entered into record and the justifications for it delivered by the chair of the committee, the floor was opened for debate. The feeding frenzy began.

A number of representatives began to speak, but after Perkins took back the floor, he yielded it to Edwin Denby of Michigan, who declared the president's language in the annual message "highly offensive" and the special message "unbefitting a state paper." About halfway through his remarks, Denby told his fellow congressmen, "To-day your special committee offers a resolution intended to make clear the attitude of this House toward the Executive when in the exercise of a constitutional privilege he strays from the path of recommendation and just criticism into the realm of personal abuse, speculation and innuendo." This was met with loud applause. Suddenly, however, the applause was interrupted, when, from the entrance to the House chamber, the loud voice of the assistant doorkeeper announced, "Mr. Speaker, a message from the President of the United States!"[5]

The House broke out in hysterics. According to the *New York Times*, "Instantly pandemonium broke loose. A loud, harsh shout of laughter went up, died down, and was renewed. The Speaker was apparently the only person who preserved an unmoved gravity of countenance. The President's secretary fidgeted uneasily in his station in the centre aisle while the doorkeeper who announced him was visibly embarrassed." Many wondered aloud if the president himself had somehow heard Mr. Denby's words and decided to interrupt and have his say. Trying to regain order, Speaker Cannon beat the desk with his gavel so hard and repeatedly that a piece of the desk to broke off and went flying. This merely brought more mirth to the chamber.[6] Eventually, order was restored and the president's letter accepted and placed on the speaker's desk, unopened. Cannon thought better of opening the letter just then, knowing full well it would only bring on another round of laughter.

Denby concluded his speech, then, to a loud and continued applause before others rose to speak. In all, there was little opposition to the resolution voiced. One of the few to do so was Representative William S. Bennet from New York, who called to his colleagues' attention the differences of attitude between members of the House and the average American. "So far as my personal communications from my district have gone," Bennet told the assembly, "none seem to have been excited over this particular portion of the President's annual message except the membership of this House." He then urged his colleagues to have some perspective. "The trouble," he told them, "is that, though we may so express it, these actions have little of historical significance, and I venture the prophecy that the student of history who, twenty-five years from now, looks up the record of Theodore Roosevelt will find that our action to-day plays no more part in the view held of him historically than the action of our predecessors here plays in the view held in history of President Tyler, or than the action of the predecessors of our colleagues in the Senate detracts from the estimate of the character of Andrew Jackson." Bennet's reasoned statement did not appear to resonate with members of the House.

The debate then focused on the ability of the Secret Service to perform its duties after the House had reduced the number of Secret Service operatives available the previous year. After some discussion, it was largely accepted that the service had been reduced by approximately twenty operatives (about the same number that had been transferred to the Bureau of Justice). Representative Bennet then reported how the Secret Service's reduced budget and manpower had affected the district attorney's office in the southern district of New York: "Since June, 1908," Bennet read from the DA's statement, "there have been important investigations in the city in which there has been serious needs for the services of the men in the Secret Service, and the Government has been handicapped by not being able to avail itself of their services."

On hearing this, fellow New York Representative John J. Fitzgerald stood and, after prevailing upon Bennet to yield the floor for a question, asked, "Does the gentlemen from New York or does the district attorney know that since the 1st of July, 1908, practically the 20 men have been taken into the Department of Justice and organized as a separate secret service; and does he not know that the department is available for use in this work, payable from the funds from which they had been paid before, subject only to the orders of the Attorney-General, and not to the Chief of the Secret Service?" Bennet pointedly ignored the question and the existence of the Bureau of Investigation, instead insisting that the attorney general's investigation had been hampered. It is possible that Representative Bennet, along with many of his colleagues, did not know of the new bureau's existence; or perhaps it was that they were simply unwilling to acknowledge it.

The debate continued with some congressmen introducing newspaper articles into the record, others discussing previous occasions on which the House had rebuked the president, and others focusing on the evidence presented by the president. Then, the four representatives Roosevelt had specifically named in his special message were recognized by the chamber. Speaker Cannon first recognized "the gentleman from Minnesota," at which point the House, hearing Tawney was about to speak, broke into a "loud and long-continued applause." It was the moment Tawney, and most of those in attendance, had waited for: Roosevelt's most ardent opponent was to speak. The members of the House settled back into their chairs, a hush fell over the chamber, and Tawney paused before launching into his speech.

He began with a grand and eloquent nod to government duty: "Mr. Speaker," he said, "the continued success and perpetuity of government depends more upon the confidence of the people in the integrity, honor, and unselfish patriotism of those charged with the duty and responsibility of government than upon any other condition connected with, or incident to, government. Without it no government can long endure. Ours would soon crumble and fall. Whatever tends to destroy this confidence, whether arising from within any of the coordinate branches of Government or coming from without, should be frankly and fearlessly met and, if possible, overcome." The House broke the reverent silence with another round of applause.

Tawney continued in this same manner before eventually arriving at the point: the president's allegations that "in adopting this provision [the Tawney amendment] the Congress of the United States intended to benefit and protect from detection and punishment those guilty of committing fraud and other violations of public law." Tawney continued to lay out all of the other charges made by the president before detailing the amendment Congress had passed. He then argued that Congress's provision had not taken away the authority of the Secret Service but that the agency had retained all its powers of investigation.

In regard to appropriations, Tawney did acknowledge that the Secret Service budget had been decreased, but he counterargued that other agencies, such as Interior and Justice, had seen their budgets increase because they were now handling their own investigations. As "proof of this fact" that no agency could possibly have been hampered in its investigation, Tawney pointed out that a new investigatory body had even been created in the previous year, which would have shared the investigative load—this, by the way, being the first time Tawney ever recognized the Bureau of Investigation. "Since the beginning of this fiscal year," Tawney told the chamber, "there existed in the Department of Justice a secret-service division, notwithstanding the provision in the sundry civil bill." He then quoted a newspaper interview Secret Service chief John E. Wilkie had given the previous December. "Since the law taking our men away from the Department of Justice went into effect," Wilkie told the paper, "that department has organized a secret service or detective force of its own." Tawney then read the newspaper article's coverage of how the new bureau had been created, noting the attorney general's previous requests that just such an agency be established.

Judging from the speech he gave the House, Tawney appears to have taken no issue with the creation of the bureau. Rather, he craftily used it to discount any claims that his amendment restricting Secret Service operations could possibly have hampered Department of Justice investigations, since Justice had its own investigatory body! "The facts conclusively prove," Tawney exulted, that "every department of the Government possess the same authority to-day it possessed before the enactment of this provision to employ that service and has more money available for the payment of that service now than it has ever had." In refuting the president's claim that the investigatory ability of the Secret Service had been hindered, Tawney failed to mention that the Department of Justice *would* have been hindered had they not created the new bureau in direct response to Congress's amendment.

Tawney then moved on to what he saw as the most egregious attack made by the president, reading aloud portions of the president's letter to Congress: "Mr. Tawney," read the president's letter, "in the debate stated that he had in his possession 'a letter from the Secretary of the Treasury received a few days ago,' in which the Secretary of the Treasury 'himself admits that the provisions under which the appropriation has been made have been violated year after year.'"[7] Tawney explained to the gallery that the message the president mentioned had been appended to Congress's record of the annual message. The president, Tawney read, had then claimed that the letter "makes no such admissions as that which Mr. Tawney alleges." In self-defense, Tawney then quoted his original statement from the record: "I have in my possession a letter from the Secretary of the Treasury, received a few days ago, in which he has pointed out to me the practice of the Treasury Department whereby he himself admits that the provisions under which this appropriation is made have been violated year after year."

This whole performance, it seems, was to point out that the president had misrepresented Tawney's statement to the assembly in omitting the word *whereby* from Tawney's statement. This was the entire argument, the cause of all of his disgruntlement with the president. "The omissions by the President of the word 'whereby,'" Tawney continued, "whether intentional or not, entirely changes the purport and meaning of my statement and conveys the impression that I deliberately misrepresented to the House that the Secretary in his letter had expressly admitted 'that the provisions under which the appropriation is made have been violated year after year for a number of years in his own department.'" Satisfied that everyone must now see things his way, Tawney concluded that "Further comment is not necessary."

After Tawney ceded the floor, Speaker Cannon named the second representative called out by the president, and J. Swagar Sherley of Kentucky took the floor: "That a grave breach of the privileges of the House, and thereby a grave injury to the country has been committed by the President, would seem to be apparent to anyone capable of understanding the English language." Sherley then addressed the president's accusations that Sherley had repeatedly claimed the Secret Service had inappropriately investigated Congress. "I did not have in my mind at any time," Sherley defended himself, "the fear of being investigated by secret-service men. I have no such fear now, but I have a pronounced repugnance to so being, and I trust the day may never come when I shall be so lacking in manhood as not to have such repugnance." For this Sherley received loud applause. His eloquent oration was repeatedly interrupted by applause, which broke out across the House chamber, as when he stated, with high flourish, "The President's stigma is gratuitous and without the shadow of an excuse."

Eventually Sherley moved to the crux of his argument. "The President," he told the assembled, "considers that a secret service department of government is not only an absolute necessity, but that the efficiency of its service is so great as to warrant its creation without restriction as to its use, trusting to the Executive to prevent abuse, and if such occurs, punishing unsparingly those guilty of the abuse. . . . I, on the contrary, believe it to be so dangerous an instrument as to warrant its creation for the use of an Executive only when it is so circumscribed as to prevent as far as possible its abuse." Unlike the president, Sherley believed it was the prerogative of Congress, through their legislative authority, to control the growing power of the executive, especially when Congress believed that power to have been abused.

After Sherley concluded his comments, the speaker called Representative Walter I. Smith of Iowa, the third of Roosevelt's villains. First, Smith said, he wished to "discuss as calmly as I can the controversy which has arisen." Though he did not defend the president, Smith did inject some sense into the debate in reviewing the history of the Secret Service. His speech focused primarily on the Secret Service's investigatory duties not just within the Treasury Department but across all federal departments, detailing how this workload had built up over time, necessitating the loaning of operatives, and how in order to pay operatives for their service various appropriation laws had been violated.

Most pointed about Smith's speech was that he tried to refocus the House's attention. "The question now," he said, "is not should a legal detective force be created in the Department of Justice, but was Congress subject to just criticism for destroying at its last session the system which had grown up of the using the counterfeiting force in the Treasury Department for miscellaneous purpose." The Bureau of Investigation had already been created by this point, so unless his use of the word *legal* was meant to differentiate this new bureau from the possibly "illegal" investigations the Secret Service had been conducting, it would seem Congressman Smith was unaware that in July of 1908 Roosevelt and Bonaparte had created the Bureau of Investigation in the Department of Justice.

Finally, Speaker Cannon called Representative John J. Fitzgerald of New York, the last of the four named by President Roosevelt. First, Fitzgerald made it very clear that he supported tabling the president's annual message. There was no excuse, he said, for Treasury's loaning out Secret Service men to perform investigations in other departments because each department had its own appropriation to pay for investigations. He argued that in no way had government investigations into wrongdoing been hampered by the Tawney amendment or the House change in budgets.

Then, Fitzgerald proceeded to tediously walk the members of the House through each department and their budgets for crime detection, including the Post Office, the Interstate Commerce Commission, and even the US Army. He summed up his exercise in budgetary politics by saying "that it has never been the policy to establish a central police or spy system in the Federal Government" and that "every department has been and now is given ample funds and authority to procure evidence and to detect criminals." In conclusion, he said, "If the criminals are not unearthed, it is not due to the provision about which the President complains, but it is due entirely to the inefficiency of his administration." This was greeted with much applause. Curiously, while Fitzgerald's list of departments and budgets appeared to be nearly exhaustive, he made no mention of the newly formed Bureau of Investigation.

And with this, the debate quickly turned to the vote and parliamentary procedure. Some members of the House asked for clarification, while others wanted the vote delayed; Representative Augustus Peabody Gardner of Massachusetts attempted to add an amendment to the resolution. In the end, the original resolution was put forth for a vote seven hours after the House had begun its deliberation. The roll call was taken, and the final vote was 212 yeas, 36 nays, five voting "present," and 135 abstaining. The resolution carried, and it was agreed that the Secret Service portion of the annual message and the entire special message would be tabled. As the *Washington Post* put it, the president's address was to be "utterly ignored by the House."[8]

As historian Gatewood explains, "The tabling of the presidential messages by the House was a method of rebuking the Chief Executive which had rarely been invoked."[9] Speaker of the House Joe Cannon himself "characterized the passage of the Perkins resolution as the most significant triumph of the legislature over the executive since Henry Clay's resolution censuring Andrew Jackson for his bank policy."[10] To the members of the House, and nearly all of Congress, the censure of a sitting president was a big deal. That sentiment, as Representative Bennet had pointed out during the debate, was not shared by the American people.

The media reported widely on the outcome the next day. "After seven hours of debate," wrote the *New York Times*, "the House this evening adopted a resolution laying on the table the references of the President to the Secret Service in his annual message and the entire text of his special message in response to a request for information from the House."[11] Tawney and the others in the House believed themselves on the winning side of not only the argument but public opinion as well. Determined not to squander his advantage, Tawney vowed to keep up the pressure on the president.

That same day, Tawney introduced his own resolution before the House, calling for a special committee to be formed for the purpose of conducting an exhaustive investigation into the Secret Service—an investigation separate from the one the

Senate was already planning to conduct.[12] With absolutely no debate, it passed by the House.[13] Although Tawney was hoping, as was traditional, to be appointed the committee's chair, on Monday, January 11, Speaker Cannon selected a more neutral party, Representative Marlin Edgar Olmsted from Pennsylvania.

But because it was Tawney who had put forth the resolution, it was he the reporters wanted to talk to. When asked if the investigation was intended as retribution against the president, Tawney told them, "I want to make it emphatic and positive that the present resolution has nothing whatever to do with the present controversy between the President and the House of Representatives or with the mention by name of myself or other members of the appropriations committee. It would seem to me that even a brief glance at the facts in the case would be convincing proof of the reasonableness of this statement." The only problem was, no one was buying it. Nearly everyone, from the average American citizen all the way up to the president, saw it for what it was: another way for the House to punish the president for his transgressions. The *Evening Star*'s editor noted that "Chairman Tawney of the appropriations committee is somewhat irritated as a result of the general impression that seems to prevail that he introduced his resolution for an investigation of all forms of public government inspection and private detective work as a result of the still warm controversy between the President and Congress."[14] Still, Tawney would not quit.

On the same day that he had introduced the resolution, Tawney had fired off copies of the letter he had been preparing to the *Duluth News-Tribune*, the *Minneapolis Journal*, the *Minneapolis Tribune*, the *Pioneer Press*, the *St. Paul Dispatch*, the *Austin Herald*, and the *Times-Enterprise*.[15] The letter, he felt, was additional proof that he was right. But to the majority of people who read his letter, it was nothing more than sour grapes.

Still one more letter was read by the public that Saturday, when the newspapers published a copy of the president's letter to the Senate before that body had even received their copy. Originally, the administration had stated it would not release a copy of Roosevelt's letter to the Senate until Monday, January 11. However, seeing the American peoples' response to the

House resolution to table the president's message, Roosevelt took full advantage of the momentum in his favor, releasing it early. Ostensibly, it was one of the notices he had sent over to Congress on Friday afternoon when his private secretary had interrupted the House session, causing such commotion.

The newspapers recognized that in breaking the administration's promise to wait until Monday, Roosevelt was proving his political savvy. As the *Washington Post* saw it, "The President, up to date, has proved himself a master in controversy, vigilant, fully equipped with facts, always on the aggressive, and commanding extraordinary facilities for setting his case before the people. Congress has certain advantages, also, which would make it irresistible in a struggle with any other antagonist than Theodore Roosevelt."[16] In other words, had Congress picked a fight with anyone other than Roosevelt, they might have proven successful. But Roosevelt had demonstrated his political agility in his sparring with the House, and he was about to outmaneuver the Senate.

There was some belief that, with the salty Benjamin Tillman, the Senate might fare better than the House had with Tawney. "There is great curiosity," wrote the *Washington Post* wrote, "as to the manner in which Senator Tillman will treat the President's charges. The South Carolinian is the possessor of the sharpest tongue in Congress. His store of invective is inexhaustible, and his faculty of coining striking and sarcastic phrases in the heat of debate makes him a dangerous opponent."[17] Yet Tillman also had more at stake than most—both because of the possibility he might perjure himself and because his health was poor after having suffered a stroke the previous year. And so it was that suspicions arose when Tillman made a particular announcement in advance of the speech he was to give the Senate on Monday, January 11.

The day before the Senate was to meet, newspapers reported that papers had been stolen from Tillman's desk in the Senate chamber, including documentary evidence that would have exonerated him from all allegations being laid upon him, particularly those the president had levied in his letter to Senator Hale. Tillman told the *New York Times* that "the papers were in my desk in a big envelope. They were there last Spring, and I had no occasion to disturb them." Though he had "made a careful search of every drawer and of every corner in which the envelope might have lodged," he insisted, "I don't know where the envelope has gone nor do I offer any suggestion," before suggestively hinting, "There are places, though, where these documents might have been eagerly desired."[18] Some thought the president's men had taken the papers, while others believed it could have been the Secret Service. Most, however, were convinced that either Tillman had misplaced the letters himself or, possibly, that it was all a ruse—the letters had never existed.

Just as the House had provided its spectacle, the Senate was about to have its own. People arrived early to claim a seat in the Senate gallery, even if it meant sitting on the stairs. As the *New York Times* reported on the spectators, "Few Senators in recent years have been greeted by so great a throng as gathered to hear the South Carolinian. Two hours before the Senate convened the corridors were packed with eager humanity striving to secure places of vantage in the galleries. Women's hats and wraps were torn and one man fainted in the press gallery. Before noon the police were forced to stop the elevators leading to the gallery floors, and to guard the stairs against crowds."[19] All eyes were now on the Senate.

When Tillman finally appeared before the body, the newspapers noted the obvious toll either his health or simply the pressure of the coming speech had been taking. "Tillman was manifestly nervous when he entered the Chamber," reported the *New York Times*, "although he protested he felt strong in his indignation. Just before entering the Senate he told some friends that he intended sticking closely to his prepared address, but he added naively that he might 'break off the reservation' under the stress of his feelings." Tillman made his way to his seat, and "Every Senator who is in Washington was in his seat when the session opened."[20]

The Senate's turn—and, more specifically Tillman's turn—had come to take on the president. The session opened with a prayer, delivered by Senate chaplain Reverend Edward E. Hale.[21] The good reverend, more widely known as Edward Everett Hale, had authored of one of America's most popular short stories, "The Man without a Country," some forty-six years prior. Long in years when he opened that session, Hale died not long after, on June 10, at the age of eighty-seven.

Almost immediately after Reverend Hale's invocation, Tillman stood up and addressed himself to the president of the Senate and to the Representative from Indiana, Vice President of the United States Charles W. Fairbanks—who during his tenure managed to transform the vice presidency from what John Adams had once called "the most insignificant office that ever the invention of man contrived."[22]

"Mr. President," Tillman began,

> I rise to a question of the highest privilege, and inasmuch as the Senate to-day occupies the attitude somewhat of a court, and inasmuch as any man who is on trial wants the indictment to which he is to answer put on record, if it is not read, I ask the permission of the Senate to have published in the Record, verbatim, seriatim, punctuation, even as it is paged, the document which I sent to the desk, which, I will explain, is the carefully prepared article for the press sent to the acting chairman of the Committee on Appropriations, in which my integrity and character are impugned. I want the charges to precede the reply.

The vice president accepted the president's letter to Senator Eugene Hale, dated January 5, 1909,[23] and it was entered into the Congressional Record. That formality complete, Tillman again addressed the assembly: "I want to say, Mr. President, that it is very irksome to me, a habit which I have never contracted, to read any speech. I would not depart from my custom to-day but for the fact that I fear I might omit, if I attempted a reply extemporaneously, some important matter." Tillman well knew the stakes were high and that he had to tread carefully lest he perjure himself.

Just as Tawney's grand, sensational opening had meant to inflate perception of the president's wrongdoing, Tillman's was positively extravagant. "For the first time in history of this Government," he began, "a member of this body has been brought to the bar of public opinion, before the Senate itself, to be judged under indictment by no less a person than the President of the United States. The manner of the doing of it and the animus and zeal displayed by the Chief Executive are worthy of consideration." Verbose though this foray was, Tillman was actually clearly playing it safe; for generally by this time in any speech he gave he would have already fired off some zinger that either undercut or insulted. This oratory, however, was rather bland in comparison.

He first discussed his grievance with the president, releasing for the record the letter to Senator Hale early on in his address. "I understood the President had notified Senator Hale that there was no need for hurry," Tillman told the Senators, "and that he would not give the papers to the press before Monday"—which was indeed true. "But on Friday morning," Tillman continued, "he changed his mind and notified Senator Hale that he had determined to give all the facts to the newspapers that evening"— also true. In light of the president's timing, while a few papers had managed to get the word out that same evening, such as the Washington *Evening Star*, most printed it on the front pages of their Saturday morning editions.[24]

Tillman then told the Senate, "It is well understood that the President is an adept at advertising and that he has used the press with more skill than any man in American politics"—a statement that no doubt was well received by the president himself. "He realizes the importance of 'getting in the first blow,' though it was below the belt and might well convict him of cowardice." While for the time and place those were no doubt fighting words, Tillman also knew that getting to the American people first was nothing more than Roosevelt playing politics. Tillman was, most likely, just upset that Roosevelt beat him to it.

Next, Tillman laid out the charges the president had made in his letter to Senator Hale, specifically the personal ones filed against Tillman, and tried to make it appear that the president had merely been retaliating against Tillman for the many things Tillman had said about the president on the Senate floor. To this point, the speech was straightforward and lacking the usual attacks for which he had earned the sobriquet "pitchfork." But that quickly changed

"I was not aware," Tillman continued,

that these darts of mine had quivered in the Executive hide and stung him so, but the eagerness and intensity with which he has presented his case against me, his making a precedent where none has existed heretofore, his taking from the committee to which he had forwarded them the papers and giving them to the press before that committee had considered them, indicate that Theodore Roosevelt enjoys to the limit the feeling of getting even with Ben Tillman, and lays on the big stick with the keenest relish, doubtless believing that the pitchfork has gone out of business.

Both laughter and loud applause broke out among the spectators in the Senate gallery, for this was the type of rhetoric everyone had come to expect from Tillman. The Senators themselves maintained their decorum, for it was against Senate rules to applaud, and the vice president had to admonish the spectators.

Tillman then got down to brass tacks, reading the president's letter, pointing out every instance in which the president had called him out by name. Despite all of Tillman's rhetorical flourish, challenging the president's interpretation of the Oregon land deals—especially where he had caught Tillman in an evident contradiction—Tillman never denied the president's allegations. More pointedly, he never denied that he'd had any interest in the purchase of land, whereas previously on the Senate floor he had insisted that he'd never been interested at all.

In order to conceal this contradiction, Tillman began introducing letters and telegrams between his land representative, various lawyers involved in the land deals, and many land circulars that had been passed around at the time. He also asked that additional documents by the president and the attorney general and regarding the Senate resolution on the Oregon and California railroad land grants—which Tillman had helped pass—be entered into the record. Of these he said, "I was not interested except as a private individual wanting to purchase, and as a Senator desiring to enable others to have the opportunity to do so."

"Of course," he continued, "the President is sure that I have done something very discreditable and outrageous. He hates me, and would destroy me if he could." Tillman's paranoia aside, in the entirety of the speech, he only once admits that he may have been "disingenuous" when he detailed his lack of interest in the land. "I court the most searching investigation," he said, nearing conclusion. "Nay, I demand it." And this insistence may very well have been Tillman's greatest mistake.

He ended with a flourish, reciting a passage from Edmund Spenser's *Faerie Queene*, before taking his seat. But "toward the close of his speech," the *New York Times* later reported, "friends of the South Carolinian feared he was about to break down." And "as he took his seat his features were contorted as though he were repressing his emotions only by violent effort, while his face was pallid. He recovered himself quickly, however, and remained for some minutes in his seat, receiving the congratulations of his colleagues."[25]

Tillman had done, and the only thing left was to pass judgment on how well he had performed. "Although the Senate avoided any such verdict," records historian Gatewood, "the press was quick to render one. And Tillman was the loser."[26]

Following Tawney's playbook, Tillman tried to remain in the news all that week in an attempt to convince the world of his righteousness. He repeatedly called for an investigation to be opened with the express purpose of helping him clear his name. "I have done all I can," he lamented to the *Evening Star* at week's end. "I have twice demanded investigation and indicated my strong desire to have every possible fact about this matter brought to light. What else can I do? If the Senate fails to do anything, I suppose it will mean that it doesn't think the charges of the President are worth investigating. I shall be disappointed, however, if there is not a thorough investigation."[27]

On same day Tillman gave his interview, January 15, the Senate created a special committee composed of Senators Gallagher, Hemenway, and Clay, who, like their House counterpart, took up consideration of whether to accept or table the portion of the president's annual message regarding the Secret Service.[28] Everyone now had to wait to see what would happen with Tawney's committee in the House to investigate the Secret Service and whether the Senate committee would follow the House in rebuking the president and open its own investigation.

Newspaper editorials, letters to the editor, and the overall assessment of public opinion affirmed that week that the president had been in the right and that Tawney and Tillman were simply making fools of themselves. As for the Tillman speech, historian Gatewood explains, "No one was more pleased with the public reaction to the exposure of Tillman than the President himself."[29] The *New York Times* noted that over at the White House "Everything was as serene as a Summer afternoon. The President, in fact, was in high good humor over what he regarded as the success of his maneuvers regarding the restriction placed on the use of the Secret Service by Congress last year. He set out to lay the whole affair before the country, and he believed that his purpose had been very thoroughly accomplished."[30]

Roosevelt expressed his deep satisfaction in a letter to his son: "I think I have knocked the paint off of Tillman, who is one of the foulest and rottenest demagogs (sic) in the whole country; and I do not see how the House can get away from what I have said about it."[31]

Roosevelt was right to feel satisfied, for the newspapers could not help but observe that the vast majority of letters and messages congressmen had received from their constituents were overwhelmingly supportive of the president.[32] Roosevelt, it seems, had not been blemished by even one of Congress's many acts to smear him, for "neither resolutions nor rhetoric by Congress prompted any substantial shift in public opinion."[33]

Not only had he managed to deflect Congress's attention away from his Bureau of Investigation, he had also gained the "popular side of the controversy." In fact, he had been such an effective political pugilist that "the more vigorously Congress reacted to his message, the more unpopular its position seemed to become."[34]

Still, the outcome was not yet final, for Roosevelt had six weeks left in office. Roosevelt was, of course, ever defiant and fully determined to ride the controversy out to the very end.

President Roosevelt on the day of Vice President William Howard Taft's inauguration on March 4, 1909. Taft remarked it would be a cold day when he became president, while Roosevelt stated there would be a blizzard going out, just the way he came in. It was indeed both cold and there was a blizzard.

Photo courtesy of the Library of Congress.

14

The Aftermath

The relationship between the executive and legislative branches during Theodore Roosevelt's administration had never been good, but after the heated battle over the Secret Service, what little goodwill that had existed was now gone. Even relationships inside the president's own political party were now rancor-filled. Less than a week after Tawney had sought to defend himself in the House of Representatives, the president sent a request from the White House to Speaker Cannon, a fellow Republican. As Roosevelt neared the end of his presidency, he had begun thinking about the transition to civilian life. "Among all the furniture and bric-à-brac in the White House," reported the *New York Times*, "the ten desk chairs in the Cabinet room and the President's own desk chair in his private office are particularly significant to the President as having been the seat of war on many critical moments in his battles with Congress and political opponents."[1]

And so the president wrote Cannon, explaining his fondness for the furniture, asking if there would be any objection to his taking it with him into retirement. The furniture was owned by the federal government, which had led Roosevelt to conclude he needed special authorization to remove it with him, and he'd believed the speaker to be the right person to whom he should address such a request. Roosevelt added that there was a "lounge for which Mrs. Roosevelt had a special liking" that he'd also like to take.[2]

The speaker received the request and immediately sent his reply. "He gave the President to understand that the legislative branch of the Government was not, properly speaking, the guardian of the White House furniture," reported the *New York Times*, "but he would gladly refer the request, with the President's letter, to the Committee on Appropriations." Representative Tawney was, of course, the chair of the committee. "Without delay," the *Times* added, "the President replied that he withdrew his request and would let the matter drop."[3]

The dispute between the president and Congress, by most public accounts, had left the president feeling good about his position, believing himself to have come out on top. Those of his aides who had seen firsthand the machinations of the White House believed the president had kept in "high good humor" regarding the affair.[4] Even his letters to his children had suggested Roosevelt believed he had gained the upper hand in the controversy. Only once, perhaps in an unguarded moment, did Roosevelt suggest otherwise. Writing to his son Kermit, he explained how "Congress of course feels that I will never again have to be reckoned with and that it is safe to be ugly with me," then adding, "I am not having an easy time."[5]

Still, most of his personal correspondence suggested that, no matter what, no matter how down he felt, he would continue to press forward in his fight with Congress. In a letter to his other son, Theodore Roosevelt Jr., the president explained in a somewhat conciliatory mood that he believed "it is a President's duty to get on with Congress if he possibly can, and that it is a reflection upon him if he and Congress come to a complete break." Yet he also believed that he had to "fight hard" or "be put in a contemptible position." So, no matter how contentious the dispute had became, it was Roosevelt's intention to fight hard "right up to the end."[6]

Initially, lighthearted public ribbing had helped bolster the president's beliefs that he'd been in the right. On January 30, 1909, a few weeks after the episodes in the House and Senate had concluded, Roosevelt and Fairbanks attended a gala at the

Gridiron Club bidding farewell to their presidency and vice presidency. The event included dinner, various speeches, and an awards ceremony, followed by a series of skits, songs, and dance numbers. One sketch, reported the *New York Times*, poked fun at the Secret Service controversy: The lights went out, a "shivery music" played, and "a sibilant and mysterious 'sh-sh-sh'" was heard. "When the lights went up, there was presented a picturesque group. In front was a large policeman, blue coat, helmet, and club complete; a black-mustached creature in a long frock coat and a big slouch hat, who looked like a stage detective; and several other members of the Music committee arrayed in evening clothes and black hats wearing domino masks across their eyes." The detective was named "Blinkerton"—a clear play on Allan Pinkerton—who was "trying to find out what Congressmen did with their $7,500 a year."[7]

"Chief Bilkie, have you detected any counterfeiters?" asked Blinkerton.[8]

"No," replied Chief Bilkie—an obvious play on Secret Service Chief John Wilkie—"but I have discovered a few four-flushers."[9] This was a reference to the Congressman who earlier that month, after reading Roosevelt's special message, had been overheard calling him a four-flusher—a welcher, piker, or braggart.[10]

Detective Blinkerton and Chief Bilkie then turned their attention to a large teddy bear that had been spotlighted on stage, and breaking into a song sung to the tune of "Tit Willow," from Gilbert and Sullivan's very popular comic opera *The Mikado*:

> On the White House front step stood a great Teddy bear
> Singing Tawney, Jim Tawney, Jim Tawney.
> His melody sad and floated forth on the air,
> Oh, Tawney, Jim Tawney, Jim Tawney.
> When we go up to Congress applying for cash,
> For a Nation that ought to be cutting a dash,
> There's a name that sends our expectations to smash:—
> It's Tawney, Jim Tawney, Jim Tawney.[11]

Roosevelt took the Gridiron Club's teasing in stride, and he soon learned that his victory in the Secret Service issue was nearly complete. The House of Representatives had not only backed down in the battle for public opinion, but they had also conceded that the creation of the Bureau of Investigation had been legal. "On February 1, 1909," historian Gatewood explains, "the House excused the Olmsted Committee, originally instituted to make a sweeping inquiry into the Secret Service, 'from all but the most perfunctory investigation.'"[12] This might not sound like much, but in the world of politics it was indeed a presidential victory.

The *New York Times* understood the implications when it reported, "The last vestige of the fight of the House on the President crumpled up to-day and fell to Earth. The surrender was disguised in the form of a resolution from Chairman Olmsted of the select committee appointed to investigate the Secret Service excusing his committee from everything but the most perfunctory investigation. The thinness of the disguise was unveiled in the fact that there was not a dissenting vote to the emasculating resolution."[13] Although the Olmsted Committee still operated, their only task left was to assess the budgetary aspects of the two agencies, debating whether there should be one central detective bureau under the Department of Justice serving all of the federal government agencies or two such agencies, as was now the case. Again, as Gatewood explained, "Members of Congress, including Tawney, conceded that although the Secret Service should be confined to its activities regarding counterfeiting and protection of the President, the attorney general 'had full power to organize a detective force under the appropriation for the prosecution and detection of crime.'"[14] The Bureau of Investigation's very existence, it was communicated through this action on the part of the House committee, was not to be challenged, leaving it on a more solid footing than it had been since its creation.

Despite these successes, politically speaking, Roosevelt was still not quite out of hot water, as members of Congress, especially in the House, were still searching for ways to undermine his stance on the issue. His decision to remain steadfast in his position was soon put to the test when, at the end of January, chief of Secret Service John Wilkie was called to testify before the House appropriations committee. They were in the process of considering the next year's budget and saw it as an opportunity to once again try to gain at least some small victory in their tiff with the president.

As the discussion of the Secret Service budget under the Sundry bill arose, Congress asked Chief Wilkie to clarify several things regarding his Secret Service operatives and their budgetary needs. One item drudged back up was whether the operatives had ever followed members of Congress in order to spy on them. "I wish to record the fact," said Wilkie, "that no member of the Secret Service or any one acting for the Secret Service, has ever shadowed a Congressman or Senator."[15]

Many of the other questions returned to whether or not the Tawney amendment had hampered any of the investigations conducted by the Secret Service. This time around, Wilkie didn't answer as succinctly, and the newspapers' takeaway was that the Tawney amendment had *not* hampered investigations, which ran counter to what the president had said in his annual message.[16] Wilkie may very well have been playing to the reality that Roosevelt would soon be out of office, the Taft administration was somewhat an unknown factor, and, however the new administration would side in the debate, Wilkie would still have to work with Congress in the future. It was, perhaps, no longer in his best interest to be antagonistic toward a Congress that was, at the time, determining his agency's budget for the next year. Answering vaguely was really the only politically expedient way he could address the question.

Roosevelt was incensed with the newspapers' reportage of Wilkie's testimony and quickly issued a statement in reply. "At no time has the President or any Administrative officer claimed that the restrictive legislation of the last session affected the Secret Service division of the Treasury Department in the matter of suppressing counterfeiting or protecting the President," the president once again insisted. He then added, "but the assertion that the restriction was harmless to the Government's interest is not correct." He continued to assert that the Tawney amendment had hampered investigations conducted by the Secret Service back when that agency had been loaning operatives to other departments for other types of investigations, including the investigation of land-fraud deals. He again advocated for an agency similar to the Secret Service to be placed under the Department of Justice "who can act against criminals anywhere, and the position of the Administration is that it is against sound public policy to discriminate in favor of criminals by discriminating against the use of the Secret Service to detect and punish them."[17]

The newspapers reported on Wilkie's "disagreement" with the president, often reprinting Wilkie's rambling response. But a few days later, one of Roosevelt's cabinet members spoke out against the president's statement. James Rudolph Garfield, son of the assassinated president, had first joined Roosevelt's administration to serve as a member of the US Civil Service Commission and then became commissioner of corporations under the Department of Commerce and Labor, until finally, in 1907, he was appointed secretary of the Interior. On most things, Garfield had agreed with the president, including exposing government fraud and the conservation of natural resources. Where Garfield disagreed with the president was regarding the Department of the Interior's dependence on Secret Service agents to conduct Interior's own investigations. Garfield believed his own men could do the job just fine and he did not need the other agency's services.

When Garfield was called before the appropriations committee for testimony regarding his department's needs under the Sundry Civil Appropriation Bill, he was asked whether Wilkie's suggestion was true that the Tawney amendment had disrupted Secret Service investigations into land-fraud cases. Garfield replied, "I took up the matter immediately after I became Secretary, March, 1907, and discussed it with the Attorney General, and we were constantly trying to find a plan by which we could eliminate the duplication of work and lack of knowledge in the public land work that existed at that time." He also added that he "wanted to keep the investigation of land frauds entirely within his own jurisdiction." When asked by Representative Smith who was doing the duplication, Garfield replied, "There was a force under the Department of Justice that was doing work of which the Land Office had no information, and I found that it was engaged upon cases upon which our own men were engaged, and there was overlapping of work, conflict, and friction between the two bodies of men."[18]

As Garfield had mentioned the new Bureau of Investigation, Congressman Smith shifted his questions to the Department of the Interior's ability to secure investigators outside of his own department, deftly ignoring Garfield's desire to only use his own men. As the *New York Times* reported, "Mr. Garfield, under persistent questioning, chiefly by Mr. Smith, was then brought to admit that although the loaning of men in the Secret Service Division of the Treasury Department was prohibited, his department was not prohibited from 'borrowing' men from the new secret force of the Department of Justice." But "Mr. Smith," the *Times* observed, "did not have any easy time getting this admission."

"You do not know of anything that would make the Department of Justice Secret Service force less available to you than the Secret Service force in the Treasury Department formerly was?" asked Smith.

"No," came Garfield's quick reply. "I do not consider that either of them is available for the Interior Department."

Smith ignored the last reply, again trying get Garfield to contradict not only the president's views expressed in the annual message but also the president's sentiments more recently expressed in his letter to the newspapers following Wilkie's testimony.

"What I am trying to get at," said Smith, clearly irritated, "is this. It now being prohibited to make loans of the men in the Secret Service of the Treasury Department, there is not anything in the law that you know of that would make it just as permissible now to loan to your department this new force in the Department of Justice as it formerly was to loan men from the Secret Service Division of the Treasury Department?"

"Yes, Sir," replied Secretary Garfield, "I think that is true."

Smith, wanting more than a "no" and a "yes" from Garfield, reworded the question.

"If you had the right to take the old men from the Treasury Secret Service you now have the right to take the men from the new Department of Justice Secret Service?"

"That is a proper statement of the situation," Garfield affirmed.

Having obtained exactly the answer he wanted, Smith and the rest of the appropriations committee moved on to other matters. "That they realized they had scored heavily on the President's charge," reported the *New York Times* the following day, "is indicated in the fact that after printing the hearings they held them for release, thus giving time for them to be mailed to all parts of the country."

When the hearing's transcript was released, newspapers like the *Washington Post* ran with the headline, "WORK IS NOT RESTRICTED," while the Washington *Evening Star* ran the headline, "UNHAMPERED BY LAW."[19] Even the *New York Times*, which noted what Smith had done in his questioning, headlined their story, "ROOSEVELT CHARGE DENIED BY GARFIELD."[20]

But Smith's was not a clean victory against the president. The only reason he'd been able to "score heavily" against the president was because of the president's own actions. If, after the passage of the Tawney amendment, the president had not created the Bureau of Investigation in response, then the Department of Interior would not have been able to borrow agents from the Department of Treasury or the Department of Justice. Assuming Interior hadn't had the investigatory capacity to make up this loss, the land-fraud investigations *would* have been hampered. So, the only reason Smith won this rhetorical victory against Roosevelt was because Roosevelt, Bonaparte, and Wilkie had worked together to create the Bureau of Investigation, which was made available to the Department of the Interior.

Meanwhile, over in the Senate, James A. Hemenway of Indiana, tasked with drafting the Senate committee's findings, was putting the finishing touches on their own Secret Service report. It was released to the press on February 11, 1909, and once again there was both an attack on the president's veracity as well as an administrative victory. Hemenway's report countered the president's claim that the Tawney amendment had hampered the Secret Service investigations, describing the president's claims as "absolutely erroneous and wrong."[21] Yet at the same time, as Gatewood explains, the report also "favored a continuation of the dual system whereby the Secret Service Division concentrated upon counterfeiting and the detective force in the Justice Department assumed responsibility for other types of investigations."[22] The Senate had given the Roosevelt administration a win when they said they also believed the creation of the Bureau of Justice was legal and that they would not dispute its very existence. While Roosevelt no doubt relished the win, there was no way he was going to let the political slight pass without a fight.

Roosevelt criticized the Hemenway report in a letter of February 21, 1909, directed to Senator Hale and publically released the next day. Roosevelt wrote, "I have seen the report presented by Senator Hemenway on behalf of your committee in reference to the Secret Service matter. The report is inaccurate and misleading in various important respects and I desire to make certain corrections in reference to statements which appear therein, and in the subsequent debate."[23] Roosevelt then offered some of the same arguments he had previously, but this time adding praise for the work of the new Bureau of Investigation. He mentioned that Congress had limited the use of the Secret Service and that, "in consequence, the Department of Justice was obliged to develop as speedily as possible its own corps of special detective agents to take the place of the Secret Service agents which it had previously used; and the nucleus of this force was made up of officers formerly connected with the Secret Service and trained in its methods. I call your special attention to the fact that if the Department of Justice had not taken this action there would have been a complete failure to enforce the law against many types of criminals."[24]

President Roosevelt then made a statement surely designed to anger Congress: "Chief Wilkie," he said, "should be transferred to the Department of Justice and placed at the head of the force therein organized."[25] As Gatewood explained, "In view of the congressional hostility toward Wilkie, it is difficult to imagine a recommendation less likely to be implemented."[26] The reaction was as expected, and Representative Tawney showed his animosity when he asserted to the newspapers that Wilkie was "the man who carried on the campaign and stirred the President against Congress, because it had interfered with the activities of his, Chief Wilkie's bureau."[27]

Despite all the rancor over Roosevelt's response, the Senate chose to simply ignore it and allowed the Hemenway report to represent "its final action in the Secret Service controversy."[28] In the end, the dispute between the president and Congress had tallied mostly as a win for the president, if infuriating nearly every member of Congress can be called a win. It was perhaps best summed up by British Ambassador James Bryce, who had come to the United States in 1907; after hearing of Roosevelt's win over Congress, the Viscount observed, "Nobody likes him now but the people."[29]

Even the newspapers were growing tired of the Secret Service controversy, and after the latest spat, they began referring to it as "a waste of time." "Congress and the President are at it again," the *Washington Post*'s editorial began. "The latest episode in the series of controversies is the 'rebuke' administered by the President of the Senate committee which has investigated the question of secret service expenditures."[30]

"These exchanges are not seemly," the editors of the *Post* observed,

> and not conducive to the proper expedition of the public business. Judging by the temper of the public as shown in the press, there is an almost universal hope that the battles and skirmishes will end without delay. The energy expended on both sides might have been employed with great benefit if joined in mutual effort by the President and Congress. There are plenty of matters demanding the attention of the legislative and executive departments in these closing days of the administration upon which no controversy need arise. It is too bad that there should be any further waste of time in controversy.[31]

That "waste of time," however, filled their newspapers and sold them to a public enjoying the spectacle. The media of the day, primarily the newspapers and weeklies, could not honestly be all that upset with Roosevelt over a controversy that had certainly increased both their sales and profits. *Harper's Weekly* was perhaps slightly more honest: "We shall miss him terribly," they editorialized. "Who will be left to supply us with exciting news after he goes away from here? Mr. Taft is a good and true man, and promises to make a good and true president. But he has no real knack for daily novelty."[32]

Despite the *Post*'s lamentations, the controversy continued. On February 19, the *New York Times* noted, when it was reported out of the appropriations committee, the Sundry Civil Appropriation Bill had retained "all the Secret Service provisions to which President Roosevelt took exception in his message to Congress." It did, however, propose increasing their budget "from $115,000 to $125,000."[33] This action moved the Sundry bill out of committee and into the full House for debate, set for February 25. This bill debate offered yet one more opportunity for the members of the House to "spank" the president—or, as Representatives Tawney, Smith, and Fitzgerald saw it, "one last opportunity to defend their honor and integrity."[34]

But the debates offered little that hadn't been covered before and were mostly spent repeating the same claims, reviewing the same history, discussing the same perceived issues with the Secret Service, and only occasionally mentioning the Bureau of Investigation. Only Smith truly went on the attack during the debates, but his aggression was mostly directed at the Secret Service, particularly Chief Wilkie. It was a vituperative attack on his part, for he charged that the Secret Service and all of its agents were worthless, and he went so far as to say, "The first requisite for a Secret Service man is that he be a common liar."[35]

This was not the worst of the inflammatory remarks, however. That dubious honor belongs to an attack on the president by Representative George Washington Cook of Colorado, who had lost his own party's nomination the previous year and was on his way out of the House after having served only one term in office. Cook railed against Roosevelt's assertion that a Secret Service operative had been killed in Colorado in the line of duty, despicably denigrating Joe Walker's honor by referring to him as nothing more than a "notorious horse thief."[36]

Cook went on to insult the president, saying, "He is almost a daily threat on the peace and prosperity of the country, and should be knocked on the head by a decision of the Supreme

Court of the United States."[37] "No citizen of the United States," Cook declared in the conclusion of his speech, "ever heard a President brag about wielding the big stick in Congress and the courts until the present crack-brained egotist came into power by the bullet of an assassin. The impudent presumption and tyrant boast of whirling a big stick over the legislative branch of the Government is the most outrageous insult that has ever been given to Congress."[38]

If the members of the House had intended to get under President Roosevelt's skin or to at least place him in an uncomfortable position, they failed. "Those critics of President Roosevelt," the *New York Times* reported the next day, "who imagine that they are giving him some unpleasant moment by their vehement denunciation, and otherwise adverse comments upon himself and his actions, miss their guess. He is having more fun out of it all than any of them, and it seems in fact only to increase his enjoyment in the course which has provoked the outbursts of wrath. A number of gentlemen who called on the President to-day had evidence of the manner in which he regards this criticism in the jokes he cracked about both the critics and the criticisms."[39] The president knew that the more the House blustered, the stronger a position it placed him in with the people and posterity on the Secret Service issue. The more they attempted to ridicule him, the harder he laughed.

Perhaps some of the members of Congress realized this, for they ceased broaching the issue. As FBI historian John F. Fox Jr. explains, "By that point, few cared to continue the political battle."[40] The majority of congressmen realized that they had lost the fight and that, the more they raised the issues, the more it looked like sour grapes on their part. Besides, Roosevelt was entering his final days in office, and all they had to do was ride out his term, and the Taft administration would be installed.

"Even so," Historian Fox adds, "some of the old opposition from Tawney's committee refused to die."[41] Tawney was perhaps the most tenacious of the appropriations committee's members. An exchange with reporters from the *New York Times* highlights his refusal to end his disagreement with the president, even when the odds were against him. The reporters asked

Tawney if he had been getting any letters on his "spanking of the President."[42]

"Oh, yes, lots of them," Tawney casually replied.

"How did they read?"

"Oh, well," Tawney replied with a wry grin, "about one in every ten I got commended me for the position I had taken."

On March 3, 1909, the Olmsted Committee delivered to the House its report on the investigation of the "Secret Service," which, as Gatewood explains, "Covered much the same ground as the various hearings and debates on the subject."[43] They concluded that "Whether the separate forces of secret service men now existing in the Treasury Department and in the Department of Justice should be combined in one, under control of the Attorney General, we do not attempt to decide, but suggest that, whether separately maintained or under one control, they should be permanently provided for and their duties clearly defined and limited by law."[44]

The only duty the committee really had left to perform was to collect the Secret Service budget for the current year and compare it with the previous year's budget, something that could have been done by a clerk, and probably was. It was clear by the report and the nebulous conclusion that the House was simply letting the problem go away. As the *Times* noted, "All Tawney's House Appropriations Committee could now do was to put up a counter of the days Roosevelt had left in office."[45] More appropriate might have been an hourglass for, Roosevelt only had hours left in office, not days.

Twenty-four hours later, on March 4, 1909, Roosevelt left office.

The weather that day offered an insightful contrast between the man leaving the executive office and the man taking it over. Overnight, an arctic cold front had moved into Washington, bringing with it below-freezing temperatures, a mixture of snow and ice, and some brutally chilly winds. By morning, ten inches of snow blanketed the ground. As conditions in the nation's capital deteriorated that morning, it was decided that the inauguration would be moved indoors, into the Senate chamber, where seating would be severely limited. Despite the weather conditions, the inaugural parade proceeded as planned, necessitating over six thousand city workers that morning to clear the snow and ice off of the parade route so that the horse-drawn carriage carrying Roosevelt and Taft could make unhindered passage to the Capitol.

When the two men arrived on Capitol Hill, both seemed to be in good spirits, laughing and telling jokes to one another. William Howard Taft was overheard commenting how he had always used to say, "It will be a cold day when I go into the White House.'"[46] Roosevelt was heard to have replied, "I knew there would be a blizzard when I went out."[47] Taft had never thought he would become president, and neither had he wanted to be; he had always preferred the idea of joining the Supreme Court. Roosevelt, however, had relished being chief executive, and, having come into Washington himself like a blizzard, would go out like one, too, and the weather would show it.

When the appointed hour arrived, Taft and Roosevelt entered the Senate chamber, with Roosevelt taking a front seat and Taft taking the podium. Roosevelt sat stoically through Taft's inaugural speech, watching his presidency come to an end. Only at the end of Taft's speech did Roosevelt become animated, when he "bounded out of his seat and ran up the steps of the rostrum to shake Taft by the hand. The two men embraced briefly, then stood talking, their hands on each other's shoulders." Roosevelt's sister Bamie recorded the scene for her sister, Corinne, in a letter. "There was not a dry eye in the place," she wrote, "and everyone's throat contracted; as he said good-bye before anyone realized what was happening he went down the steps from the speakers desk and bowing and smiling went out the little side door. . . . It was the simplest most dramatic exit imaginable & left the whole packed Senate with a tremor going through it."[48]

The snowstorm outside had died down by the end of the inauguration ceremony, but a new storm was brewing in the Taft administration. The new president had promised a continuation of Roosevelt's policies, saying, "I should be untrue to myself, to my promises, and to the dedications of the party platform on which I was elected if I did not make the maintenance and enforcement of these reforms a most important feature of my administration."[49] However, Taft did not live up to his words, and even among his first cabinet there was only James Wilson, the secretary of agriculture, who was a holdover from the Roosevelt administration. That unto itself communicated to the world, and especially to Roosevelt, that Taft had every intention of going his own way.

One of the first changes that came with Taft's new leadership was the appointment of a new head of the Department of Justice. George W. Wickersham, Taft's friend and a partner in the law firm of Strong and Cadwalader, served as the forty-seventh attorney general. In 1914, after stepping down, he returned to the law firm, which was then named Cadwalader, Wickersham and Taft, the president's brother Henry W. Taft having joined the firm. The day after being appointed attorney general, Wickersham was asked pointedly if he were prepared to give both the Secret Service and the Bureau of Investigation the "permanent authority of law." Wickersham merely replied that he would "give the matter his consideration."[50]

Wickersham, however, had his own plans, and within days, on March 6, he issued an order that officially established the Bureau of Investigation, and he placed Stanley Finch in the role of director, a role he served until stepping down on April 30, 1912.[51] What Wickersham had left open, however, was the question of which specific types of investigations the Bureau of Investigation was authorized to conduct, leaving the agency to search for its own proper role in government.

"The Bureau's first criminal cases were of a somewhat makeshift character," writes FBI historian Max Lowenthal. "The Justice detectives investigated crimes committed on Indian and other Government reservations; they prepared some District of Columbia cases involving false purchases and sales of securities; they handled a few peonage and bankruptcy fraud cases."[52] For the most part, their cases now tended to be lower profile, mostly bureaucratic in nature. That soon changed, however—not because of the new presidential administration but, ironically, because of a new law passed by Congress.

In light of America's Progressive movement, Congress was beginning to assert more power in the area of the Constitution's interstate-commerce clause, which gave them the power to regulate commerce between states. Congress was fully aware of their power to regulate, but a large part of regulation is enforcement, and until the creation of the Bureau of Investigation, they'd had little means by which they could enforce their laws.[53] Now that the Bureau was officially established, they could include enforcement measures in bills related to interstate commerce. So Congress "passed a number of laws which enabled the Bureau of Investigation to work on crimes in this category" such as "interstate shipment of stolen goods, contraceptives, obscene books, and prizefight films, and the transportation of liquor into dry States."[54]

Most importantly, however, was the passage of the Mann Act of 1910, introduced by Representative James Robert Mann of Illinois. The White-Slave Traffic Act, as it was also known, made it illegal to transport women across state lines for "immoral purposes." One of the earliest cases of the enforcement of this law came when boxing's heavyweight champion, Jack Johnson, a black man, was arrested for transporting Lucille Cameron, his white girlfriend, across state lines on October 12, 1912. Found guilty, Johnson fled the country with Cameron and married her, but he eventually returned to the States, where he surrendered to authorities. On May 24, 2018, President Donald Trump pardoned Jack Johnson for his crime.

Despite its controversial nature, the Mann Act was the law that, according to FBI historian Lowenthal, "gave the Bureau of Investigation its first big push toward and important place in the detective world."[55] Congress had passed a law with a strong enforcement element to it, and the Bureau of Investigation was able to give it teeth. The bureau now had a mission, one that has continued to expand ever since.

As both the bureau's and Roosevelt's reputations continued to expand in the aftermath of the Secret Service controversy, two others reputations rapidly diminished. House Representative James A. Tawney and Senator Benjamin "Pitchfork" Tillman did not fare as well over the public dispute with Roosevelt. The following year found Tawney once again up for reelection, but his reputation had been badly tarnished by his controversy with the president and his unwillingness to move on. "During the Congressional campaign of 1910, when Tawney was fighting for political survival," Gatewood writes, "Roosevelt hastened his demise by publicly criticizing him for his role in the Secret Service incident."[56] Tawney lost his party's nomination in the primaries; he was ousted from his congressional seat. "Looking back a bit," the Washington *Evening Star* editorialized in the aftermath, "Mr. Tawney can and does attribute most of his recent political troubles . . . to his big row with President Roosevelt over the Secret Service."[57] The *Star* could not have been more accurate.

As Roosevelt's tenure in office had been winding down, Tawney had gone against the advice of his own lawyers and decided to move forward with his lawsuit against the *Albert Lea Tribune*. He saw *Tawney* v. *Simonson, Whitcomb, & Hurley Co.* as his last means of keeping the row with Roosevelt alive in the hopes he would one day be personally vindicated. After the judge in the case heard the evidence Tawney submitted as defamation of character, the case was dismissed as "frivolous" and "without foundation."[58]

Tawney was, once again, indignant. In a letter to his lawyers dated January 14, 1910, he wrote how he believed "the Tribune was the aggressor" in the case and that "my principal object in authorizing suit to be brought was to vindicate myself, not only against the Tribune but against the false charge made by Mr. Roosevelt, then President of the United States."[59] Believing the judge had been biased, Tawney filed an appeal to the Minnesota State Supreme Court, which, in the end, did rule the *Tribune*'s words had been "libelous per se."[60] But it was too little too late. By that point, Tawney was already serving what would be his last days in Congress.

Senator Tillman's reputation fared little better, but unlike Tawney, he knew when to give up the fight. "For all his animosity toward Roosevelt," noted Gatewood, Tillman "chose not to make good his threat to expose the 'long list of abuses' committed by the Secret Service." Although "his failure to pursue the issue allowed the President the personal satisfaction of having the last word in the public quarrel," Tillman did manage to retain his Senate seat.[61] He ran for reelection in 1912 and, through a series of political maneuvers, closely won his bid for renomination. Despite announcing his retirement at the end of the 1913–1919 term and the ratification of the Seventeenth Amendment, which allowed the direct election of senators, Tillman believed he could still win and planned to run once more in the fall of 1918. He never had the chance to run, though, for shortly before the election, on July 3, 1918, he died of a cerebral hemorrhage.

In the end, Theodore Roosevelt came out the winner in the Secret Service controversy, and because of his success the Federal Bureau of Investigation has become part of his legacy. It was journalist H. L. Mencken who wrote that Roosevelt "didn't believe in democracy; he believed simply in government."[62] There is much truth in saying that Roosevelt believed in good government, for it was clearly a key element to the Progressive movement Roosevelt had made possible. It was not so much that Roosevelt did not believe in democracy but that he believed democracy was created through good government. Roosevelt saw the potential for government to be a force for good, which he believed helped establish and maintain democratic principles. Good government, he believed, allows democracy to thrive.

Mencken also noted that Roosevelt "was not in favor of unlimited experiment" but that "he was in favor of a rigid control from above, a despotism of inspired prophets and policemen."[63] Roosevelt did believe in the prophets of science and the good that could come of both their research and their advocacy, but he also believed in the human penchant for corruption, and he knew good government needed good police to enforce the laws and to investigate and arrest those who would take advantage of the system for their own personal gain.

That was part and parcel to Roosevelt's good-government plan from his earliest days as a member of the New York State Assembly to his time as a civil service commissioner and to his service as New York City's police commissioner. In the Secret Service controversy, Roosevelt saw the need for that agency's services across the entire federal bureaucracy in order to fight corruption and enforce the laws for the sake of good government and democracy. When that agency was denied by

Congress its ability to investigate corruption across the board, Roosevelt became instrumental in creating an agency that could do just that—today's Federal Bureau of Investigation.

Historian Gatewood, who wrote of President Roosevelt's deft ability to navigate controversy, explained that "Roosevelt appealed to the public conscience with the argument that federal detectives were necessary to combat the lawlessness and corruption which menaced the very institutions essential to democracy."[64] The key reason that Roosevelt won the day was that he had won over the people. They saw on a daily basis how the corrupt abused the system, denying any sense that democracy was for everyone but merely for the elite and the criminal-minded. By taking the fight against corruption publically to the people, Roosevelt knew that his fight for a law-enforcement agency that could root out lawlessness and stop corruption was their fight as well.

Once the American people had sided with Roosevelt, there was nothing Congress could do to alter or stop Roosevelt's new Bureau of Investigation from fighting corruption and keeping lawlessness in check for democracy.

Epilogue

The greatest myth in US politics outside of the belief that the Supreme Court is an apolitical branch of government is that the Federal Bureau of Investigation is a professional, apolitical governmental bureaucracy. Nothing could be further from the truth.

The FBI was born out of a political controversy, a fight over the balance of power between the executive and legislative branches of government, and both its birth and early fight for survival were wholly wrapped up in that political battle. Once firmly established by Attorney General Wickersham under the Taft Administration, the FBI then had to find its purpose. But finding its grounding in the enforcement of the Mann Act, did not mean the organization no longer had to play politics to fight for its survival.[1]

Although today's FBI does try to preserve a sense of professionalism, adhere to the rule of law, and maintain impartiality in its actions, it still engages in politics because by its very nature: as part of the federal bureaucracy under the executive branch of government, it is a part of the political system. Added to this is the fact that the FBI is the leading law-enforcement agency in the federal government, meaning so high-profile criminal cases, especially those having political implications, will be investigated by that agency, further entrenching the organization in politics.

Dozens of books have been written about the FBI's history, and nearly all of them—save perhaps some of those written by retired agents—detail the agency's politics across time.[2] When America joined the "war to end all wars," it not only went after German spies, it also targeted Americans who had not registered for the draft and investigated immigrants, especially Germans, as possible subversives.[3] Much of this was politically motivated, not legally based. This then evolved into the first of America's Red Scares: radical immigrants who declared themselves to be Communists and Socialists and who had memberships in the Community Party and the Industrial Workers of the World, the "Wobblies," were infiltrated, investigated, and eventually rounded up during the Palmer Raids, ordered by Attorney General A. Mitchell Palmer, and deported. This was done for political reasons, and the Bureau of Investigation was at the forefront of the political assault.[4]

Then came the Teapot Dome Scandal of the early 1920s, in which oilman Harry Sinclair was found to be selling oil from US Naval oil reserves and funneling the money into bribes. The bureau helped expose the lucrative arrangement but was also caught up in the corruption itself.[5] Attorney General Harlan Stone realized "the Bureau had become a political police force" and was now "lawless, maintaining many activities which were without any authority in federal statutes, and engaging in many practices which were brutal and tyrannical in the extreme."[6] This led Stone to appoint J. Edgar Hoover as first interim and then permanent director of the bureau, because he was a hardworking bureaucrat who lived at home with his mother—which, ironically, was supposed to mean he was safe and apolitical.[7] Hoover, however, went on to become one of the most powerful political operatives of the twentieth century, and dozens of books recount this in detail.[8]

Whether Hoover was going after Gangsters in the 1930s, German and Japanese subversives in the 1940s, Communists in the 1950s, or members of the civil-rights movement in the 1960s, the Federal Bureau of Investigation, as it was rechristened in 1935, was always engaged in some aspect of political intrigue.[9] Hoover famously compiled dossiers on members of Congress and other important people whom he could later blackmail with the information contained in those files, a notorious example of how at least Director Hoover used the agency for political purposes.[10]

Yet even after Hoover's death in 1972, the FBI continued to find itself at the center of many political conspiracies and controversies. Deep Throat in the Watergate Scandal was of course the FBI's number-two man, Mark Felt, who helped to bring down the corrupt Nixon administration.[11] The FBI played a political role in the Whitewater Scandal involving President Bill Clinton, and then-director Louis Freeh (1993–2001) was often criticized for engaging in politics throughout his tenure.[12] And one need only look at the political intrigue of the two most recent FBI directors—Robert Mueller (2001–2013) and James Comey (2013–2017)—to find political controversy not only during their tenures with the agency but also after leaving, where they continue to find themselves at the center of politics revolving around President Barack Obama, Senator Hillary Clinton, and President Donald Trump.[13]

While the special agents of the FBI may conduct their investigations by the rule of law, the high-profile nature of many of their investigations often place them in the middle of political controversies. Born out of political controversy roiling between the executive and legislative branches of government, the early bureau was merely a pawn in a game. Since then, the FBI has continually found itself involved in politics because they are a political agency conducting investigations in a political world. They are a law-enforcement agency born out of politics—as hopefully this book has demonstrated—and they have been, and no doubt will be, a political agency well into the future.

Notes

Prologue

1. Bryan Burrough, *Public Enemies: America's Greatest Crime Wave and the Birth of the FBI, 1933–34* (New York: The Penguin Press, 2004); and David Grann, *Killers of the Flower Moon: The Osage Murders and the Birth of the FBI* (New York: Vintage, 2018).

Chapter 1. Federal Law Enforcement

1. Lawrence M. Friedman, *Crime and Punishment in American History* (New York: Basic Books, 1993), 261.
2. David T. Courtwright, *Forces of Habit: Drugs and the Making of the Modern World* (Cambridge, MA: Harvard University Press, 2001).
3. Samuel Walker, *Popular Justice: A History of American Criminal Justice*, 2nd ed. (New York: Oxford University Press, 1998), 25.
4. Bruce Smith, *Rural Crime Control* (New York: Institute of Public Administration, Columbia University, 1933).
5. Walker, *Popular Justice*, 25.
6. Roger Lane, *Policing the City: Boston, 1822–1855* (New York, NY: Atheneum, 1971), 8.
7. William J. Bopp and Donald O. Schultz, *A Short History of American Law Enforcement* (Springfield, IL: Charles C. Thomas, 1977); Robert M. Fogelson, *Big-City Police* (Cambridge, MA: Harvard Uni-

versity Press, 1977); Law Enforcement Assistance Association, *Two Hundred Years of American Criminal Justice: An LEAA Bicentennial Study*, ed. Joseph Foote (Washington, DC: US Department of Justice, 1976).

8. Boston City Council, *Ordinances and Rules and Orders of the City of Boston: Together with the General and Special Statutes of the Massachusetts Legislature Relating to the City* (Boston: Alfred Mudge and Son Printers, 1869), 524.

9. Willard M. Oliver and James F. Hilgenberg Jr., *A History of Crime and Criminal Justice in America*, 2nd ed. (Durham, NC: Carolina Academic Press, 2010), 47.

10. Oliver and Hilgenberg, *History of Crime.*

11. Lane, *Policing the City*; Walker, *Popular Justice.*

12. William Shakespeare, *Much Ado about Nothing* (New York: Oxford University Press, 1999), 79.

13. Benjamin Franklin, *The Autobiography of Benjamin Franklin* (Mineola, NY: Dover Thrift Editions, [1791] 1996), 81.

14. James F. Richardson, *Urban Police in the United States* (Port Washington, NY: Kennikat Press, 1974), 10.

15. Eric H. Monkkonen, *Police in Urban America, 1860–1920* (New York: Cambridge University Press, 1981), 32.

16. George Washington Walling, *Recollections of a New York Chief of Police: An Official Record of Thirty-Eight Years as Patrolman, Detective, Captain, Inspector and Chief of the New York Police* (New York: Caxton Book Concern, 1887), 32.

17. Edwin G. Burrows and Mike Wallace, *Gotham: A History of New York City to 1898* (New York: Oxford University Press, 1999), 637; Wilbur R. Miller, *Cops and Bobbies: Police Authority in New York and London, 1830–1870*, 2nd ed. (Columbus: The Ohio State University Press, 1997), 4.

18. James Madison, "Notes on the Debates in the Federal Convention," transcript, August 30, 1787, available at http://avalon.law.yale.edu/18th_century/debates_830.asp.

19. David R. Johnson, *American Law Enforcement: A History* (Wheeling, IL: Forum Press, 1981); Madison, "Notes on the Debates."

20. Sean Condon, *Shays's Rebellion: Authority and Distress in Post-Revolutionary America* (Baltimore: Johns Hopkins University Press, 2015); Leonard L. Richards, *Shays's Rebellion: The American Revolution's Final Battle* (Philadelphia: University of Pennsylvania Press, 2002).

21. John Willard Hahn, *The Background of Shays's Rebellion: A Study of Massachusetts History, 1780–1787* (Madison: University of Wisconsin–

Madison, 1946), 33; Broadus Mitchell, *Heritage from Hamilton* (New York: Columbia University Press, 1957), 26.

22. Condon, *Shays's Rebellion*; Richards, *Shays's Rebellion*.
23. Madison, "Notes on the Debates."
24. U.S. Const. art. IV, § 4, text available online at https://uscon .mobi/usc/4/4.html.
25. Richards, *Shays's Rebellion*.
26. Alexander Hamilton, essay no. 17, in Alexander Hamilton, James Madison, and John Jay, *The Federalist: A Collection of Essays, Written in Favour of the New Constitution*, 2 vols. (New York: J. and A. McLean, 1787).
27. Ibid.
28. Gordon S. Wood, *Empire of Liberty: A History of the Early Republic, 1789–1815* (New York: Oxford University Press, 2009), 409.
29. Johnson, *American Law Enforcement*.
30. Wood, *Empire of Liberty*, 409.
31. Ibid.
32. Ibid., 410.
33. Frederick S. Calhoun, *The Lawmen: United States Marshals and Their Deputies, 1789–1989* (New York: Penguin Books, 1991), 13.
34. Robert Sabbag, *Too Tough to Die: Down and Dangerous with the U.S. Marshals* (New York: Simon and Schuster, 1992), 39.
35. An Act to Establish the Judicial Courts of the United States, Public Law 1, U.S. Statutes at Large 73, § 27 (1789), text available at https://www.ourdocuments.gov/doc.php?flash=false&doc=12&page =transcript. This act is informally known as the Judiciary Act of 1789.
36. Calhoun, *Lawmen*, 3.
37. Ibid.; Sabbag, *Too Tough to Die*.
38. Mark Edward Lender and Garry Wheeler Stone, *Fatal Sunday: George Washington, the Monmouth Campaign, and the Politics of Battle* (Norman: University of Oklahoma Press, 2016).
39. US Marshals Service, "History—The First Generation of United States Marshals: The First Marshal of Maryland; Nathanial [sic] Ramsay," accessed August 9, 2016, https://www.usmarshals.gov/history/ firstmarshals/ramsay.htm.
40. Calhoun, *Lawmen*, 12 and 15.
41. John C. Fitzpatrick, ed., *The Writings of George Washington from the Original Manuscript Sources, 1745–1799: Prepared under the Direction of the United States George Washington Bicentennial Commission and Published by Authority of Congress* (Washington, DC: US Government Printing Office, 1939), 336.

42. Calhoun, *Lawmen*, 3.

43. Calhoun, *Lawmen*.

44. William Hogeland, *The Whisky Rebellion: George Washington, Alexander Hamilton, and the Frontier Rebels Who Challenged America's Newfound Sovereignty* (New York: Simon and Schuster, 2010).

45. Jeffrey B. Bumgarner, *Federal Agents: The Growth of Federal Law Enforcement in America* (Westport, CT: Praeger, 2006); Calhoun, *Lawmen*.

46. Calhoun, *Lawmen*.

47. Ibid; Robin Langley Sommer, *The History of the U.S. Marshals: The Proud Story of America's Legendary Lawmen* (Philadelphia: Courage Books, 1993).

48. U.S. Const. art. I, § 2.

49. An Act Providing for the Enumeration of the Inhabitants of the United States, United States Statute at Large, Vol. 1, First Congress, 2nd Session, Chap. II, Stat. 101, § 1 (1790), text available online at https://en.wikisource.org/wiki/United_States_Statutes_at_Large/Volume_1/1st_Congress/2nd_Session/Chapter_2.

50. Calhoun, *Lawmen*; Nancy E. Marion and Willard M. Oliver, *Federal Law Enforcement Agencies in America* (Frederick, MD: Wolters Kluwer Law and Business), 2015; Sommer, *History*.

51. David S. Turk, "Conclusion: Retired Deputy U.S. Marshal Follows the Trail of Robert Forsyth's Murderer," History, *US Marshals Service* (website), accessed August 10, 2016, https://www.usmarshals.gov/history/forsyth.htm.

52. Officer Down Memorial Page, "Deputy U.S. Marshal John Gatewood," accessed August 10, 2016, https://www.odmp.org/officer/21996-deputy-us-marshal-john-gatewood.

53. Jane H. Pease and William H. Pease, *The Fugitive Slave Law and Anthony Burns: A Problem in Law Enforcement* (New York: Lippincott, 1975).

54. Thomas P. Slaughter, *Bloody Dawn: The Christiana Riot and Racial Violence in the Antebellum North* (New York: Oxford University Press, 1991).

55. Pease and Pease, *Fugitive Slave Law*.

56. Calhoun, *Lawmen*; James Mackay, *Allan Pinkerton: The First Private Eye* (New York: John Wiley and Sons, Inc., 1996); Frank Morn, *"The Eye That Never Sleeps": A History of the Pinkerton National Detective Agency* (Bloomington: Indiana University Press, 1982).

Chapter 2. Pinkerton's Detectives

1. Allan Pinkerton, *Professional Thieves and the Detective: Containing Numerous Detective Sketches Collected from Private Records* (New York: G. W. Dillingham Co., Publishers, 1880), 17 and 19.
2. Morn, *Eye That Never Sleeps*.
3. Ibid., 21.
4. Pinkerton, *Professional Thieves*, 24.
5. Mackay, *Allan Pinkerton*, 59.
6. Pinkerton, *Professional Thieves*, 24 and 25.
7. Ibid.
8. Mackay, *Allan Pinkerton*, 60.
9. Pinkerton, *Professional Thieves*, 26.
10. Ibid., 54.
11. Mackay, *Allan Pinkerton*; Morn, *Eye That Never Sleeps*.
12. As quoted in ibid., 27.
13. As quoted in Morn, *Eye That Never Sleeps*, 19.
14. Mackay, *Allan Pinkerton*; Morn, *Eye That Never Sleeps*.
15. Mackay, *Allan Pinkerton*, 49 and passim.
16. As quoted in ibid., 53.
17. As quoted in ibid., 54.
18. Ibid.
19. Ibid.; Morn, *Eye That Never Sleeps*.
20. As quoted in Mackay, *Allan Pinkerton*, 68.
21. James D. Horan, *The Pinkertons: The Detective Dynasty That Made History* (New York: Crown Publishers, Inc., 1967); James D. Horan and Howard Swiggett, *The Pinkerton Story* (New York: G. P. Putnam's Sons, 1951); Mackay, *Allan Pinkerton*.
22. Pinkerton, "Our History," accessed August 17, 2016, https://www.pinkerton.com/our-difference/history.
23. Morn, *Eye That Never Sleeps*, 22.
24. Mackay, *Allan Pinkerton*; Morn, *Eye That Never Sleeps*.
25. *Chicago Press*, July 2, 1855.
26. Morn, *Eye That Never Sleeps*, 54.
27. Ibid., 24.
28. Donald, *Lincoln*.
29. U.S. Const. art. II, § 1, cl. 8. See also David Herbert Donald, *Lincoln* (New York: Simon and Schuster, 1995).
30. Doris Kearns Goodwin, *Team of Rivals: The Political Genius of Abraham Lincoln* (New York: Simon and Schuster, 2005).
31. Oliver and Marion, *Killing the President*, 162.

32. Morn, *Eye That Never Sleeps*.

33. Ward Hill Lamon, *Recollections of Abraham Lincoln, 1847–1865*, ed. Dorothy Lamon Teillard (Washington, DC: Dorothy Lamon Teillard, 1911), 33.

34. Michael J. Kline, *The Baltimore Plot: The First Conspiracy to Assassinate Abraham Lincoln* (Yardley, PA: Westholme, 2008).

35. Ibid. Norma C. Cuthbert, ed., *Lincoln and the Baltimore Plot, 1861: From Pinkerton Records and Related Papers* (San Marino, CA: The Huntington Library, 1949).

36. Cuthbert, *Lincoln*.

37. Sometimes written *Cipriano*.

38. John G. Nicolay and John Hay, *Abraham Lincoln: A History* (New York: The Century Co., 1890), 306.

39. Kline, *Baltimore Plot*.

40. Morn, *Eye That Never Sleeps*, 40.

41. Goodwin, *Team of Rivals*, 310.

42. Lamon, *Recollections*, 39.

43. Ibid.

44. Walter Stahr, *Seward: Lincoln's Indispensable Man* (New York: Simon and Schuster, 2012).

45. Frederick William Seward, *Seward at Washington, as Senator and Secretary of State: A Memoir of His Life, with Selections from His Letters*, vol. 2, *1861–1872* (New York: Derby and Miller, 1891), 509.

46. Ibid., 509–10.

47. Goodwin, *Team of Rivals*; Kline, *Baltimore Plot*.

48. Oliver and Marion, *Killing the President*.

49. Kline, *Baltimore Plot*, 268.

50. Kline, *Baltimore Plot*; Morn, *Eye That Never Sleeps*.

51. Goodwin, *Team of Rivals*; Kline, *Baltimore Plot*; Stahr, *Seward*.

52. Morn, *Eye That Never Sleeps*.

53. *Chicago Democrat*, March 5, 1861.

54. George Templeton Strong, *The Diary of George Templeton Strong*, vol. 3, *The Civil War 1860–1865*, ed. Allan Nevins and Milton Halsey Thomas (New York: Macmillan Company, 1952), 102.

55. Goodwin, *Team of Rivals*.

56. Cuthbert, *Lincoln*; Kline, *Baltimore Plot*.

57. Mackay, *Allan Pinkerton*, 110.

58. Ibid., 114.

59. Horan, *The Pinkertons*, 67.

60. Carl Sandburg, *Storm over the Land: A Profile of the Civil War Taken Mainly from Abraham Lincoln; The War Years* (New York: Harcourt, Brace and Company, 1942), 62.

61. Mackay, *Allan Pinkerton*; Morn, *Eye That Never Sleeps*.

62. Morn, *Eye That Never Sleeps*.

63. "Young Napoleon" and "Little Mac" were common nicknames for General McClellan, who was very popular with the soldiers.

64. Morn, *Eye That Never Sleeps*, 45.

65. Mackay, *Allan Pinkerton*; Morn, *Eye That Never Sleeps*.

66. Thomas J. Craughwell, *Stealing Lincoln's Body* (Cambridge, MA: The Belknap Press, 2007); Morn, *Eye That Never Sleeps*.

67. Morn, *Eye That Never Sleeps*, 106.

68. Arthur D. Burgoyne, *The Homestead Strike of 1892* (Pittsburgh: University of Pittsburgh Press, 1979).

69. Les Standiford, *Meet You in Hell: Andrew Carnegie, Henry Clay Frick, and the Bitter Partnership That Transformed America* (New York: Three Rivers Press, 2005).

70. George Harvey, *Henry Clay Frick: The Man* (New York: Beard Books, 1928), 177.

71. Burgoyne, *Homestead Strike*.

72. Standiford, *Meet You in Hell*.

73. Burgoyne, *Homestead Strike*, 41.

74. Standiford, *Meet You in Hell*.

75. "What a Boatman Saw; His Story of the Trip on the Steamer Little Bill," *New York Times*, July 7, 1892, https://www.nytimes.com/1892/07/07/archives/what-a-boatman-saw-his-story-of-the-trip-on-the-steamer-little-bill.html.

76. Paul Kahan, *The Homestead Strike: Labor, Violence, and American Industry* (New York: Routledge, 2014).

77. Burgoyne, *Homestead Strike*, 84.

78. Morn, *Eye That Never Sleeps*, 107.

79. Morn, *Eye That Never Sleeps*.

80. Willard B. Gatewood Jr., *Theodore Roosevelt and the Art of Controversy: Episodes of the White House Years* (Baton Rouge: Louisiana State University Press, 1970); J. Anthony Lukas, *Big Trouble: A Murder in a Small Western Town Sets Off a Struggle for the Soul of America* (New York: Simon and Schuster, 1997); Morn, *Eye That Never Sleeps*; Thomas A. Reppetto, *American Police: The Blue Parade, 1845–1945; A History* (New York: Enigma Books, 2010).

Chapter 3. Counterfeiters

1. U.S. Const. art I, § 8, text available online at https://uscon.mobi/usc/1/8.html.

2. Adam Smith, *An Inquiry into the Nature and Causes of the Wealth of Nations* (New York: MetaLibri, [1776] 2007), 37 and 39.

3. Ibid.

4. David R. Johnson, *Illegal Tender: Counterfeiting and the Secret Service in Nineteenth-Century America* (Washington, DC: Smithsonian Institution Press, 1995).

5. Alexander Del Mar, *The History of Money in America: From the Earliest Times to the Establishment of the Constitution* (New York: Burt Franklin, [1899] 1968).

6. Ibid.; A. Barton Hepburn, *A History of Currency in the United States* (New York: Augustus M. Kelley Publishers, 1967).

7. Del Mar, *History of Money*, 79.

8. Ben Tarnoff, *Moneymakers: The Wicked Lives and Surprising Adventures of Three Notorious Counterfeiters* (New York: The Penguin Press, 2011).

9. Stephen E. Lankenau, "Smoke 'Em if You Got 'Em: Cigarette Black Markets in U.S. Prisons and Jails," *The Prison Journal* 81, no. 2 (2001): 142–61, https://www.ncbi.nlm.nih.gov/pmc/articles/PMC2117377/; R. A. Radford, "The Economic Organisation of a P.O.W. Camp," *Economica* 12, no. 48 (1945): 189–201.

10. Del Mar, *History of Money*; Hepburn, *History of Currency*.

11. Tarnoff, *Moneymakers*, 4.

12. Eric P. Newman, *The Early Paper Money of America: An Illustrated, Historical, and Descriptive Compilation of Data Relating to American Paper Currency from Its Inception in 1686 to the Year 1800. . . .* 5th ed. (Iola, WI: Krause Publications, 2008), 11. See also Tarnoff, *Moneymakers*, 3.

13. Tarnoff, *Moneymakers*, 4.

14. Franklin, *Autobiography*, 33.

15. Smith, *Wealth of Nations*.

16. Charles Rappleye, *Robert Morris: Financier of the American Revolution* (New York: Simon and Schuster, 2010), 4.

17. Oswald Tilghman, "Robert Morris, the Oxford Merchant, 1711–1750," *History of Talbot County, Maryland, 1661–1861: Compiled Principally from the Literary Relics of . . . Samuel Alexander Harrison*, vol. 1 (Baltimore: Wilkins and Wilkins Co., 1915), available online at http://www.tcfl.org/mdroom/worthies/morris.html.

18.   Marla R. Miller, *Betsy Ross and the Making of America* (New York: Henry Holt and Company, 2010), 170.

19.   Bray Hammond, *Banks and Politics in America: From the Revolution to the Civil War* (Princeton: Princeton University Press, 1957), 66.

20.   Johnson, *Illegal Tender*.

21.   US Department of the Treasury, "Resource Center: Denominations," last updated June 15, 2018, https://www.treasury.gov/resource-center/faqs/Coins/Pages/denominations.aspx.

22.   Johnson, *Illegal Tender*, x.

23.   Quoted in Wood, *Empire of Liberty*, 293–94.

24.   Hepburn, *History of Currency*.

25.   Stephen Mihm, *A Nation of Counterfeiters: Capitalists, Con Men, and the Making of the United States* (Cambridge, MA: Harvard University Press, 2007).

26.   Johnson, *Illegal Tender*.

27.   Hepburn, *History of Currency*.

28.   Hugh Howard, *Mr. and Mrs. Madison's War: America's First Couple and the War of 1812* (New York: Bloomsbury Press, 2012).

29.   Mihm, *Nation of Counterfeiters*.

30.   Hepburn, *History of Currency*.

31.   Paul Kahan, *The Bank War: Andrew Jackson, Nicholas Biddle, and the Fight for American Finance* (Yardley, PA: Westholme Publishing, 2015).

32.   Martin Van Buren, *The Autobiography of Martin Van Buren*, vol. 2, *Annual Report of the American Historical Association for the Year 1918*, ed. John C. Fitzpatrick (Washington, DC: US Government Printing Office, 1920), 625.

33.   Daniel Walker Howe, *What Hath God Wrought: The Transformation of America, 1815–1848* (New York: Oxford University Press, 2007), 391.

34.   Ibid., 388.

35.   Jessica M. Lepler, *The Many Panics of 1837: People, Politics, and the Creation of a Transatlantic Financial Crisis* (New York: Cambridge University Press, 2013); Alasdair Roberts, *America's First Great Depression: Economic Crisis and Political Disorder after the Panic of 1837* (Ithaca, NY: Cornell University Press, 2012).

36.   Tarnoff, *Moneymakers*, 5.

37.   Craughwell, *Stealing Lincoln's Body*, 36.

38.   Peter L. Bernstein, *Wedding of the Waters: The Erie Canal and the Making of a Great Nation* (New York: W. W. Norton and Co., 2005).

39.   Johnson, *Illegal Tender*, ix.

40. Ibid., 3.
41. Lynn Glaser, *Counterfeiting in America: The History of an American Way to Wealth* (New York: Clarkson N. Potter, Inc., 1968), 12. See also Craughwell, *Stealing Lincoln's Body*.
42. Tarnoff, *Moneymakers*, 3.
43. Kenneth Scott, *Counterfeiting in Colonial America*, with a foreword by U. E. Baughman (New York: Oxford University Press, 1957), 24.
44. Johnson, *Illegal Tender*, 4.
45. Scott, *Counterfeiting*.
46. Ibid., 25.
47. Johnson, *Illegal Tender*, 4.
48. Glaser, *Counterfeiting in America*; Mihm, *Nation of Counterfeiters*; Scott, *Counterfeiting*.
49. Tarnoff, *Moneymakers*, 4.
50. Mihm, *Nation of Counterfeiters*, 35.
51. Ibid.; Scott, *Counterfeiting*; Tarnoff, *Moneymakers*.
52. Johnson, *Illegal Tender*.
53. Mihm, *Nation of Counterfeiters*, 34.
54. Tarnoff, *Moneymakers*.
55. Craughwell, *Stealing Lincoln's Body*, 34–35.
56. Ibid., 35.
57. Rappleye, *Robert Morris*.
58. Glaser, *Counterfeiting in America*, 78.
59. "Scraps—About Banks and Banking," *Niles' Weekly Register*, September 19, 1818, p. 58, available online at https://hdl.handle.net/2027/nnc1.cu04016602?urlappend=%3Bseq=72.
60. Glaser, *Counterfeiting in America*, 78.
61. John Jay Knox, *A History of Banking in the United States*, ed. Bradford Rhodes and Elmer H. Youngman (New York: Bradford Rhodes and Company, 1900), 747.
62. "The Fountain of Evil: With Notes and Illustrations; and Facts and Remarks," *Niles' Weekly Register*, July 4, 1818, 314–15, https://babel.hathitrust.org/cgi/pt?id=umn.319510028101807;view=1up;seq=328, emphasis original.
63. Mihm, *Nation of Counterfeiters*, 6.
64. See chapter 2 for a full discussion of Allan Pinkerton.
65. For a full discussion of the lack of a federal oversight mechanism, see chapter 1.
66. Johnson, *Illegal Tender*, 41.
67. Oliver and Hilgenberg, *History of Crime*.
68. Johnson, *Illegal Tender*, 40.

69. Bray Hammond, *Sovereignty and an Empty Purse: Banks and Politics in the Civil War* (Princeton: Princeton University Press, 1970).

70. George A. Nikolaieff, ed., *Taxation and the Economy* (New York: H. W. Wilson Co., 1968), 104.

71. Craughwell, *Stealing Lincoln's Body*, 39.

72. Hepburn, *History of Currency*.

73. Johnson, *Illegal Tender*, 66.

74. U.S. Const. art. II, § 8, text available online at https://uscon. mobi/usc/1/8.html.

75. Johnson, *Illegal Tender*, 66.

76. Mihm, *Nation of Counterfeiters*, 309.

77. Craughwell, *Stealing Lincoln's Body*, 41.

78. Johnson, *Illegal Tender*.

79. Walter S. Bowen and Harry Edward Neal, *The United States Secret Service* (New York: Popular Library, 1960), 26; Glaser, *Counterfeiting in America*, 106.

80. Willard M. Oliver and Nancy E. Marion, *Killing the President: Assassinations, Attempts, and Rumored Attempts on U.S. Commanders-in-Chief* (Santa Barbara, CA: Praeger, 2010); James L. Swanson, *Manhunt: The Twelve-Day Chase for Lincoln's Killer* (New York: HarperCollins, 2006).

Chapter 4. Assassinations

1. Catherine Drinker Bowen, *Miracle at Philadelphia: The Story of the Constitutional Convention, May to September 1787* (Boston: Back Bay Books, 1986).

2. Carlos E. Godfrey, *The Commander-in-Chief's Guard: Revolutionary War* (Washington, DC: Stevenson-Smith Company, 1904).

3. Ron Chernow, *Washington: A Life* (New York: Penguin Books, 2010).

4. Godfrey, *Commander-in-Chief's Guard*; Harry M. Ward, *George Washington's Enforcers: Policing the Continental Army* (Carbondale: Southern Illinois University Press, 2006).

5. Ward, *George Washington's Enforcers*, 59.

6. Ibid., 99–100.

7. Gary Shattuck, "Plotting the 'Sacracide' of George Washington," *Journal of the American Revolution* (July 25, 2014): 10, https://allthings liberty.com/2014/07/plotting-the-sacricide-of-george-washington/.

8. Ibid., 11.

9. National Archives, "Arrest Warrant from a Secret Committee of the New York Provincial Congress, 21 June 1776," *Founders Online*, last modified June 13, 2018, https://founders.archives.gov/documents/Washington/03-05-02-0042. [Original source: George Washington, "Arrest Warrant from a Secret Committee of the New York Provincial Congress, 21 June 1776," *The Papers of George Washington*, Revolutionary War Series, vol. 5, *16 June 1776–12 August 1776*, 72–74, ed. Philander D. Chase (Charlottesville: University Press of Virginia, 1993).]

10. Northern Illinois University, University Libraries, "Court Martial for the Trial of Thomas Hickey and Others, v6:1084," *American Archives: Documents of the American Revolutionary Period, 1774–1776* (website), 2015, http://amarch.lib.niu.edu/islandora/object/niu-amarch%3A85258.

11. Shattuck, "Sacracide," 3.

12. Northern Illinois University, University Libraries, "Court Martial."

13. Shattuck, "Sacracide," 12.

14. Chernow, *Washington*.

15. Ward, *George Washington's Enforcers*, 59.

16. Warren Commission, *Report of the President's Commission on the Assassination of President John F. Kennedy* (Washington, DC: US Government Printing Office, 1964), 504, text available online at https://www.archives.gov/research/jfk/warren-commission-report/appendix7.html.

17. For a vivid description of the Madisons' peril and flight, see Anthony S. Pitch, "The Burning of Washington," *White House History* 4 (Fall 1998), available at The White House Historical Association (website), https://www.whitehousehistory.org/the-burning-of-washington.

18. Oliver and Marion, *Killing the President*.

19. Robert V. Remini, *Andrew Jackson: The Course of American Democracy, 1833–1845*, vol. 3 (New York: Harper and Row, 1984), 227.

20. James G. Barber, *Andrew Jackson: A Portrait Study* (Seattle: University of Washington Press, 1991); Jon Meacham, *American Lion: Andrew Jackson in the White House* (New York: Random House, 2008).

21. Meacham, *American Lion*, 254.

22. Remini, *Andrew Jackson*, 227.

23. Warren Commission, *Report*, 505, text available online at https://www.archives.gov/research/jfk/warren-commission-report/appendix7.html.

24. James W. Clarke, *American Assassins: The Darker Side of Politics* (Princeton: Princeton University Press, 1982).

25. John Davidson Lawson, ed., *American State Trials: A Collection of the Important and Interesting Criminal Trials Which Have Taken Place in the United States, from the Beginning of Our Government to the Present Day; with Notes and Annotations*, vol. 3 (Saint Louis: F. H. Thomas Law Book Co., 1915), https://hdl.handle.net/2027/hvd.32044055052633.

26. Oliver and Marion, *Killing the President*, 5.

27. Lawson, *American State Trials*, 539.

28. Oliver and Marion, *Killing the President*, 5.

29. Clarke, *American Assassins*, 197.

30. Ibid.

31. Lawson, *American State Trials*, 539.

32. Oliver and Marion, *Killing the President*.

33. Ibid.

34. Ibid., 7; Harriet Martineau, *Retrospect of Western Travel*, 2 vols. (London: Saunders and Otley, 1838), 161.

35. Remini, *Andrew Jackson*, 228.

36. H. W. Brands, *Andrew Jackson: His Life and Times* (New York: Doubleday, 2005), 503.

37. Oliver and Marion, *Killing the President*, 8.

38. Clarke, *American Assassins*, 195.

39. John William Ward, *Andrew Jackson, Symbol for an Age* (New York: Oxford University Press, 1955), 114.

40. Remini, *Andrew Jackson*, 227.

41. Oliver and Marion, *Killing the President*.

42. Van Buren, *Autobiography*, 353.

43. Oliver and Marion, *Killing the President*.

44. Andrew Burstein, *The Passions of Andrew Jackson* (New York: Alfred A. Knopf, 2003), 202.

45. Brands, *Andrew Jackson*.

46. Philip H. Melanson, *The Secret Service: The Hidden History of an Enigmatic Agency*, with Peter F. Stevens (New York: Carroll and Graff Publishers, 2002).

47. Oliver and Marion, *Killing the President*, 14.

48. Ibid., 185.

49. Michael Parenti, "The Strange Death of President Zachary Taylor: A Case Study in the Manufacture of Mainstream History," *New Political Science* 20, no. 2 (1998): 144.

50.   James C. Whorton, *The Arsenic Century: How Victorian Britain Was Poisoned at Home, Work, and Play* (New York: Oxford University Press, 2010).

51.   Oliver and Marion, *Killing the President*, 189.

52.   James M. McPherson, *Battle Cry of Freedom: The Civil War Era* (New York: Oxford University Press, 1988).

53.   Kearns, *Team of Rivals*, 731.

54.   Bowen and Neal, *United States Secret Service*.

55.   Donald, *Lincoln*, 593.

56.   Ibid.; Kearns, *Team of Rivals*, 733.

57.   Donald, *Lincoln*, 593.

58.   O. J. Hollister, *Life of Schuyler Colfax* (New York: Funk and Wagnalls, 1886), 253.

59.   Margarita Spalding Gerry, ed., *Through Five Administrations: Reminiscences of Colonel William H. Crook, Body-Guard to President Lincoln* (New York: Harper and Brothers Publishers, 1910), 67.

60.   Gerry, *Five Administrations*.

61.   Paul Martin, "Lincoln's Missing Bodyguard," *Smithsonian Magazine*, April 7, 2010, https://www.smithsonianmag.com/history/lincolns-missing-bodyguard-12932069/.

62.   Lloyd Lewis, *The Assassination of Lincoln: History and Myth* (Lincoln: University of Nebraska Press, 1929), 297.

63.   Kearns, *Team of Rivals*.

64.   Martin, "Lincoln's Missing Bodyguard."

65.   Donald, *Lincoln*; Kearns, *Team of Rivals*; Swanson, *Manhunt*.

66.   Kearns, *Team of Rivals*, 739.

67.   Warren Commission, *Report*, 506–507, text available online at https://www.archives.gov/research/jfk/warren-commission-report/appendix7.html.

68.   Kenneth D. Ackerman, *Dark Horse: The Surprise Election and Political Murder of President James A. Garfield* (Falls Church, VA: Viral History Press, 2011).

69.   Daniel J. Vermilya, *James Garfield and the Civil War: For Ohio and the Union* (Charleston, SC: History Press, 2015).

70.   Candice Millard, *Destiny of the Republic: A Tale of Madness, Medicine and the Murder of a President* (New York: Doubleday, 2011).

71.   Oliver and Marion, *Killing the President*, 40.

72.   Millard, *Destiny of the Republic*.

73.   Oliver and Marion, *Killing the President*, 43.

74.   Millard, *Destiny of the Republic*, 131.

75.   Oliver and Marion, *Killing the President*, 45.

76.   Warren Commission, *Report*, 508, text online at https://www
.archives.gov/research/jfk/warren-commission-report/appendix7
.html.

77.   Ibid.

78.   Ivan Musicant, *Empire by Default: The Spanish-American War and the Dawn of the American Century* (New York: Henry Holt and Company, 1998).

79.   Scott Miller, *The President and the Assassin: McKinley, Terror, and Empire at the Dawn of the American Century* (New York: Random House, 2011).

80.   Ibid., 301.

81.   Oliver and Marion, *Killing the President*, 59.

82.   Ibid., 62.

83.   Miller, *President and the Assassin*, 301.

84.   Miller, *President and the Assassin*.

85.   Oliver and Marion, *Killing the President*, 67.

Chapter 5. The Secret Service

1.   Gatewood, *Theodore Roosevelt*, 239.

2.   For a more in-depth look at the history of American banking and currency, see chapter 3.

3.   For more on Allan Pinkerton, see chapter 2.

4.   Melanson, *Secret Service*, 5.

5.   Norman Ansley, "The United States Secret Service: An Administrative History," *Journal of Criminal Law, Criminology, and Police Science* 47, no. 1 (1956): 93–109; Gatewood, *Theodore Roosevelt*.

6.   Jacob Mogelever, *Death to Traitors: The Story of General Lafayette C. Baker, Lincoln's Forgotten Secret Service Chief* (New York: Doubleday, 1960), 17.

7.   Lafayette Charles Baker, *The Secret Service in the Late War: Comprising the Author's . . . etc.* (Philadelphia: John E. Potter and Company, 1874), 45.

8.   Melanson, *Secret Service*, 5.

9.   Bowen and Neal, *United States Secret Service*, 23.

10.   Curtis Carroll Davis, "The 'Old Capitol' and Its Keeper: How William P. Wood Ran a Civil War Prison," *Records of the Columbia Historical Society* 52 (1989): 211.

11. "Col. William P. Wood Dead: Veteran of Wars and Friend of Edwin M. Stanton; Unearthed Brockway; Secured Plates of Noted 7.30 Bond Counterfeit; Performed Many Important Missions For Government and Life Was a Continuous Melodrama," Washington *Evening Star*, March 21, 1903, p. 8, available online at https://chroniclingamerica.loc.gov/lccn/sn83045462/1903-03-21/ed-1/seq-8/.

12. Craughwell, *Stealing Lincoln's Body*, 42.

13. Bowen and Neal, *United States Secret Service*, 23.

14. Mihm, *Nation of Counterfeiters*, 341.

15. Davis, "Old Capitol," 210.

16. Bowen and Neal, *United States Secret Service*, 24.

17. Mihm, *Nation of Counterfeiters*, 342.

18. Davis, "Old Capitol," 234.

19. Johnson, *Illegal Tender*.

20. Mihm, *Nation of Counterfeiters*, 344.

21. Glaser, *Counterfeiting in America*, 105–6.

22. Bowen and Neal, *United States Secret Service*, 25–26.

23. For more on this reported exchange, see chapter 3, and for details of Lincoln's fateful engagement, see chapter 4.

24. Mihm, *Nation of Counterfeiters*, 345.

25. Johnson, *Illegal Tender*, 69.

26. US Secret Service, "USSS History," Department of Homeland Security (website), accessed October 25, 2017, https://www.secretservice.gov/about/history/events/.

27. Tarnoff, *Moneymakers*, 245.

28. Davis, "Old Capitol," 234; Mihm, *Nation of Counterfeiters*, 345–46.

29. Tarnoff, *Moneymakers*, 246.

30. Mihm, *Nation of Counterfeiters*, 353.

31. Johnson, *Illegal Tender*, 73.

32. Johnson, *Illegal Tender*.

33. Tarnoff, *Moneymakers*, 246.

34. Mihm, *Nation of Counterfeiters*, 352 and 353.

35. Melanson, *Secret Service*, 12.

36. Allan Pinkerton, *Thirty Years a Detective: A Thorough and Comprehensive Exposé of Criminal Practices of All Grades and Classes. . .* (New York: G. W. Carleton and Co., Publishers, 1884), 460.

37. Glaser, *Counterfeiting in America*, 125.

38. "Counterfeiters in the Employ of Government," *New York Times*, June 28, 1867, https://www.nytimes.com/1867/06/28/archives/counterfeiters-in-the-employ-of-the-government.html, emphasis mine.

39. Ibid.

40. Tarnoff, *Moneymakers*, 248.

41. Johnson, *Illegal Tender*, 77.

42. Curtis Carroll Davis, "The Craftiest of Men: William P. Wood and the Establishment of the United States Secret Service," *Maryland Historical Magazine* 83 (1988): 121.

43. Tarnoff, *Moneymakers*.

44. Bowen and Neal, *United States Secret Service*.

45. Johnson, *Illegal Tender*, 80.

46. Glaser, *Counterfeiting in America*, 129.

47. Johnson, *Illegal Tender*, 82.

48. Gatewood, *Theodore Roosevelt*, 240.

49. Johnson, *Illegal Tender*, 96.

50. Melanson, *Secret Service*, 22.

51. Johnson, *Illegal Tender*, 103.

52. Gatewood, *Theodore Roosevelt*, 240. And for more on the Pinkerton riots, see chapter 2.

53. Melanson, *Secret Service*, 23–24.

54. Richard B. Sherman, "Presidential Protection during the Progressive Era: The Aftermath of the McKinley Assassination," *The Historian* 46, no. 1 (1983): 1–20.

55. Johnson, *Illegal Tender*, xvii and 145.

56. Frederick M. Kaiser, "Origins of Secret Service Protection of the President: Personnel, Interagency, and Institutional Conflict," *Presidential Studies Quarterly* 18, no. 1 (1988): 101–27.

57. Melanson, *Secret Service*, 24.

58. Sherman, "Presidential Protection," 2.

59. Melanson, *Secret Service*, 26 and 27.

60. Ibid., 27.

61. Gatewood, *Theodore Roosevelt*, 240.

62. Melanson, *Secret Service*, 28.

63. Melanson, *Secret Service*.

64. Don Wilkie, *American Secret Service Agent*, as told to Mark Lee Luther (New York: Frederick A. Stokes Company, 1934), 11.

65. Kaiser, "Secret Service Protection," 110.

66. Gatewood, *Theodore Roosevelt*, 241 and then 240.

67. Sherman, "Presidential Protection."

68. Edmund Morris, *Theodore Rex* (New York: The Modern Library, 2002), 122.

69. Doris Kearns Goodwin, *The Bully Pulpit: Theodore Roosevelt, William Howard Taft, and the Golden Age of Journalism* (New York: Simon and Schuster, 2013), 286.

70. Officer Down Memorial Page, "Operative William Craig," accessed October 18, 2017, https://www.odmp.org/officer/3571-operative-william-craig.

71. Morris, *Theodore Rex*, 137; Officer Down Memorial Page, "William Craig."

72. Albert B. Southwick, "William Craig's Last Interview," *Worchester Telegram*, September 5, 2013, http://www.telegram.com/article/20130905/COLUMN21/309059975.

73. Goodwin, *Bully Pulpit*, 308. And *Washington Times*, September 4, 1902.

74. Goodwin, *Bully Pulpit*, 308; *Washington Times*, September 4, 1902.

75. Goodwin, *Bully Pulpit*, 308; *New York World*, September 4, 1902.

76. Morris, *Theodore Rex*, 142; Southwick, "Last Interview."

77. Melanson, *Secret Service*, 29.

78. Sherman, "Presidential Protection."

79. The Sundry Civil Expenses Act of 1907, Pub. L. No. 253, 59th Cong., 2nd. sess., 1315 (1906), text available online at https://en.wikisource.org/wiki/Page:United_States_Statutes_at_Large_Volume_34_Part_1.djvu/1345.

80. Sherman, "Presidential Protection," 4.

81. Morris, *Theodore Rex*.

82. Candice Millard, *The River of Doubt: Theodore Roosevelt's Darkest Journey* (New York: Broadway Books, 2005), 265.

83. Morris, *Theodore Rex*, 8.

84. Theodore Roosevelt Center, "Abraham Lincoln's Funeral Procession," Theodore Roosevelt Birthplace National Historic Site, Dickinson State University, accessed October 27, 2017, http://www.theodorerooseveltcenter.org/Research/Digital-Library/Record.aspx?libID=o284880; Edmund Morris, *The Rise of Theodore Roosevelt* (New York: The Modern Library, 2001), 128.

85. Morris, *Theodore Rex*, 266.

86. Morris, *Rise*, xx.

87. Melanson, *Secret Service*, 31.

Chapter 6. The Making of President Theodore Roosevelt

1. Kathleen Dalton, *Theodore Roosevelt: A Strenuous Life* (New York: Vintage, 2004), 5.

2. Morris, *Rise*, xv and 213.

3. William Henry Harbaugh, *Power and Responsibility: The Life and Times of Theodore Roosevelt* (New York: Farrar, Straus and Cudahy, 1961), 303.

4. Goodwin, *Bully Pulpit*, 34.

5. Morris, *Rise*.

6. Corinne Roosevelt Robinson, *My Brother, Theodore Roosevelt* (New York: Charles Scribner's Sons, 1921), 1.

7. *New York World*, November 16, 1902; Theodore Roosevelt to Edward S. Martin, November 26, 1900, in Theodore Roosevelt, *The Letters of Theodore Roosevelt*, ed. Elting Elmore Morison (Cambridge, MA: Harvard University Press, 1951–1954), 2:1443.

8. William Draper Lewis, *The Life of Theodore Roosevelt* (Philadelphia: John C. Winston Co., 1919), 36.

9. Robinson, *My Brother*, 50. See also Dalton, *Theodore Roosevelt*.

10. Roosevelt, *Letters*, 1:13.

11. Lewis, *Life*, 51.

12. Goodwin, *Bully Pulpit*, 45.

13. February 12, 1878, in Theodore Roosevelt, "Diaries and Notebooks of the American President Theodore Roosevelt," archives spanning 1868–1914, maintained by HOLLIS Archive, Harvard University, https://hollisarchives.lib.harvard.edu/repositories/24/resources/6304.

14. January 25, 1880, ibid.

15. Roosevelt, *Letters of Theodore Roosevelt*, 1:43.

16. Theodore Roosevelt, *The Naval War of 1812*, 2 vols. (New York: G. P. Putnam's Sons, 1900); *New York Times*, June 5, 1882.

17. Hermann Hagedorn, *The Boy's Life of Theodore Roosevelt* (New York: Harper and Brothers, 1918), 66–67.

18. Goodwin, *Bully Pulpit*, 67.

19. H. W. Brands, *T. R.: The Last Romantic* (New York: Basic Books, 1997), 372.

20. Morris, *Rise*, 223.

21. Goodwin, *Bully Pulpit*, 69.

22. Edward P. Kohn, "'A Most Revolting State of Affairs': Theodore Roosevelt's Aldermanic Bill and the New York Assembly City Investigating Committee of 1884," *American Nineteenth Century History*

10, no. 1 (2009): 71–92; Nathan Miller, *Theodore Roosevelt: A Life* (New York: Quill, 1992).

23. Goodwin, *Bully Pulpit*, 69.

24. Miller, *Theodore Roosevelt*, 140.

25. Kohn, "Most Revolting State of Affairs."

26. Miller, *Theodore Roosevelt*, 155.

27. Ibid., 154.

28. David McCullough, *Mornings on Horseback: The Story of an Extraordinary Family, a Vanished Way of Life, and the Unique Child Who Became Theodore Roosevelt* (New York: Simon and Schuster, 2001).

29. Henry F. Pringle, *Theodore Roosevelt: A Biography* (New York: Harcourt, Brace, and Co., 1931), 51.

30. Morris, *Rise*.

31. February 14, 1884, in Roosevelt, "Diaries."

32. Morris, *Rise*, 418.

33. Ibid., 397.

34. Pringle, *Theodore Roosevelt*, 123.

35. Ibid.

36. Goodwin, *Bully Pulpit*, 139.

37. *Washington Post*, May 6, 1890.

38. E. W. Halford, "Roosevelt's Introduction to Washington," *Frank Leslie's Illustrated Weekly* 128, no. 3312 (March 1, 1919): 314.

39. Roosevelt, *Letters of Theodore Roosevelt*, 1:167 and then 237.

40. Goodwin, *Bully Pulpit*, 141.

41. Miller, *Theodore Roosevelt*, 221.

42. A. G. Gardiner, *Pillars of Society* (London: James Nisbet and Co., Limited, 1913), 238.

43. Theodore Roosevelt, *Theodore Roosevelt: An Autobiography* (New York: The Macmillan Company, 1916), 172.

44. Ibid., 174.

45. Lincoln Steffens, *The Autobiography of Lincoln Steffens* (New York: Harcourt, Brace, and Co., 1936), 257.

46. Ibid., 257–58.

47. Ibid.

48. Jay Stuart Berman, *Police Administration and Progressive Reform: Theodore Roosevelt as Police Commissioner of New York* (Westport, CT: Greenwood Publishing Group, 1987), 47.

49. Miller, *Theodore Roosevelt*, 229.

50. Steffens, *Autobiography*, 258.

51. Miller, *Theodore Roosevelt*, 229.

52. Roosevelt, *Autobiography*, 175.

53. Roosevelt, *Letters of Theodore Roosevelt*, 1:457.

54. Charles H. Parkhurst, *Our Fight with Tammany* (New York: Charles Scribner's Sons, 1895).

55. Mike Dash, *Satan's Circus: Murder, Vice, Police Corruption, and New York's Trial of the Century* (New York: Three Rivers Press, 2007), 63.

56. James Lardner and Thomas Reppetto, *NYPD: A City and Its Police* (New York: Henry Holt and Company, 2000), 64–65.

57. Dash, *Satan's Circus*, 65–66.

58. H. Paul Jeffers, *Commissioner Roosevelt: The Story of Theodore Roosevelt and the New York City Police, 1895–1897* (New York: John Wiley and Sons, Inc., 1994), 81.

59. Ibid., 82 and 83.

60. Morris, *Rise*, 512; Richard Zacks, *Island of Vice: Theodore Roosevelt's Doomed Quest to Clean up Sin-Loving New York* (New York: Doubleday, 2012), 94.

61. Jeffers, *Commissioner Roosevelt*, 107 and 110.

62. Roosevelt, *Autobiography*, 177. 193–94.

63. Roosevelt, *Letters of Theodore Roosevelt*, 1:466.

64. *New York Times*, July 17, 1895.

65. Roosevelt, *Autobiography*, 196.

66. Edward P. Kohn, *Hot Time in the Old Town: The Great Heat Wave of 1896 and the Making of Theodore Roosevelt* (New York: Basic Books, 2010), 24.

67. Kohn, *Hot Time*.

68. Mrs. Bellamy Storer, "How Theodore Roosevelt Was Appointed Assistant Secretary of the Navy," *Harper's Weekly*, 56 (June 1, 1912): 8–9, archived online at https://babel.hathitrust.org/cgi/pt?id=mdp.39015033848121;view=1up;seq=616.

69. Musicant, *Empire*.

70. Edmund Morris, *Colonel Roosevelt* (New York: Random House, 2010); Theodore Roosevelt, *The Rough Riders* (Lincoln: University of Nebraska Press, 1998).

71. For an expanded look at Leon Czolgosz and the assassination of President William McKinley, see chapter 4.

72. Miller, *Theodore Roosevelt*, 348.

73. Roosevelt, *Letters of Theodore Roosevelt*, 3:139.

74. Morris, *Theodore Rex*, 3.

75. Ibid., 7.

76. Ibid., 11.

77. Goodwin, *Bully Pulpit*, 281.

Chapter 7. Conservation

1. Halford, "Introduction," 314.
2. David McCullough, *The Path between the Seas: The Creation of the Panama Canal, 1870–1914* (New York: Simon and Schuster, 1978).
3. National Park Service, "Theodore Roosevelt and Conservation," last updated November 16, 2017, https://www.nps.gov/thro/learn/historyculture/theodore-roosevelt-and-conservation.htm.
4. Ibid.
5. Douglas Brinkley, *The Wilderness Warrior: Theodore Roosevelt and the Crusade for America* (New York: HarperCollins Publishers, 2009), 528.
6. Roosevelt, *Autobiography*, 6–7.
7. Miller, *Theodore Roosevelt*, 40.
8. Ibid., 40 and 58–59.
9. Ibid., 39.
10. Brinkley, *Wilderness Warrior*, 32.
11. Miller, *Theodore Roosevelt*, 40.
12. Roosevelt, *Autobiography*, 15.
13. Darrin Lunde, *The Naturalist: Theodore Roosevelt, a Lifetime of Exploration, and the Triumph of American Natural History* (New York: Crown Publishers, 2016), 10.
14. Roosevelt, *Autobiography*, 15.
15. Ibid.; Brinkley, *Wilderness Warrior*.
16. Roosevelt, *Autobiography*, 15 and 19.
17. McCullough, *Mornings*, 119.
18. Roosevelt, *Autobiography*, 20.
19. Jonathan Rosen, *The Life of the Skies: Birding at the End of Nature* (New York: Farrar, Straus and Giroux, 2008), 128.
20. Roosevelt, *Autobiography*, 20.
21. Theodore Roosevelt Association, "The Hunter," accessed November 29, 2017, http://www.theodoreroosevelt.org/site/c.elKSIdOWIiJ8H/b.8344379/k.2B69/The_Hunter.htm.
22. Roosevelt, *Autobiography*, 23.
23. Brinkley, *Wilderness Warrior*, 97.
24. Miller, *Theodore Roosevelt*, 74.
25. Roosevelt, *Autobiography*, 32.
26. Brinkley, *Wilderness Warrior*, 119.
27. Roosevelt, *Autobiography*, 36.
28. Miller, *Theodore Roosevelt*, 166.
29. Ibid.

30. Morris, *Rise*, 388.
31. Theodore Roosevelt, "The Boone and Crockett Club," *Harper's Weekly*, March 18, 1893, 267, archived online at https://babel.hathitrust.org/cgi/pt?id=pst.000020243371;view=1up;seq=281.
32. Morris, *Rise*, 389–90.
33. Roosevelt, *Autobiography*, 299 and then 408–36.
34. Brinkley, *Wilderness Warrior*, 356.
35. Ibid., 356–57.
36. Roosevelt, *Autobiography*, 324–25 and then 323.
37. Ibid.
38. Brinkley, *Wilderness Warrior*, 1.
39. Millard, *River*, 23.
40. Salt Lake City *Desert Evening News*, March 28, 1903.
41. John Burroughs, *Camping and Tramping with Roosevelt* (Boston: Houghton, Mifflin and Company, 1907), 4 and 80–81.
42. Roosevelt, *Autobiography*, 410.
43. Ibid.
44. Ibid.
45. Miller, *Theodore Roosevelt*, 381.
46. Donald R. Wolfensberger, *Congress and the People: Deliberative Democracy on Trial* (Baltimore: The Johns Hopkins University Press, 2000), 48.
47. Timothy Egan, *The Big Burn: Teddy Roosevelt and the Fire That Saved America* (Boston: Houghton Mifflin Harcourt, 2009), 68.
48. Goodwin, *Bully Pulpit*, 352.
49. Miller, *Theodore Roosevelt*, 469–70 and 472.
50. Egan, *Big Burn*.
51. Roosevelt, *Autobiography*, 409.
52. Egan, *Big Burn*.
53. Roosevelt, *Autobiography*, 409.
54. Egan, *Big Burn*; Bibi Gaston, ed., *Gifford Pinchot and the First Foresters: The Untold Story of the Brave Men and Women Who Launched the American Conservation Movement* (New Milford, CT: Baked Apple Club Productions, 2016).
55. Wister once dedicated a work of Western fiction to Roosevelt (*The Virginian* [New York: Macmillan, 1902]). The above quotation is from Owen Wister, *Roosevelt: The Story of a Friendship, 1880–1919* (New York: Macmillan, 1930), 174.
56. Morris, *Rise*, 486.
57. Roosevelt, *Autobiography*, 418–19.
58. Morris, *Rise*, 487.

59. Roosevelt, *Autobiography*, 420.

60. George E. Mowry, *The Era of Theodore Roosevelt: 1900–1912* (New York: Harper and Row Publishers, 1958), 215.

61. Egan, *Big Burn*, 70.

62. Morris, *Rise*, 487.

63. Roosevelt, *Autobiography*, 419.

64. Mowry, *Era*, 215.

65. Egan, *Big Burn*, 70.

66. Leroy G. Dorsey, *Theodore Roosevelt, Conservation, and the 1908 Governors' Conference* (College Station: Texas A&M University Press, 2016). 1, 22, and 51.

67. Roosevelt, *Autobiography*, 420.

68. Theodore Roosevelt, *African Game Trails: An Account of the African Wanderings of an American Hunter-Nationalist* (New York: Safari Press, 1909).

69. Theodore Roosevelt, "Our Vanishing Wild Life," *The Outlook*, January 25, 1913, 161, text archived online at https://babel.hathitrust .org/cgi/pt?id=coo.31924066372842;view=1up;seq=223.

70. Brinkley, *Wilderness Warrior*, 817.

Chapter 8. Land Thieves

1. Bowen and Neal, *United States Secret Service*, 93.

2. Roosevelt, *Autobiography*, 425 and 378.

3. Matthew Josephson, *The Robber Barons: The Great American Capitalists, 1861–1901* (New York: Harcourt Brace and Company, 1934).

4. Roosevelt, *Autobiography*, 384.

5. National Archives, "The Homestead Act of 1862," last reviewed October 3 2016, https://www.archives.gov/education/lessons/home stead-act.

6. Ibid.

7. Ibid.

8. Ibid.

9. Ibid.

10. Greg Bradsher, "How the West Was Settled: The 150-Year-Old Homestead Act Lured Americans Looking for a New Life and New Opportunities," *Prologue* 44, no. 4 (2012): 31–32.

11. Ibid., 33.

12. Bowen and Neal, *United States Secret Service*, 93.

13. Henry S. Brown, "Punishing the Land-Looters," *The Outlook*, February 23, 1907, 437.

14. Richard H. Byrd, "Foils the Land Thieves: Secretary Hitchcock's Relentless Pursuit of Land Grabbing Thieves," *Amador Ledger*, January 12, 1906, available online at https://cdnc.ucr.edu/cgi-bin/cdnc?a=d&d=AL19060112.2.63.8&e=-------en--20--1--txt-txIN--------1.

15. Roosevelt, *Autobiography*, 374.

16. S. A. D. Puter, *Looters of the Public Domain* (Portland: The Portland Printing House, 1908).

17. Brown, "Punishing the Land-Looters."

18. Oliver Tatom, "Binger Hermann (1843–1926)," in *The Oregon Encyclopedia*, The Oregon Historical Society, 2008–, article last updated March 17, 2018, https://oregonencyclopedia.org/articles/hermann_binger_1843_1926_/.

19. Roosevelt, *Autobiography*, 425.

20. Jerry A. O'Callaghan, "Senator Mitchell and the Oregon Land Frauds, 1905," *Pacific Historical Review* 21, no. 3 (1952): 256.

21. O'Callaghan, "Senator Mitchell."

22. Egan, *Big Burn*, 67.

23. O'Callaghan, "Senator Mitchell," 261.

24. Egan, *Big Burn*, 67–68.

25. Oliver Tatom, "Oregon Land Fraud Trials (1904–1910)," in *The Oregon Encyclopedia*, The Oregon Historical Society, 2008–, article last updated March 17, 2018, https://oregonencyclopedia.org/articles/oregon_land_fraud_trials_1904_1910_/.

26. Melanson and Stevens, *Secret Service*, 33.

27. Wilkie, *American Secret Service Agent*, 61.

28. "Inspector Jos. A. Walker Was Shot in the Back: Prominent Government Official Filled Full of Backshot while Investigating Hesperus Coal Mine," *Durango Democrat*, November 5, 1907, p. 1, available online at https://newspaperarchive.com/durango-democrat-nov-05-1907-p-1/.

29. Carol Turner, *Notorious San Juans: Wicked Tales from Ouray, San Juan and La Plata Counties* (Charleston, SC: History Press, 2011), 17.

30. Ibid., 14.

31. Bowen and Neal, *United States Secret Service*, 93.

32. Melanson and Stevens, *Secret Service*, 33.

33. Turner, *Notorious San Juans*, 13.

34. Melanson and Stevens, *Secret Service*, 34.

35. Wilkie, *American Secret Service Agent*, 61.

36. Ibid.

37. Bowen and Neal, *United States Secret Service*, 94.

38. Ibid.

39. Wilkie, *American Secret Service Agent*, 61.

40. Melanson and Stevens, *Secret Service*, 33–34.

41. Turner, *Notorious San Juans*, 13.

42. Bowen and Neal, *United States Secret Service*, 94.

43. Turner, *Notorious San Juans*, 13.

44. Bowen and Neal, *United States Secret Service*, 94.

45. Wilkie, *American Secret Service Agent*, 61–62.

46. Bowen and Neal, *United States Secret Service*, 95.

47. Ibid.

48. Wilkie, *American Secret Service Agent*, 62.

49. Ibid.

50. Bowen and Neal, *United States Secret Service*, 96–97.

51. Bowen and Neal, *United States Secret Service*.

52. Turner, *Notorious San Juans*, 16.

53. *Durango Democrat*, April 28, 1908.

54. US Secret Service, "Ordinary People, Extraordinary Times," Department of Homeland Security (website), accessed January 26, 2018, https://www.secretservice.gov/about/history/honor/.

55. "Secret Service Agent Killed by a Miner," *San Francisco Call*, November 4, 1907.

56. "Killing of Officer Walker," New York *Independent*, November 14, 1907, 1138.

57. Turner, *Notorious San Juans*, 21–22.

58. Wilkie, *American Secret Service Agent*, 64.

59. Bowen and Neal, *United States Secret Service*, 97.

60. Ibid., 97–98.

61. *United States, Plff. in Err., v. William R. Mason and Joseph Vanderweide*, 213 U.S. 115 (1909).

62. Wilkie, *American Secret Service Agent*, 63.

63. Officer Down Memorial Page, "Operative Joseph A. Walker," accessed January 18, 2018, http://www.odmp.org/officer/13759-operative-joseph-a-walker.

64. John Peel, "Sisters on the Trail of 1907 Killing," *Durango Herald*, updated October 25, 2010, https://durangoherald.com/articles/15448. John Peel, "Guilty or Innocent? Agent's Killers Faced Trial in 1908," *Durango Herald*, October 31, 2010, https://durangoherald.com/articles/15698-guilty-or-innocent-agents-killers-faced-trial-in-1908.

65. Tom Morton, "Marker for Secret Service Agent," Fairmont Cemetery (website), November 11, 2010, http://fairmount-cemetery.com/new-marker-for-secret-service-agent/.

66. Wilkie, *American Secret Service Agent*, 65.

67. Ibid.

Chapter 9. Chairman James A. Tawney

1. Congressional Record, May 4, 1908, 5685.

2. Wilkie, *American Secret Service Agent*, 65.

3. Gatewood, *Theodore Roosevelt*.

4. Ibid., 238.

5. James A. Tawney, Papers, Minnesota Historical Society; US Congress, "Tawney, James Albertus, (1855–1919)," *Biographical Directory of the United States Congress, 1774–Present*, accessed March 2, 2016, http://bioguide.congress.gov/scripts/biodisplay.pl?index=T000060.

6. Tawney Papers; US Congress, "Tawney."

7. Tawney Papers; US Congress, "Tawney."

8. Roger E. Wyman, "Insurgency in Minnesota: The Defeat of James A. Tawney in 1910," *Minnesota History* 40, no. 7 (1967): 318.

9. Wyman, "Insurgency."

10. Ibid., 319.

11. Tawney Papers; US Congress, "Tawney."

12. Gatewood, *Theodore Roosevelt*, 246 and then 245.

13. Wyman, "Insurgency."

14. US House of Representatives, Hearings before Subcommittee of House Committee on Appropriations, Consisting of . . . the Legislative, Executive, and Judicial Appropriation Bill for 1907 (Washington, DC: US Government Printing Office, 1906), available online at https://babel.hathitrust.org/cgi/pt?id=nyp.33433019658206;view=1up;seq=7. The following description of the exchange is taken from this source.

15. For further discussion of the formation of the Secret Service, see chapter 5.

16. John F. Fox Jr., "The Birth of the Federal Bureau of Investigation," Federal Bureau of Investigation (website), July 2003, https://www.fbi.gov/history/history-publications-reports/the-birth-of-the-federal-bureau-of-investigation.

17. For further detail on this case, see chapter 8.

18. Wilkie, *American Secret Service Agent*, 66.
19. Joseph Bucklin Bishop, *Charles Joseph Bonaparte: His Life and Public Service* (New York: Charles Scribner's Sons, 1922).
20. Gatewood, *Theodore Roosevelt*, 244.
21. US Department of Justice, *The Annual Report of the Attorney-General of the United States for the Year 1907*, vol. 1 (Washington, DC: US Government Printing Office, 1907), available online at (vol. 1) https:// babel.hathitrust.org/cgi/pt?id=osu.32437010220560.
22. Ibid., 10.
23. Fox, "Birth of the Federal Bureau of Investigation."
24. US House of Representatives, Subcommittee of House Committee on Appropriations, records, January 17, 1908.
25. Athan G. Theoharis and John Stuart Cox, *The Boss: J. Edgar Hoover and the Great American Inquisition* (Philadelphia: Temple University Press, 1988), 42.
26. "Loan of Detectives," Washington *Evening Star*, April 21, 1908. Unless explicitly cited otherwise, the entire following account of the exchange between Tawney and Moran detailed in this chapter is taken from this source.
27. For a detailed account of the Homestead Strike, see chapter 2.
28. Fox, "Birth of the Federal Bureau of Investigation."
29. Theoharis and Cox, *Boss*, 42.
30. Wilkie, *American Secret Service Agent*, 66.
31. Gatewood, *Theodore Roosevelt*, 247.
32. L. White Busbey, *Uncle Joe Cannon: The Story of a Pioneer American* (New York: Henry Holt and Company, 1927), 231.
33. Roosevelt, *Letters*, vol. 5, letter 4705.
34. Gatewood, *Theodore Roosevelt*, 247.
35. Tawney Papers, box 3.
36. *Congressional Record*, May 1, 1908, 5554.
37. Ibid.
38. *Congressional Record*, May 1, 1908, 5555.
39. Ibid., 5556.
40. Ibid., 5557.
41. Washington *Evening Star*, May 2, 1908.
42. Wilkie, *American Secret Service Agent*, 66.
43. Theoharis and Cox, *Boss*, 42–43.
44. Gatewood, *Theodore Roosevelt*, 247–48.
45. "Tool of Thieves," *New York Times*, May 6, 1908, https://www.nytimes.com/1908/05/06/archives/tools-of-thieves.html.
46. *New York Tribune*, May 6, 1908.

47. Fox, "Birth of the Federal Bureau of Investigation."
48. Gatewood, *Theodore Roosevelt*, 251.
49. Fox, "Birth of the Federal Bureau of Investigation."
50. Ibid.
51. *Chicago Tribune*, May 23, 1908.
52. Pringle, *Theodore Roosevelt*, 339.
53. Gatewood, *Theodore Roosevelt*, 252.
54. Max Lowenthal, *The Federal Bureau of Investigation* (New York: William Sloane Associates, Inc., 1950); Theoharis and Cox, *Boss*.

Chapter 10. The Bureau of Investigation

1. U.S. Const. art. 2, § 3, text available online at https://uscon.mobi/usc/2/3.html.
2. Arthur S. Miller, *Presidential Power* (Saint Paul, MN: West Publishing Company, 1977), 105.
3. Don Whitehead, *The FBI Story: A Report to the People*, foreword by J. Edgar Hoover (New York: Random House, 1956), 21.
4. Gatewood, *Theodore Roosevelt*, 252.
5. Friedman, *Crime and Punishment*, 270.
6. Mark Twain, *Mark Twain's Letters*, arranged with comment by Albert Bigelow Paine (New York: Harper and Brothers, 1919), 766.
7. Congressional Record, June 22, 1870, 162.
8. Gatewood, *Theodore Roosevelt*, 252–53.
9. Ibid., 252.
10. Whitehead, *FBI Story*, 21.
11. Ibid.
12. Tim Weiner, *Enemies: A History of the FBI* (New York: Random House, 2012), 11.
13. Fox, "Birth of the Federal Bureau of Investigation."
14. Henry M. Holden, *FBI: 100 Years; An Unofficial History* (Minneapolis: Zenith Press, 2008), 13; Tawney Papers, box 2; Athan G. Theoharis, *The FBI and American Democracy: A Brief Critical History* (Lawrence: University Press of Kansas, 2004), 3.
15. Gatewood, *Theodore Roosevelt*, 253.
16. Weiner, *Enemies*, puts the number at eight operatives; Holden, *FBI*, on the other hand, says ten.
17. Holden, *FBI*, 13.
18. Theoharis, *American Democracy*, 3.

19. Weiner, *Enemies*, 11–12.
20. Gatewood, *Theodore Roosevelt*, 253.
21. Tawney Papers, box 2.
22. Ibid.
23. Gatewood, *Theodore Roosevelt*, 253.
24. Steven E. Barkan and George J. Bryjak, *Fundamentals of Criminal Justice: A Sociological View*, 2nd ed. (Sudbury, MA: Jones and Bartlett Learning, 2011), 207; Steven G. Brandl, *Criminal Investigation*, 4th ed. (Thousand Oaks, CA: Sage, 2018), 31; Matt Donnelly, *Theodore Roosevelt: Larger Than Life* (North Haven, CT: Linnet Books, 2002), 133; Joshua Dressler, ed., *Encyclopedia of Crime and Justice*, 2nd ed., vol. 2, *Delinquent and Criminal Subcultures–Juvenile Justice: Institutions* (New York: Macmillan Reference USA, 2002), 687; Diana Lambdin Meyer, *Kansas Myths and Legends: The True Stories behind History's Mysteries*, 2nd ed. (Guilford, CT: TwoDot, 2017), 161; Thomas A. Reppetto, *American Mafia: A History of Its Rise to Power* (New York: Henry Holt, 2004), 183; Schultz and Vile, *Encyclopedia*, 2:355.
25. Fox, "Birth of the Federal Bureau of Investigation"; Friedman, *Crime and Punishment*, 270; Wolters Kluwer Law and Business, *The Department of Justice Manual*, 3rd ed. (New York: Aspen Publishers, 2016), 1.2000C; Kenneth Mayer, *With the Stroke of a Pen: Executive Orders and Presidential Power* (Princeton: Princeton University Press, 2001), 164; Theoharis and Cox, *Boss*, 43; Weiner, *Enemies*, 11; Whitehead, *FBI Story*, 21.
26. *Grapevine*, January 1954.
27. Howard Blum, *American Lightning: Terror, Mystery, the Birth of Hollywood, and the Crime of the Century* (New York: Crown Publishers, 2008).
28. Gatewood, *Theodore Roosevelt*, 254.
29. Ibid.
30. Weiner, *Enemies*, 11.
31. Gatewood, *Theodore*, 255.
32. Fox, "Birth of the Federal Bureau of Investigation."
33. Rebecca Jenkins, *The First London Olympics, 1908: The Definitive Story of London's Most Sensational Olympics to Date* (London: Hachette Digital, 2008).
34. Morris, *Theodore Rex*.
35. Ibid., 529.
36. Washington *Evening Star*, September 18, 1908.
37. Ibid.
38. Ibid.

39. Washington *Evening Star*, September 8, 1908.
40. Ibid.
41. *New York Times*, September 9, 1908.
42. Morris, *Theodore Rex*, 534 and 536.
43. Ibid., 539.
44. Ibid., 543; Goodwin, *Bully Pulpit*, 564.
45. Fox, "Birth of the Federal Bureau of Investigation."
46. US Department of Justice, *The Annual Report of the Attorney-General of the United States for the Year 1908* (Washington, DC: US Government Printing Office, 1908), page 1, available online at https://babel.hathitrust.org/cgi/pt?id=uc1.b5145516;view=1up;seq=11.
47. Ibid., 3–7.
48. Ibid., 7.
49. Lowenthal, *Federal Bureau of Investigation*, 5.
50. Theoharis, *American Democracy*, 3.

Chapter 11. Born in Controversy

1. Busbey, *Uncle Joe Cannon*, 231.
2. Ibid., 232.
3. Jim Rasenberger, *America, 1908: The Dawn of Flight, the Race to the Pole, the Invention of the Model T, and the Making of a Modern Nation* (New York: Scribner, 2007), 259–60.
4. Theodore Roosevelt, "Eighth Annual Message," letter to the US Senate and House of Representatives, issued from the White House, Washington, DC, December 8, 1908, text archived by the American Presidency Project at https://www.presidency.ucsb.edu/node/206223.
5. Rasenberger, *America*, 260.
6. Roosevelt, "Eighth Annual Message."
7. Ibid.
8. Rasenberger, *America*, 261.
9. *New York Times*, December 8, 1908.
10. Gatewood, *Theodore Roosevelt*, 255.
11. Miller, *Theodore Roosevelt*, 385 and then 255.
12. Morris, *Theodore Rex*, 16.
13. Gatewood, *Theodore Roosevelt*, 255–56.
14. Ibid., 256.

15. Lawrence F. Abbott, ed., *The Letters of Archie Butt* (Garden City, NY: Doubleday, 1924), 239.

16. Ibid., 239–40.

17. Gatewood, *Theodore Roosevelt*, 256.

18. Theoharis, *American Democracy*, 3.

19. Gatewood, *Theodore Roosevelt*, 259.

20. *Washington Post*, December 9, 1908.

21. Busbey, *Uncle Joe Cannon*, 231–32.

22. Ibid., 233.

23. Ibid., 233–34.

24. US Congress, *Congressional Record: Containing the Proceedings and Debates of the Sixtieth Congress, Second Session*, vol. 43 (Washington, DC: Government Printing Office, 1909), 140, emphasis original, available at https://books.google.com/books?id=LQlRWQ8ET58C.

25. US Congress, *Congressional Record*, 140.

26. Ibid.

27. Ibid.

28. Ibid., 141.

29. Busbey, *Uncle Joe Cannon*, 234.

30. US Congress, *Congressional Record*, 311 and 312.

31. Ibid., 312.

32. Ibid.

33. Stephen Kantrowitz, *Ben Tillman and the Reconstruction of White Supremacy* (Chapel Hill: The University of North Carolina Press, 2000).

34. US Congress, *Congressional Record*, 313.

35. Ibid.

36. Ibid.

37. Clemson University, "Benjamin Ryan Tillman," 2018, https://www.clemson.edu/about/history/bios/ben-tillman.html.

38. US Congress, *Congressional Record*, 313.

39. Ibid., 314.

40. Ibid.

41. Ibid., 373.

42. Ibid., 373.

43. Washington *Evening Star*, December 17, 1908.

44. Busbey, *Uncle Joe Cannon*, 235, 236, and 237.

45. *Washington Post*, December 16, 1908.

46. Busbey, *Uncle Joe Cannon*, 237.

47. Roosevelt, *Autobiography*, 366–67.

48. Ibid., 367.

49. Gatewood, *Theodore Roosevelt*, 263.

50. "Senate Will Order Full Investigation of Secret Service," Washington *Evening Star*, December 16, 1908, p. 1, available online at https://chroniclingamerica.loc.gov/lccn/sn83045462/1908-12-16/ed-1/seq-1/. Also see *Zion's Herald*, December 22, 1908.

51. "Abolition of the Secret Service May Be Proposed," Washington *Evening Star*, December 21, 1908, p. 1, text archived at https://chroniclingamerica.loc.gov/lccn/sn83045462/1908-12-21/ed-1/seq-1.pdf.

52. "Plans Sleuth Merge," *Washington Post*, December 22, 1908. Also see *New York Times*, December 22, 1908.

53. "Roosevelt Out of It: Need Not Testify regarding Secret Service Operations," Washington *Evening Star*, December 31, 1908, page 2, text available online at https://chroniclingamerica.loc.gov/lccn/sn83045462/1908-12-31/ed-1/seq-2/. Also see *New York Times*, January 1, 1909.

54. "The President and Congress," editorial, *New York Observer*, vol. 86, December 24, 1908, text available online at https://books.google.com/books?id=DX5PAAAAYAAJ&dq.

55. Edward P. Crapol, *John Tyler: The Accidental President* (Chapel Hill: The University of North Carolina Press, 2012).

56. Brands, *Andrew Jackson*; Meacham, *American Lion*.

57. "The President and Congress," editorial, *New-York Observer*, vol. 86, December 24, 1908, text available online at https://books.google.com/books?id=DX5PAAAAYAAJ&dq.

58. "The President Will Reply," *Washington Post*, December 19, 1908.

59. "Roosevelt Shaping Evidence; To Submit to Congress on His Secret Service Statements," *New York Times*, December 19, 1908, https://www.nytimes.com/1908/12/19/archives/roosevelt-shaping-evidence-to-submit-to-congress-on-his-secret.html.

60. "Work of Detectives: Cabinet Officers Preparing Reports for the President," Washington *Evening Star*, December 29, 1908, page 1, text available online at https://chroniclingamerica.loc.gov/lccn/sn83045462/1908-12-29/ed-1/seq-1/.

Chapter 12. The Battle over the Bureau

1. Roosevelt, *Letters*, 6:1492.
2. Gatewood, *Theodore Roosevelt*, 265.

3. Arthur Wallace Dunn, *From Harrison to Harding: A Personal Narrative Covering a Third of a Century, 1881–1921* (New York: Putnam, 1922), 2:89.

4. Gatewood, *Theodore Roosevelt*, 267.

5. "Tawney Is Censured, Secret Service Praised," Washington *Evening Star*, January 4, 1909, p. 1, text available online at https://chroniclingamerica.loc.gov/lccn/sn83045462/1909-01-04/ed-1/seq-1.pdf.

6. Theodore Roosevelt, "Special Message," letter to the US House of Representatives, issued from the White House, Washington, DC, January 4, 1909, text archived by the American Presidency Project at http://www.presidency.ucsb.edu/ws/index.php?pid=69655.

7. For an extensive review of Congress's resolution, see chapter 11.

8. Roosevelt, "Special Message."

9. Ibid.

10. Ibid.

11. Ibid.

12. Ibid.

13. Ibid.

14. Ibid.

15. Ibid.

16. Ibid.

17. Ibid.

18. Ibid.

19. "President's Reply Angers the House: 'Knaves Before, but Fools Now,' Says Keifer of Secret Service Message; Tawney the Hardest Hit; Denial of Intent to Slander House, but No Retraction of Remarks in Annual Message," *New York Times*, January 5, 1909, https://www.nytimes.com/1909/01/05/archives/presidents-reply-angers-the-house-knaves-before-but-fools-now-says.html.

20. *Washington Post*, January 5, 1909.

21. "President's Reply Angers the House: 'Knaves Before, but Fools Now,' Says Keifer of Secret Service Message; Tawney the Hardest Hit; Denial of Intent to Slander House, but No Retraction of Remarks in Annual Message," *New York Times*, January 5, 1909, https://www.nytimes.com/1909/01/05/archives/presidents-reply-angers-the-house-knaves-before-but-fools-now-says.html.

22. "Riled Up by Message," Washington *Evening Star*, January 5, 1909, page 1, text available online at https://chroniclingamerica.loc.gov/lccn/sn83045462/1909-01-05/ed-1/seq-1/.

23. Vincent Joseph Monteleone, *Criminal Slang: The Vernacular of the Underworld Lingo* (Clark, NJ: Lawbook Exchange, 2003), 90.

24. "Riled Up by Message," Washington *Evening Star*, January 5, 1909, page 1, text available online at https://chroniclingamerica.loc .gov/lccn/sn83045462/1909-01-05/ed-1/seq-1/.

25. Ibid.

26. *Washington Post*, January 6, 1909.

27. Ibid.

28. Gatewood, *Theodore Roosevelt*, 268.

29. Busbey, *Uncle Joe Cannon*, 232, 240–41.

30. *Atlanta Constitution*, January 5, 1909.

31. Washington *Evening Star*, January 5, 1909.

32. Gatewood, *Theodore Roosevelt*, 269.

33. For a full reprint of the letter, see January 11, 1909, in US Congress, *Congressional Record*, 720–25.

34. Ibid., 720.

35. Ibid., 720–21.

36. Ibid., 721.

37. Ibid., 722.

38. Ibid.

39. *Washington Post*, January 9, 1909.

40. *New York Times*, January 8, 1909.

41. Tawney Papers, box 3.

42. Ibid.

43. Ibid.

44. Ibid.

45. Ibid.

46. Ibid.

47. Ibid.

48. Oscar H. Hawley, *Musical Courier*, January 6, 1909.

49. "Who Are These Men?" *Albert Lea Evening Tribune*, January 6, 1909.

Chapter 13. Sore Losers and Petty Politics

1. Gatewood, *Theodore Roosevelt*, 236.

2. Ellen Maury Slayden, *Washington Wife: Journal of Ellen Maury Slayden from 1897–1919* (New York: Harper, 1962), 116.

3. The details from this January 8, 1909, session of Congress, unless explicitly cited otherwise, can be found in US Congress, *Congressional Record*, 645–78.

4. Roosevelt, "Special Message."

5. "Long Debate in the House: Restraint Shown by Critics of the President; Galleries Are Crowded; House Returns Roosevelt Blow," *New York Times*, January 9, 1909, page 2, https://www.nytimes.com/1909/01/09/archives/long-debate-in-the-house-restraint-shown-by-critics-of-the.html.

6. Ibid.

7. *Congressional Record*, January 8, 1909, 664.

8. *Washington Post*, January 9, 1909.

9. Gatewood, *Theodore Roosevelt*, 271.

10. Ibid.

11. *New York Times*, January 9, 1909.

12. The events of January 9, 1909, recorded in US Congress, *Congressional Record*, begin on page 687.

13. Washington *Evening Star*, January 9, 1909.

14. Washington *Evening Star*, January 11, 1909.

15. Tawney Papers, box 3.

16. *Washington Post*, January 10, 1909.

17. Ibid.

18. *New York Times*, January 10, 1909.

19. *New York Times*, January 12, 1909.

20. Ibid.

21. Hereafter, unless explicitly cited otherwise, recounting of the Senate's proceedings of January 11, 1909, are taken from US Congress, *Congressional Record*, beginning on page 718.

22. John Adams to Abigail Adams, December 19, 1793, *Adams Family Papers: An Electronic Archive*, Massachusetts Historical Society, https://www.masshist.org/digitaladams/archive/doc?id=L17931219ja.

23. For more on Roosevelt's letter to Hale, see chapter 12.

24. Washington *Evening Star*, January 8, 1909; *Washington Post*, January 9, 1909.

25. "Tillman Replies, Asks an Inquiry: And Promises That He Will Here-After Disclose Roosevelt to the People; Told No Lie, Broke No Law', Harriman, President's Friend, He Says, Unlawfully Holds 2,000,000 Acres of Oregon's Best Land," *New York Times*, January 12, 1909, https://www.nytimes.com/1909/01/12/archives/tillman-replies-asks-an-inquiry-and-promises-that-he-will-hereafter.html.

26. Gatewood, *Theodore Roosevelt*, 275.

27. Washington *Evening Star*, January 16, 1909.
28. *New York Times*, January 16, 1909.
29. Gatewood, *Theodore Roosevelt*, 276.
30. *New York Times*, January 10, 1909.
31. Roosevelt, *Letters*, 3:1472.
32. *New York Times*, January 9, 1909; *New York Times*, January 10, 1909.
33. *New York Times*, January 10, 1909.
34. Gatewood, *Theodore Roosevelt*, 271.

Chapter 14. The Aftermath

1. *New York Times*, January 17, 1909.
2. Ibid.
3. Ibid.
4. *New York Times*, January 10, 1909.
5. Roosevelt, *Letters*, 6:1475.
6. Ibid., 1498 and 1499.
7. *New York Times*, January 31, 1909.
8. Ibid.
9. Ibid.
10. Monteleone, *Criminal Slang*, 90. For a fuller discussion of the incident, see chapter 12.
11. *New York Times*, January 31, 1909.
12. Gatewood, *Theodore Roosevelt*, 280.
13. *New York Times*, February 2, 1909.
14. Gatewood, *Theodore Roosevelt*, 280.
15. *New York Times*, February 4, 1909.
16. *New York Times*, January 27, 1909.
17. *New York Times*, February 4, 1909.
18. The following coverage of Congress's questioning of Garfield is borrowed from "Roosevelt Charge Denied by Garfield: Land Fraud Hunt Not Hindered by Secret Service Law, Secretary Admits . . ." *New York Times*, February 8, 1909, https://www.nytimes.com/1909/02/08/archives/roosevelt-charge-denied-by-garfield-land-fraud-hunt-not-hindered-by.html.
19. "Work Is Not Restricted," *Washington Post*, February 8, 1909; "Unhampered by Law," Washington *Evening Star*, February 8, 1909.

20. "Roosevelt Charge Denied by Garfield: Land Fraud Hunt Not Hindered by Secret Service Law, Secretary Admits . . ." *New York Times*, February 8, 1909, https://www.nytimes.com/1909/02/08/archives/roosevelt-charge-denied-by-garfield-land-fraud-hunt-not-hindered-by.html.

21. *New York Times*, February 12, 1909.

22. Gatewood, *Theodore Roosevelt*, 281.

23. *New York Times*, February 22, 1909; Washington *Evening Star*, February 22, 1909.

24. *New York Times*, February 22, 1909; Washington *Evening Star*, February 22, 1909.

25. *New York Times*, February 22, 1909. See also Roosevelt, *Letters*, 6:1533.

26. Gatewood, *Theodore Roosevelt*, 281.

27. *Washington Post*, February 26, 1909.

28. Gatewood, *Theodore Roosevelt*, 281.

29. Morris, *Theodore Rex*, 547.

30. *Washington Post*, February 12, 1909.

31. Ibid.

32. Rasenberger, *America 1908*, 261.

33. *New York Times*, February 20, 1909.

34. Gatewood, *Theodore Roosevelt*, 282.

35. *New York Times*, February 26, 1909.

36. *Washington Post*, February 26, 1909.

37. Washington *Evening Star*, February 25, 1909.

38. *New York Times*, February 26, 1909.

39. *New York Times*, February 27, 1909.

40. Fox, "Birth of the Federal Bureau of Investigation."

41. Ibid.

42. This following exchange with Tawney is taken from the *New York Times*, February 2, 1909.

43. Gatewood, *Theodore Roosevelt*, 282.

44. March 3, 1909, US Congress, *Congressional Record*, 3801.

45. *New York Times*, March 3, 1909.

46. Morris, *Theodore Rex*, 550.

47. *New York Times*, March 5, 1909.

48. Morris, *Theodore Rex*, 552.

49. Henry F. Pringle, *The Life and Times of William Howard Taft: A Biography* (Hamden, CT: Archon Books, 1964), 393.

50. Gatewood, *Theodore Roosevelt*, 283.

51. Sanford J. Ungar, *FBI: An Uncensored Look behind the Walls* (Boston: Little, Brown, 1976).

52. Lowenthal, *Federal Bureau of Investigation*, 12.

53. For a more extensive look at the history of law enforcement in the United States, see chapter 1.

54. Lowenthal, *Federal Bureau of Investigation*, 13.

55. Ibid.

56. Gatewood, *Theodore Roosevelt*, 286.

57. Washington *Evening Star*, September 21, 1910.

58. *Tribune Albert Lea, Minnesota*, May 18, 1909.

59. Tawney Papers, box 4.

60. *Times-Enterprise*, January 5, 1910.

61. Gatewood, *Theodore Roosevelt*, 286.

62. H. L. Mencken, *Prejudices: Second Series* (New York: Alfred A. Knopf, 1920), 123.

63. Ibid.

64. Gatewood, *Theodore Roosevelt*, 286.

Epilogue

1. Jessica R. Pliley, *Policing Sexuality: The Mann Act and the Making of the FBI* (Cambridge, MA: Harvard University Press, 2014).

2. Burrough, *Public Enemies*; Grann, *Killers*; Holden, *FBI*; Rhodri Jeffreys-Jones, *The FBI: A History* (New Haven: Yale University Press, 2007); Ronald Kessler, *The Secrets of the FBI* (New York: Broadway Paperbacks, 2012); Richard Gid Powers, *Broken: The Troubled Past and Uncertain Future of the FBI* (New York: Free Press, 2004); Athan G. Theoharis, ed., *The FBI: A Comprehensive Reference Guide* (New York: Checkmark Books, 2000); Theoharis, *American Democracy*; Weiner, *Enemies*.

3. Jeffreys-Jones, *FBI*; Kessler, *Secrets*; Powers, *Broken*; Weiner, *Enemies*.

4. Kenneth D. Ackerman, *Young J. Edgar: Hoover, the Red Scare, and the Assault on Civil Liberties* (New York: Carroll and Graf Publishers, 2007); Edwin Palmer Hoyt, *The Palmer Raids, 1919–1920: An Attempt to Suppress Dissent* (New York: Seabury Press, 1969).

5. Laton McCartney, *The Teapot Dome Scandal: How Big Oil Bought the Harding White House and Tried to Steal the Country* (New York: Random House, 2008); David H. Stratton, *Tempest over Teapot Dome: The Story of Albert B. Fall* (Norman: University of Oklahoma Press, 1998).

6. Holden, *FBI*, 25–26.

7. Ackerman, *Young J. Edgar.*

8. Ibid.; Curt Gentry, *J. Edgar Hoover: The Man and the Secrets* (New York: W. W. Norton and Company, 1991); Richard Hack, *Puppetmaster: The Secret Life of J. Edgar Hoover* (Beverly Hills: Phoenix Books, 2007); Betty L. Medsger, *The Burglary: The Discovery of J. Edgar Hoover's Secret FBI* (New York: Vintage Books, 2014); Anthony Summers, *Official and Confidential: The Secret Life of J. Edgar Hoover* (New York: Open Road Integrated Media, Inc., 2013); Theoharis and Cox, *Boss*; Weiner, *Enemies.*

9. Burrough, *Public Enemies*; David J. Garrow, *The FBI and Martin Luther King, Jr.: From "Solo" to Memphis* (New York: Open Road Media, 2015); J. Edgar Hoover, *On Communism* (New York: Random House, 1969); Medsger, *Burglary*; Weiner, *Enemies.*

10. Hack, *Puppetmaster*; Athan G. Theoharis, ed. with commentary, *From the Secret Files of J. Edgar Hoover* (Chicago: Elephant Paperbacks, 1993).

11. Mark W. Felt and John O'Connor, *Mark Felt: The Man Who Brought Down the White House* (New York: PublicAffairs, 2006); Bob Woodward and Carl Bernstein, *The Secret Man: The Story of Watergate's Deep Throat* (New York: Pocket Books, 2005).

12. Louis J. Freeh, *My FBI: Bringing Down the Mafia, Investigating Bill Clinton, and Fighting the War on Terror* (New York: St. Martin's Press, 2005); Elsa Walsh, "Louis Freeh's Last Case," *The New Yorker*, May 14, 2001, https://www.newyorker.com/magazine/2001/05/14/louis-freehs-last-case; *Washington Post*, May 2, 2001; Weiner, *Enemies.*

13. James B. Comey, *A Higher Loyalty: Truth, Lies, and Leadership* (New York: Flatiron Books, 2018); Garrett M. Graff, *The Threat Matrix: Inside Robert Mueller's FBI and the War on Global Terror* (New York: Little, Brown and Company, 2011).

Bibliography

Abbott, Lawrence F., ed. *The Letters of Archie Butt*. Garden City, NY: Doubleday, 1924.

Ackerman, Kenneth D. *Dark Horse: The Surprise Election and Political Murder of President James A. Garfield*. Falls Church, VA: Viral History Press, 2011.

———. *Young J. Edgar: Hoover, the Red Scare, and the Assault on Civil Liberties*. New York: Carroll and Graf Publishers, 2007.

Adams, John. Letter to Abigail Adams. December 19, 1793. *Adams Family Papers: An Electronic Archive*. Massachusetts Historical Society. https://www.masshist.org/digitaladams/archive/doc?id=L17931219ja.

Ansley, Norman. "The United States Secret Service: An Administrative History." *Journal of Criminal Law, Criminology, and Police Science* 47, no. 1 (1956): 93–109.

Baker, Lafayette Charles. *The Secret Service in the Late War: Comprising the Author's . . . etc*. Philadelphia: John E. Potter and Company, 1874.

Barber, James G. *Andrew Jackson: A Portrait Study*. Seattle: University of Washington Press, 1991.

Barkan, Steven E., and George J. Bryjak. *Fundamentals of Criminal Justice: A Sociological View*. 2nd ed. Sudbury, MA: Jones and Bartlett Learning, 2011.

Berman, Jay Stuart. *Police Administration and Progressive Reform: Theodore Roosevelt as Police Commissioner of New York*. Westport, CT: Greenwood Publishing Group, 1987.

Bernstein, Peter L. *Wedding of the Waters: The Erie Canal and the Making of a Great Nation.* New York: W. W. Norton and Co., 2005.

Bishop, Joseph Bucklin. *Charles Joseph Bonaparte: His Life and Public Service.* New York: Charles Scribner's Sons, 1922.

Blum, Howard. *American Lightning: Terror, Mystery, the Birth of Hollywood, and the Crime of the Century.* New York: Crown Publishers, 2008.

Bopp, William J., and Donald O. Schultz. *A Short History of American Law Enforcement.* Springfield, IL: Charles C. Thomas, 1977.

Boston City Council. *Ordinances and Rules and Orders of the City of Boston: Together with the General and Special Statutes of the Massachusetts Legislature Relating to the City.* Boston: Alfred Mudge and Son Printers, 1869.

Bowen, Catherine Drinker. *Miracle at Philadelphia: The Story of the Constitutional Convention, May to September 1787.* Boston: Back Bay Books, 1986.

Bowen, Walter S., and Harry Edward Neal. *The United States Secret Service.* New York: Popular Library, 1960.

Bradsher, Greg. "How the West Was Settled: The 150-Year-Old Homestead Act Lured Americans Looking for a New Life and New Opportunities." *Prologue* 44, no. 4 (2012): 26–35.

Brandl, Steven G. *Criminal Investigation.* 4th ed. Thousand Oaks, CA: Sage, 2018.

Brands, H. W. *Andrew Jackson: His Life and Times.* New York: Doubleday, 2005.

———. *T. R.: The Last Romantic.* New York: Basic Books, 1997.

Brinkley, Douglas. *The Wilderness Warrior: Theodore Roosevelt and the Crusade for America.* New York: HarperCollins Publishers, 2009.

Brown, Henry S. "Punishing the Land-Looters." *The Outlook,* February 23, 1907, 427–39.

Bumgarner, Jeffrey B. *Federal Agents: The Growth of Federal Law Enforcement in America.* Westport, CT: Praeger, 2006.

Burgoyne, Arthur D. *The Homestead Strike of 1892.* Pittsburgh: University of Pittsburgh Press, 1979.

Burrough, Bryan. *Public Enemies: America's Greatest Crime Wave and the Birth of the FBI, 1933–34.* New York: The Penguin Press, 2004.

Burroughs, John. *Camping and Tramping with Roosevelt.* Boston: Houghton, Mifflin and Company, 1907.

Burrows, Edwin G., and Mike Wallace. *Gotham: A History of New York City to 1898.* New York: Oxford University Press, 1999.

Burstein, Andrew. *The Passions of Andrew Jackson*. New York: Alfred A. Knopf, 2003.

Busbey, L. White. *Uncle Joe Cannon: The Story of a Pioneer American*. New York: Henry Holt and Company, 1927.

Calhoun, Frederick S. *The Lawmen: United States Marshals and Their Deputies, 1789–1989*. New York: Penguin Books, 1991.

Chernow, Ron. *Washington: A Life*. New York: Penguin Books, 2010.

Clarke, James W. *American Assassins: The Darker Side of Politics*. Princeton: Princeton University Press, 1982.

Clemson University. "Benjamin Ryan Tillman." 2018. https://www.clemson.edu/about/history/bios/ben-tillman.html.

Comey, James B. *A Higher Loyalty: Truth, Lies, and Leadership*. New York: Flatiron Books, 2018.

Condon, Sean. *Shays's Rebellion: Authority and Distress in Post-Revolutionary America*. Baltimore: Johns Hopkins University Press, 2015.

Courtwright, David T. *Forces of Habit: Drugs and the Making of the Modern World*. Cambridge, MA: Harvard University Press, 2001.

Crapol, Edward P. *John Tyler: The Accidental President*. Chapel Hill: The University of North Carolina Press, 2012.

Craughwell, Thomas J. *Stealing Lincoln's Body*. Cambridge, MA: The Belknap Press, 2007.

Cuthbert, Norma C., ed. *Lincoln and the Baltimore Plot, 1861: From Pinkerton Records and Related Papers*. San Marino, CA: The Huntington Library, 1949.

Dalton, Kathleen. *Theodore Roosevelt: A Strenuous Life*. New York: Vintage, 2004.

Dash, Mike. *Satan's Circus: Murder, Vice, Police Corruption, and New York's Trial of the Century*. New York: Three Rivers Press, 2007.

Davis, Curtis Carroll. "The Craftiest of Men: William P. Wood and the Establishment of the United States Secret Service." *Maryland Historical Magazine* 83 (1988): 111–26.

———. "The 'Old Capitol' and Its Keeper: How William P. Wood Ran a Civil War Prison." *Records of the Columbia Historical Society* 52 (1989): 206–34.

Del Mar, Alexander. *The History of Money in America: From the Earliest Times to the Establishment of the Constitution*. New York: Burt Franklin, [1899] 1968.

Donald, David Herbert. *Lincoln*. New York: Simon and Schuster, 1995.

Donnelly, Matt. *Theodore Roosevelt: Larger Than Life*. North Haven, CT: Linnet Books, 2002.

Dorsey, Leroy G. *Theodore Roosevelt, Conservation, and the 1908 Governors' Conference*. College Station: Texas A&M University Press, 2016.

Dressler, Joshua, ed. *Encyclopedia of Crime and Justice*. 2nd ed. Vol. 2, *Delinquent and Criminal Subcultures–Juvenile Justice: Institutions*. New York: Macmillan Reference USA, 2002.

Dunn, Arthur Wallace. *From Harrison to Harding: A Personal Narrative Covering a Third of a Century, 1881–1921*. 2 vols. New York: Putnam, 1922.

Egan, Timothy. *The Big Burn: Teddy Roosevelt and the Fire That Saved America*. Boston: Houghton Mifflin Harcourt, 2009.

Felt, Mark W., and John O'Connor. *Mark Felt: The Man Who Brought Down the White House*. New York: PublicAffairs, 2006.

Fitzpatrick, John C., ed. *The Writings of George Washington from the Original Manuscript Sources, 1745–1799: Prepared under the Direction of the United States George Washington Bicentennial Commission and Published by Authority of Congress*. Washington, DC: US Government Printing Office, 1939.

Fogelson, Robert M. *Big-City Police*. Cambridge, MA: Harvard University Press, 1977.

Fox, John F., Jr. "The Birth of the Federal Bureau of Investigation." Federal Bureau of Investigation (website). July 2003. https://www.fbi.gov/history/history-publications-reports/the-birth-of-the-federal-bureau-of-investigation.

Franklin, Benjamin. *The Autobiography of Benjamin Franklin*. Mineola, NY: Dover Thrift Editions, [1791] 1996.

Freeh, Louis J. *My FBI: Bringing Down the Mafia, Investigating Bill Clinton, and Fighting the War on Terror*. New York: St. Martin's Press, 2005.

Friedman, Lawrence M. *Crime and Punishment in American History*. New York: Basic Books, 1993.

Gardiner, A. G. *Pillars of Society*. London: James Nisbet and Co., Limited, 1913.

Garrow, David J. *The FBI and Martin Luther King, Jr.: From "Solo" to Memphis*. New York: Open Road Media, 2015.

Gaston, Bibi, ed. *Gifford Pinchot and the First Foresters: The Untold Story of the Brave Men and Women Who Launched the American Conservation Movement*. New Milford, CT: Baked Apple Club Productions, 2016.

Gatewood, Willard B., Jr. *Theodore Roosevelt and the Art of Controversy: Episodes of the White House Years*. Baton Rouge: Louisiana State University Press, 1970.

Gentry, Curt. *J. Edgar Hoover: The Man and the Secrets*. New York: W. W. Norton and Company, 1991.

Gerry, Margarita Spalding, ed. *Through Five Administrations: Reminiscences of Colonel William H. Crook, Body-Guard to President Lincoln.* New York: Harper and Brothers Publishers, 1910.

Glaser, Lynn. *Counterfeiting in America: The History of an American Way to Wealth.* New York: Clarkson N. Potter, Inc., 1968.

Godfrey, Carlos E. *The Commander-in-Chief's Guard: Revolutionary War.* Washington, DC: Stevenson-Smith Company, 1904.

Goodwin, Doris Kearns. *The Bully Pulpit: Theodore Roosevelt, William Howard Taft, and the Golden Age of Journalism.* New York: Simon and Schuster, 2013.

———. *Team of Rivals: The Political Genius of Abraham Lincoln.* New York: Simon and Schuster, 2005.

Graff, Garrett M. *The Threat Matrix: Inside Robert Mueller's FBI and the War on Global Terror.* New York: Little, Brown and Company, 2011.

Grann, David. *Killers of the Flower Moon: The Osage Murders and the Birth of the FBI.* New York: Vintage, 2018.

Hack, Richard. *Puppetmaster: The Secret Life of J. Edgar Hoover.* Beverly Hills: Phoenix Books, 2007.

Hagedorn, Hermann. *The Boy's Life of Theodore Roosevelt.* New York: Harper and Brothers, 1918.

Hahn, John Willard. *The Background of Shays's Rebellion: A Study of Massachusetts History, 1780–1787.* Madison: University of Wisconsin–Madison, 1946.

Halford, E. W. "Roosevelt's Introduction to Washington." *Frank Leslie's Illustrated Weekly* 128, no. 3312 (March 1, 1919): 314–17.

Hamilton, Alexander, James Madison, and John Jay. *The Federalist: A Collection of Essays, Written in Favour of the New Constitution.* 2 vols. New York: J. and A. McLean, 1787.

Hammond, Bray. *Banks and Politics in America: From the Revolution to the Civil War.* Princeton: Princeton University Press, 1957.

———. *Sovereignty and an Empty Purse: Banks and Politics in the Civil War.* Princeton: Princeton University Press, 1970.

Harbaugh, William Henry. *Power and Responsibility: The Life and Times of Theodore Roosevelt.* New York: Farrar, Straus and Cudahy, 1961.

Harvey, George. *Henry Clay Frick: The Man.* New York: Beard Books, 1928.

Hepburn, A. Barton. *A History of Currency in the United States.* New York: Augustus M. Kelley Publishers, 1967.

Hogeland, William. *The Whisky Rebellion: George Washington, Alexander Hamilton, and the Frontier Rebels Who Challenged America's Newfound Sovereignty.* New York: Simon and Schuster, 2010.

Holden, Henry M. *FBI: 100 Years; An Unofficial History*. Minneapolis: Zenith Press, 2008.

Hollister, O. J. *Life of Schuyler Colfax*. New York: Funk and Wagnalls, 1886.

Hoover, J. Edgar. *On Communism*. New York: Random House, 1969.

Horan, James D. *The Pinkertons: The Detective Dynasty That Made History*. New York: Crown Publishers, Inc., 1967.

Horan, James D., and Howard Swiggett. *The Pinkerton Story*. New York: G. P. Putnam's Sons, 1951.

Howard, Hugh. *Mr. and Mrs. Madison's War: America's First Couple and the War of 1812*. New York: Bloomsbury Press, 2012.

Howe, Daniel Walker. *What Hath God Wrought: The Transformation of America, 1815–1848*. New York: Oxford University Press, 2007.

Hoyt, Edwin Palmer. *The Palmer Raids, 1919–1920: An Attempt to Suppress Dissent*. New York: Seabury Press, 1969.

Jeffers, H. Paul. *Commissioner Roosevelt: The Story of Theodore Roosevelt and the New York City Police, 1895–1897*. New York: John Wiley and Sons, Inc., 1994.

Jeffreys-Jones, Rhodri. *The FBI: A History*. New Haven: Yale University Press, 2007.

Jenkins, Rebecca. *The First London Olympics, 1908: The Definitive Story of London's Most Sensational Olympics to Date*. London: Hachette Digital, 2008.

Johnson, David R. *American Law Enforcement: A History*. Wheeling, IL: Forum Press, 1981.

———. *Illegal Tender: Counterfeiting and the Secret Service in Nineteenth-Century America*. Washington, DC: Smithsonian Institution Press, 1995.

Josephson, Matthew. *The Robber Barons: The Great American Capitalists, 1861–1901*. New York: Harcourt Brace and Company, 1934.

Kahan, Paul. *The Bank War: Andrew Jackson, Nicholas Biddle, and the Fight for American Finance*. Yardley, PA: Westholme Publishing, 2015.

———. *The Homestead Strike: Labor, Violence, and American Industry*. New York: Routledge, 2014.

Kaiser, Frederick M. "Origins of Secret Service Protection of the President: Personnel, Interagency, and Institutional Conflict." *Presidential Studies Quarterly* 18, no. 1 (1988): 101–27.

Kantrowitz, Stephen. *Ben Tillman and the Reconstruction of White Supremacy*. Chapel Hill: The University of North Carolina Press, 2000.

Kessler, Ronald. *The Secrets of the FBI*. New York: Broadway Paperbacks, 2012.

Kline, Michael J. *The Baltimore Plot: The First Conspiracy to Assassinate Abraham Lincoln*. Yardley, PA: Westholme, 2008.

Knox, John Jay. *A History of Banking in the United States*. Edited by Bradford Rhodes and Elmer H. Youngman. New York: Bradford Rhodes and Company, 1900.

Kohn, Edward P. "'A Most Revolting State of Affairs': Theodore Roosevelt's Aldermanic Bill and the New York Assembly City Investigating Committee of 1884." *American Nineteenth Century History* 10, no. 1 (2009): 71–92.

———. *Hot Time in the Old Town: The Great Heat Wave of 1896 and the Making of Theodore Roosevelt*. New York: Basic Books, 2010.

Lamon, Ward Hill. *Recollections of Abraham Lincoln, 1847–1865*. Edited by Dorothy Lamon Teillard. Washington, DC: Dorothy Lamon Teillard, 1911.

Lane, Roger. *Policing the City: Boston, 1822–1855*. New York, NY: Atheneum, 1971.

Lankenau, Stephen E. "Smoke 'Em if You Got 'Em: Cigarette Black Markets in U.S. Prisons and Jails." *The Prison Journal* 81, no. 2 (2001): 142–61. https://www.ncbi.nlm.nih.gov/pmc/articles/PMC2117377/.

Lardner, James, and Thomas Reppetto. *NYPD: A City and Its Police*. New York: Henry Holt and Company, 2000.

Law Enforcement Assistance Association. *Two Hundred Years of American Criminal Justice: An LEAA Bicentennial Study*. Edited by Joseph Foote. Washington, DC: US Department of Justice, 1976.

Lawson, John Davidson, ed. *American State Trials: A Collection of the Important and Interesting Criminal Trials Which Have Taken Place in the United States, from the Beginning of Our Government to the Present Day; with Notes and Annotations*. Vol. 3. Saint Louis: F. H. Thomas Law Book Co., 1915. https://hdl.handle.net/2027/hvd.32044055052633.

Lender, Mark Edward, and Garry Wheeler Stone. *Fatal Sunday: George Washington, the Monmouth Campaign, and the Politics of Battle*. Norman: University of Oklahoma Press, 2016.

Lepler, Jessica M. *The Many Panics of 1837: People, Politics, and the Creation of a Transatlantic Financial Crisis*. New York: Cambridge University Press, 2013.

Lewis, Lloyd. *The Assassination of Lincoln: History and Myth*. Lincoln: University of Nebraska Press, 1929.

Lewis, William Draper. *The Life of Theodore Roosevelt*. Philadelphia: John C. Winston Co., 1919.

Lowenthal, Max. *The Federal Bureau of Investigation*. New York: William Sloane Associates, Inc., 1950.

Lukas, J. Anthony. *Big Trouble: A Murder in a Small Western Town Sets Off a Struggle for the Soul of America*. New York: Simon and Schuster, 1997.

Lunde, Darrin. *The Naturalist: Theodore Roosevelt, a Lifetime of Exploration, and the Triumph of American Natural History*. New York: Crown Publishers, 2016.

Mackay, James. *Allan Pinkerton: The First Private Eye*. New York: John Wiley and Sons, Inc., 1996.

Madison, James. "Notes on the Debates in the Federal Convention." Transcript. August 30, 1787. Available at http://avalon.law.yale.edu/18th_century/debates_830.asp.

Marion, Nancy E., and Willard M. Oliver. *Federal Law Enforcement Agencies in America*. Frederick, MD: Wolters Kluwer Law and Business, 2015.

Martin, Paul. "Lincoln's Missing Bodyguard." *Smithsonian Magazine*, April 7, 2010. https://www.smithsonianmag.com/history/lincolns-missing-bodyguard-12932069/.

Martineau, Harriet. *Retrospect of Western Travel*. 2 vols. London: Saunders and Otley, 1838.

Mayer, Kenneth. *With the Stroke of a Pen: Executive Orders and Presidential Power*. Princeton: Princeton University Press, 2001.

McCartney, Laton. *The Teapot Dome Scandal: How Big Oil Bought the Harding White House and Tried to Steal the Country*. New York: Random House, 2008.

McCullough, David. *Mornings on Horseback: The Story of an Extraordinary Family, a Vanished Way of Life, and the Unique Child Who Became Theodore Roosevelt*. New York: Simon and Schuster, 2001.

———. *The Path between the Seas: The Creation of the Panama Canal, 1870–1914*. New York: Simon and Schuster, 1978.

McPherson, James M. *Battle Cry of Freedom: The Civil War Era*. New York: Oxford University Press, 1988.

Meacham, Jon. *American Lion: Andrew Jackson in the White House*. New York: Random House, 2008.

Medsger, Betty L. *The Burglary: The Discovery of J. Edgar Hoover's Secret FBI*. New York: Vintage Books, 2014.

Melanson, Philip H. *The Secret Service: The Hidden History of an Enigmatic Agency*. With Peter F. Stevens. New York: Carroll and Graff Publishers, 2002.

Mencken, H. L. *Prejudices: Second Series*. New York: Alfred A. Knopf, 1920.

Meyer, Diana Lambdin. *Kansas Myths and Legends: The True Stories behind History's Mysteries*. 2nd ed. Guilford, CT: TwoDot, 2017.

Mihm, Stephen. *A Nation of Counterfeiters: Capitalists, Con Men, and the Making of the United States*. Cambridge, MA: Harvard University Press, 2007.

Millard, Candice. *Destiny of the Republic: A Tale of Madness, Medicine and the Murder of a President*. New York: Doubleday, 2011.

———. *The River of Doubt: Theodore Roosevelt's Darkest Journey*. New York: Broadway Books, 2005.

Miller, Arthur S. *Presidential Power*. Saint Paul, MN: West Publishing Company, 1977.

Miller, Marla R. *Betsy Ross and the Making of America*. New York: Henry Holt and Company, 2010.

Miller, Nathan. *Theodore Roosevelt: A Life*. New York: Quill, 1992.

Miller, Scott. *The President and the Assassin: McKinley, Terror, and Empire at the Dawn of the American Century*. New York: Random House, 2011.

Miller, Wilbur R. *Cops and Bobbies: Police Authority in New York and London, 1830–1870*. 2nd ed. Columbus: The Ohio State University Press, 1997.

Mitchell, Broadus. *Heritage from Hamilton*. New York: Columbia University Press, 1957.

Mogelever, Jacob. *Death to Traitors: The Story of General Lafayette C. Baker, Lincoln's Forgotten Secret Service Chief*. New York: Doubleday, 1960.

Monkkonen, Eric H. *Police in Urban America, 1860–1920*. New York: Cambridge University Press, 1981.

Monteleone, Vincent Joseph. *Criminal Slang: The Vernacular of the Underworld Lingo*. Clark, NJ: Lawbook Exchange, 2003.

Morn, Frank. *"The Eye That Never Sleeps": A History of the Pinkerton National Detective Agency*. Bloomington: Indiana University Press, 1982.

Morris, Edmund. *Colonel Roosevelt*. New York: Random House, 2010.

———. *The Rise of Theodore Roosevelt*. New York: The Modern Library, 2001.

———. *Theodore Rex*. New York: The Modern Library, 2002.

Morton, Tom. "Marker for Secret Service Agent." Fairmont Cemetery (website). November 11, 2010. http://fairmount-cemetery.com/new-marker-for-secret-service-agent/.

Mowry, George E. *The Era of Theodore Roosevelt: 1900–1912.* New York: Harper and Row Publishers, 1958.

Musicant, Ivan. *Empire by Default: The Spanish-American War and the Dawn of the American Century.* New York: Henry Holt and Company, 1998.

National Archives. "Arrest Warrant from a Secret Committee of the New York Provincial Congress, 21 June 1776." *Founders Online.* Last modified June 13, 2018. https://founders.archives.gov/documents/Washington/03-05-02-0042. [Original source: Washington, George. "Arrest Warrant from a Secret Committee of the New York Provincial Congress, 21 June 1776." *The Papers of George Washington,* Revolutionary War Series. Vol. 5, *16 June 1776–12 August 1776,* 72–74. Edited by Philander D. Chase. Charlottesville: University Press of Virginia, 1993.]

———. "The Homestead Act of 1862." Last reviewed October 3, 2016. https://www.archives.gov/education/lessons/homestead-act.

National Park Service. "Theodore Roosevelt and Conservation." Last updated November 16, 2017. https://www.nps.gov/thro/learn/historyculture/theodore-roosevelt-and-conservation.htm.

Newman, Eric P. *The Early Paper Money of America: An Illustrated, Historical, and Descriptive Compilation of Data Relating to America Paper Currency from Its Inception in 1686 to the Year 1800. . . .* 5th ed. Iola, WI: Krause Publications, 2008.

Nicolay, John G., and John Hay. *Abraham Lincoln: A History.* New York: The Century Co., 1890.

Nikolaieff, George A., ed. *Taxation and the Economy.* New York: H. W. Wilson Co., 1968.

Northern Illinois University, University Libraries. "Court Martial for the Trial of Thomas Hickey and Others, v6:1084." *American Archives: Documents of the American Revolutionary Period, 1774–1776* (website). 2015. http://amarch.lib.niu.edu/islandora/object/niuamarch%3A85258.

O'Callaghan, Jerry A. "Senator Mitchell and the Oregon Land Frauds, 1905." *Pacific Historical Review* 21, no. 3 (1952): 255–61.

Officer Down Memorial Page. "Deputy U.S. Marshal John Gatewood." Accessed August 10, 2016. https://www.odmp.org/officer/21996-deputy-us-marshal-john-gatewood.

———. "Operative Joseph A. Walker." Accessed January 18, 2018. http://www.odmp.org/officer/13759-operative-joseph-a-walker.

———. "Operative William Craig." Accessed October 18, 2017. https://www.odmp.org/officer/3571-operative-william-craig.

Oliver, Willard M., and James F. Hilgenberg Jr. *A History of Crime and Criminal Justice in America*. 2nd ed. Durham, NC: Carolina Academic Press, 2010.

Oliver, Willard M., and Nancy E. Marion. *Killing the President: Assassinations, Attempts, and Rumored Attempts on U.S. Commanders-in-Chief*. Santa Barbara, CA: Praeger, 2010.

Parenti, Michael. "The Strange Death of President Zachary Taylor: A Case Study in the Manufacture of Mainstream History." *New Political Science* 20, no. 2 (1998): 141–58.

Parkhurst, Charles H. *Our Fight with Tammany*. New York: Charles Scribner's Sons, 1895.

Pease, Jane H., and William H. Pease. *The Fugitive Slave Law and Anthony Burns: A Problem in Law Enforcement*. New York: Lippincott, 1975.

Pinkerton. "Our History." Accessed August 17, 2016. https://www.pinkerton.com/our-difference/history.

Pinkerton, Allan. *Professional Thieves and the Detective: Containing Numerous Detective Sketches Collected from Private Records*. New York: G. W. Dillingham Co., Publishers, 1880.

———. *Thirty Years a Detective: A Thorough and Comprehensive Exposé of Criminal Practices of All Grades and Classes. . . .* New York: G. W. Carleton and Co., Publishers, 1884.

Pitch, Anthony S. "The Burning of Washington." *White House History* 4 (Fall 1998). Available at The White House Historical Association (website), https://www.whitehousehistory.org/the-burning-of-washington.

Pliley, Jessica R. *Policing Sexuality: The Mann Act and the Making of the FBI*. Cambridge, MA: Harvard University Press, 2014.

Powers, Richard Gid. *Broken: The Troubled Past and Uncertain Future of the FBI*. New York: Free Press, 2004.

Pringle, Henry F. *The Life and Times of William Howard Taft: A Biography*. Hamden, CT: Archon Books, 1964.

———. *Theodore Roosevelt: A Biography*. New York: Harcourt, Brace, and Co., 1931.

Puter, S. A. D. *Looters of the Public Domain*. Portland: The Portland Printing House, 1908.

Radford, R. A. "The Economic Organisation of a P.O.W. Camp." *Economica* 12, no. 48 (1945): 189–201.

Rappleye, Charles. *Robert Morris: Financier of the American Revolution.* New York: Simon and Schuster, 2010.

Rasenberger, Jim. *America, 1908: The Dawn of Flight, the Race to the Pole, the Invention of the Model T, and the Making of a Modern Nation.* New York: Scribner, 2007.

Remini, Robert V. *Andrew Jackson: The Course of American Democracy, 1833–1845.* Vol. 3. New York: Harper and Row, 1984.

Reppetto, Thomas A. *American Mafia: A History of Its Rise to Power.* New York: Henry Holt, 2004.

———. *American Police: The Blue Parade, 1845–1945; A History.* New York: Enigma Books, 2010.

Rich, Burdett A., ed. *The Lawyers Reports Annotated.* Jointly edited by Henry P. Farnham. Rochester, NY: The Lawyers Co-Operative Publishing Company, 1910.

Richards, Leonard L. *Shays's Rebellion: The American Revolution's Final Battle.* Philadelphia: University of Pennsylvania Press, 2002.

Richardson, James F. *Urban Police in the United States.* Port Washington, NY: Kennikat Press, 1974.

Roberts, Alasdair. *America's First Great Depression: Economic Crisis and Political Disorder after the Panic of 1837.* Ithaca, NY: Cornell University Press, 2012.

Robinson, Corinne Roosevelt. *My Brother, Theodore Roosevelt.* New York: Charles Scribner's Sons, 1921.

Roosevelt, Theodore. *African Game Trails: An Account of the African Wanderings of an American Hunter-Nationalist.* New York: Safari Press, 1909.

———. "The Boone and Crockett Club." *Harper's Weekly*, March 18, 1893, 267. Archived online at https://babel.hathitrust.org/cgi/pt?id=pst.000020243371;view=1up;seq=281.

———. "Diaries and Notebooks of the American President Theodore Roosevelt." Archives spanning 1868–1914. Maintained by HOLLIS Archive, Harvard University. https://hollisarchives.lib.harvard.edu/repositories/24/resources/6304.

———. "Eighth Annual Message." Letter to the US Senate and House of Representatives. Issued from the White House, Washington, DC. December 8, 1908. Text archived by the American Presidency Project at https://www.presidency.ucsb.edu/node/206223.

———. *The Letters of Theodore Roosevelt.* 8 vols. Edited by Elting Elmore Morison. Cambridge, MA: Harvard University Press, 1951–1954.

———. *The Naval War of 1812*. 2 vols. New York: G. P. Putnam's Sons, 1900.

———. "Our Vanishing Wild Life." *The Outlook*, January 25, 1913, 161–62. Text archived online at https://babel.hathitrust.org/cgi/pt?id=coo.31924066372842;view=1up;seq=223.

———. *The Rough Riders*. Lincoln: University of Nebraska Press, 1998.

———. "Special Message." Letter to the US House of Representatives. Issued from the White House, Washington, DC. January 4, 1909. Text archived by the American Presidency Project at http://www.presidency.ucsb.edu/ws/index.php?pid=69655.

———. *Theodore Roosevelt: An Autobiography*. New York: The Macmillan Company, 1916.

Rosen, Jonathan. *The Life of the Skies: Birding at the End of Nature*. New York: Farrar, Straus and Giroux, 2008.

Sabbag, Robert. *Too Tough to Die: Down and Dangerous with the U.S. Marshals*. New York: Simon and Schuster, 1992.

Sandburg, Carl. *Storm over the Land: A Profile of the Civil War Taken Mainly from Abraham Lincoln; The War Years*. New York: Harcourt, Brace and Company, 1942.

Schultz, David, and John R. Vile, eds. *The Encyclopedia of Civil Liberties in America*. 3 vols. New York: Routledge, 2015.

Scott, Kenneth. *Counterfeiting in Colonial America*. With a foreword by U. E. Baughman. New York: Oxford University Press, 1957.

Seward, Frederick William. *Seward at Washington, as Senator and Secretary of State: A Memoir of His Life, with Selections from His Letters*. Vol. 2, *1861–1872*. New York: Derby and Miller, 1891.

Shakespeare, William. *Much Ado about Nothing*. New York: Oxford University Press, 1999.

Shattuck, Gary. "Plotting the 'Sacracide' of George Washington." *Journal of the American Revolution* (July 25, 2014): 1–17. https://allthingsliberty.com/2014/07/plotting-the-sacricide-of-george-washington/.

Sherman, Richard B. "Presidential Protection during the Progressive Era: The Aftermath of the McKinley Assassination." *The Historian* 46, no. 1 (1983): 1–20.

Slaughter, Thomas P. *Bloody Dawn: The Christiana Riot and Racial Violence in the Antebellum North*. New York: Oxford University Press, 1991.

Slayden, Ellen Maury. *Washington Wife: Journal of Ellen Maury Slayden from 1897–1919*. New York: Harper, 1962.

Smith, Adam. *An Inquiry into the Nature and Causes of the Wealth of Nations*. New York: MetaLibri, [1776] 2007.

Smith, Bruce. *Rural Crime Control*. New York: Institute of Public Administration, Columbia University, 1933.

Sommer, Robin Langley. *The History of the U.S. Marshals: The Proud Story of America's Legendary Lawmen*. Philadelphia: Courage Books, 1993.

Southwick, Albert B. "William Craig's Last Interview." *Worchester Telegram*, September 5, 2013. http://www.telegram.com/article/20130905/COLUMN21/309059975.

Stahr, Walter. *Seward: Lincoln's Indispensable Man*. New York: Simon and Schuster, 2012.

Standiford, Les. *Meet You in Hell: Andrew Carnegie, Henry Clay Frick, and the Bitter Partnership That Transformed America*. New York: Three Rivers Press, 2005.

Steffens, Lincoln. *The Autobiography of Lincoln Steffens*. New York: Harcourt, Brace, and Co., 1936.

Storer, Mrs. Bellamy. "How Theodore Roosevelt Was Appointed Assistant Secretary of the Navy." *Harper's Weekly*, 56 (June 1, 1912): 8–9. Archived online at https://babel.hathitrust.org/cgi/pt?id=mdp.39015033848121;view=1up;seq=616.

Stratton, David H. *Tempest over Teapot Dome: The Story of Albert B. Fall*. Norman: University of Oklahoma Press, 1998.

Strong, George Templeton. *The Diary of George Templeton Strong*. Vol. 3, *The Civil War 1860–1865*. Edited by Allan Nevins and Milton Halsey Thomas. New York: Macmillan Company, 1952.

Summers, Anthony. *Official and Confidential: The Secret Life of J. Edgar Hoover*. New York: Open Road Integrated Media, Inc., 2013.

Swanson, James L. *Manhunt: The Twelve-Day Chase for Lincoln's Killer*. New York: HarperCollins, 2006.

Tarnoff, Ben. *Moneymakers: The Wicked Lives and Surprising Adventures of Three Notorious Counterfeiters*. New York: The Penguin Press, 2011.

Tatom, Oliver. "Binger Hermann (1843–1926)." In *The Oregon Encyclopedia*. The Oregon Historical Society, 2008–. Article last updated March 17, 2018. https://oregonencyclopedia.org/articles/hermann_binger_1843_1926_/.

———. "Oregon Land Fraud Trials (1904–1910)." In *The Oregon Encyclopedia*. The Oregon Historical Society, 2008–. Article last updated March 17, 2018. https://oregonencyclopedia.org/articles/oregon_land_fraud_trials_1904_1910_/.

Tawney, James A., Papers. Minnesota Historical Society.

Theodore Roosevelt Association. "The Hunter." Accessed November 29, 2017. http://www.theodoreroosevelt.org/site/c.elKSIdOWIiJ8H/b.8344379/k.2B69/The_Hunter.htm.

Theodore Roosevelt Center. "Abraham Lincoln's Funeral Procession." Theodore Roosevelt Birthplace National Historic Site, Dickinson State University. Accessed October 27, 2017. http://www.theodorerooseveltcenter.org/Research/Digital-Library/Record.aspx?libID=o284880.

Theoharis, Athan G., ed. *The FBI: A Comprehensive Reference Guide*. New York: Checkmark Books, 2000.

———. *The FBI and American Democracy: A Brief Critical History*. Lawrence: University Press of Kansas, 2004.

———, ed. with commentary. *From the Secret Files of J. Edgar Hoover*. Chicago: Elephant Paperbacks, 1993.

Theoharis, Athan G., and John Stuart Cox. *The Boss: J. Edgar Hoover and the Great American Inquisition*. Philadelphia: Temple University Press, 1988.

Tilghman, Oswald. "Robert Morris, the Oxford Merchant, 1711–1750." *History of Talbot County, Maryland, 1661–1861: Compiled Principally from the Literary Relics of . . . Samuel Alexander Harrison*, vol. 1. Baltimore: Wilkins and Wilkins Co., 1915. Available online at http://www.tcfl.org/mdroom/worthies/morris.html.

Turk, David S. "Conclusion: Retired Deputy U.S. Marshal Follows the Trail of Robert Forsyth's Murderer." History. *US Marshals Service* (website). Accessed August 10, 2016. https://www.usmarshals.gov/history/forsyth.htm.

Turner, Carol. *Notorious San Juans: Wicked Tales from Ouray, San Juan and La Plata Counties*. Charleston, SC: History Press, 2011.

Twain, Mark. *Mark Twain's Letters*. Arranged with comment by Albert Bigelow Paine. New York: Harper and Brothers, 1919.

Ungar, Sanford J. *FBI: An Uncensored Look behind the Walls*. Boston: Little, Brown, 1976.

US Congress. *Congressional Record: Containing the Proceedings and Debates of the Sixtieth Congress, Second Session*. Vol. 43. Washington, DC: Government Printing Office, 1909. Text available online at https://books.google.com/books?id=LQlRWQ8ET58C.

———. The Sundry Civil Expenses Act of 1907. Pub. L. No. 253, 59th Cong., 2nd. sess., 1315. 1906. Text available online at https://en.wikisource.org/wiki/Page:United_States_Statutes_at_Large_Volume_34_Part_1.djvu/1345.

———. "Tawney, James Albertus, (1855–1919)." *Biographical Directory of the United States Congress, 1774–Present*. Accessed March 2, 2016. http://bioguide.congress.gov/scripts/biodisplay.pl?index=T000060.

US Department of Justice. *The Annual Report of the Attorney-General of the United States for the Year 1907*. 2 vols. Washington, DC: US Government Printing Office, 1907. Available online at (vol. 1) https://babel.hathitrust.org/cgi/pt?id=osu.32437010220560 and (vol. 2) https://babel.hathitrust.org/cgi/pt?id=hvd.hl0j9a;view=1up;seq=10.

———. *The Annual Report of the Attorney-General of the United States for the Year 1908*. Washington, DC: US Government Printing Office, 1908. Available online at https://babel.hathitrust.org/cgi/pt?id=ucl.b5145516;view=1up;seq=1.

US Department of the Treasury. "Resource Center: Denominations." Last updated June 15, 2018. https://www.treasury.gov/resource-center/faqs/Coins/Pages/denominations.aspx.

US House of Representatives. Hearings before Subcommittee of House Committee on Appropriations, Consisting of . . . the Legislative, Executive, and Judicial Appropriation Bill for 1907. Washington, DC: US Government Printing Office, 1906. Available online at https://babel.hathitrust.org/cgi/pt?id=nyp.33433019658206;view=1up;seq=7.

———. Subcommittee of House Committee on Appropriations. Records. January 17, 1908.

US Marshals Service. "History—The First Generation of United States Marshals: The First Marshal of Maryland; Nathaniel Ramsay." Accessed August 9, 2016. https://www.usmarshals.gov/history/firstmarshals/ramsay.htm.

US Secret Service. "Ordinary People, Extraordinary Times." Department of Homeland Security (website). Accessed January 26, 2018. https://www.secretservice.gov/about/history/honor/.

———. "USSS History." Department of Homeland Security (website). Accessed October 25, 2017. https://www.secretservice.gov/about/history/events/.

Van Buren, Martin. *The Autobiography of Martin Van Buren*. Vol. 2, *Annual Report of the American Historical Association for the Year 1918*. Edited by John C. Fitzpatrick. Washington, DC: US Government Printing Office, 1920.

Vermilya, Daniel J. *James Garfield and the Civil War: For Ohio and the Union*. Charleston, SC: History Press, 2015.

Walker, Samuel. *Popular Justice: A History of American Criminal Justice.* 2nd ed. New York: Oxford University Press, 1998.

Walling, George Washington. *Recollections of a New York Chief of Police: An Official Record of Thirty-Eight Years as Patrolman, Detective, Captain, Inspector and Chief of the New York Police.* New York: Caxton Book Concern, 1887.

Walsh, Elsa. "Louis Freeh's Last Case." *The New Yorker*, May 14, 2001. https://www.newyorker.com/magazine/2001/05/14/louis-freehs-last-case.

Ward, Harry M. *George Washington's Enforcers: Policing the Continental Army.* Carbondale: Southern Illinois University Press, 2006.

Ward, John William. *Andrew Jackson, Symbol for an Age.* New York: Oxford University Press, 1955.

Warren Commission. *Report of the President's Commission on the Assassination of President John F. Kennedy.* Washington, DC: US Government Printing Office, 1964. Text available online at https://www.archives.gov/research/jfk/warren-commission-report.

Weiner, Tim. *Enemies: A History of the FBI.* New York: Random House, 2012.

Whitehead, Don. *The FBI Story: A Report to the People.* Foreword by J. Edgar Hoover. New York: Random House, 1956.

Whorton, James C. *The Arsenic Century: How Victorian Britain Was Poisoned at Home, Work, and Play.* New York: Oxford University Press, 2010.

Wilkie, Don. *American Secret Service Agent.* As told to Mark Lee Luther. New York: Frederick A. Stokes Company, 1934.

Wister, Owen. *Roosevelt: The Story of a Friendship, 1880–1919.* New York: Macmillan, 1930.

———. *The Virginian.* New York: Macmillan, 1902.

Wolfensberger, Donald R. *Congress and the People: Deliberative Democracy on Trial.* Baltimore: The Johns Hopkins University Press, 2000.

Wolters Kluwer Law and Business. *The Department of Justice Manual.* 3rd ed. New York: Aspen Publishers, 2016.

Wood, Gordon S. *Empire of Liberty: A History of the Early Republic, 1789–1815.* New York: Oxford University Press, 2009.

Woodward, Bob, and Carl Bernstein. *The Secret Man: The Story of Watergate's Deep Throat.* New York: Pocket Books, 2005.

Wyman, Roger E. "Insurgency in Minnesota: The Defeat of James A. Tawney in 1910." *Minnesota History* 40, no. 7 (1967): 317–29.

Zacks, Richard. *Island of Vice: Theodore Roosevelt's Doomed Quest to Clean up Sin-Loving New York.* New York: Doubleday, 2012.

Index

About the Author

Willard M. Oliver is professor of criminal justice at Sam Houston State University in Huntsville, Texas. He received his PhD in political science from West Virginia University. His areas of research interest include policing, criminal-justice history, and policy of federal-crime control. He is author of two dozen books, a retired major from the US Army Reserves, and a former police officer. He resides in Huntsville with his family.